D1030761

WITHDRAWN
FROM THE
INSTITUTE LIBRARY
PRATT INSTITUTE LIBRARY

369
93

FILM

FILM
The Front Line 1983

BY JONATHAN ROSENBAUM

ARDEN PRESS, INC.
Denver, Colorado
1983

791.43
R813

Copyright ©1983 Jonathan Rosenbaum
All Rights Reserved

Book design by Stephanie Van Bogart

Published in the United States of America
Arden Press, Inc.
Denver, Colorado

Publisher's Note

The 1983 volume of *Film: The Front Line* is the first in an annual series meant to bring a greater prominence to the work of experimental and personal filmmakers, whose access to the film press has been severely limited. The range of work is broad—from the barely narrative to the purely structural—but as the number of volumes increases we will try to move repeatedly along the edge of the art. The selection of artists to be covered in each volume will, of course, indicate the critical inclinations of the compiler, but by opening the series each year to a critic with an opposing view, we hope *Film* will begin to generate not only a broad portrait of the front line, but also a critical dialogue that will bring the political and aesthetic issues of the avant-garde into sharper focus.

Table of Contents

Acknowledgements

For her 40 handwritten pages of judicious notes, I'm particularly grateful to Bérénice Reynaud, whose generosity with her time, erudition, and editorial acumen played a crucial role in helping me bring this book into its final form. On many of the early chapters, Sandy Flitterman was no less helpful. I'd also like to thank Steven Soba and Fabiano Canosa of the Public Theater, Anthology Film Archives, the Center for Public Cinema, the Museum of Modern Art's Film Study Center, Amy Gateff and Bibi Wein (for use of their desks and typewriters and the company of their cats), and the 18 filmmakers I've devoted chapters to, nearly all of whom have assisted me concretely in studying their work.

A few portions of this book have been adapted (with revisions and updates) from previously published articles or reviews in *Afterimage, American Film, Artforum, Film Comment, Millennium Film Journal, Sight and Sound, Soho News,* and *Take One;* my thanks also to the editors of those magazines.

Jonas Mekas in *Paradise Not Yet Lost*

TENANTS OF THE HOUSE:
A Conversation with Jonas Mekas

> Tenants of the house,
> Thoughts of a dry brain in a dry season.
> T.S. Eliot, *Gerontion*

Preface: When I was approached last year about inaugurating a series of volumes surveying recent avant-garde film, I immediately started to wonder about how this could be done. Having lived nearly eight years in Paris and London and about as long in New York, I've had several opportunities to note the relative degree of information flow between these and other centers of avant-garde film activity, and the growing isolation of New York from these other centers made my own fixed vantage point less than ideal in some ways. When a colleague told me that Jonas Mekas had recently said that it was no longer possible to know what was happening in experimental film as a whole, a bell of recognition rang in my head, and I knew at once that Mekas was the only available oracle I could turn to. The Lithuanian patron saint of the American avant-garde film, now 60, has been an American filmmaker for at least half of his life, and a chronicler of the avant-garde film in New York—mainly in *The Village Voice* and (more briefly) *Soho News*—for at least 15 years. If *he* no longer knew with confidence where we were, a consideration of the nature of the very problem of our ignorance was clearly in order.

Out of this need and curiosity, the two following conversations took shape, with Mekas's kind consent, at the temporary headquarters of Anthology Film Archives on Broadway in lower Manhattan, in late July and early November 1982. Robert Haller, executive director of Anthology, was present at both discussions, and some of his remarks are also included. The second dialogue, longer and somewhat more polemical than the first, occurred during a two-week season at the Public Theater devoted to

11

Jean-Marie Straub and Danièle Huillet and filmmakers they admire (about two dozen films in all) that I was involved in curating at the time, and which became a logical reference point for part of our discussion. The results have been edited by Mekas as well as myself.

I.

JONATHAN ROSENBAUM: If someone were writing a survey of recent avant-garde film 10 or 20 years ago, he'd have a much easier task. Things were much more centralized then. If someone came to New York from, say, Kansas with an avant-garde film and he or she wanted it to be shown, that person would have gone to see you, probably.

JONAS MEKAS: Yes, between about 1960 and 1970. Before that, between 1950 and 1960, they went to see Amos Vogel* or the Museum of Modern Art. In a few other big cities, like San Francisco, you could count on one place where you could go.

JR: But if someone came from Kansas with an avant-garde film today, he or she would be likelier to search out an institution, not an individual. And the person in charge at the institution might think, "Do I like this?" But he or she would be just as likely to think, "Would the audience for the Collective for Living Cinema go for this?" "Would the audience for Film Forum like this?"

JM: Today, New York is split into a dozen showcases. Why did these different showcases develop? Because, beginning with the Seventies, there were no longer 20 or 30 filmmakers to deal with, but literally thousands, making thousands of films. No one showcase could deal with that; so that different showcases developed with preferences for different filmmakers. Actually, some of the showcases were started by filmmakers who felt excluded from other showcases. And, of course, filmgoing people as well as filmmakers became familiar with the preferences of the different showcases. Like somebody who is making abstract, personal films wouldn't necessarily go to see Karen Cooper at Film Forum—unless they were cutely animated.

The field is too big now; no one can cover it all. Amos Vogel could cover all the varieties of avant-garde, experimental, and documentary. In the Sixties, the Filmmakers' Cinematheque was already neglecting a lot of documentaries. Today, it's impossible for any single showcase to show everything—unless you had three or four different programs every day. It's not only that you have to catch up so constantly; you also have to give

---

*Founder of the pioneering film society, Cinema 16, and co-founder of the New York Film Festival. (J.R.)

some background and show what went before, which is harder and harder. That's why the Museum of Modern Art introduced their series "What's Happening?" to show the documentaries that no one was showing. And of course the feminist groups also have a purpose—to cover a certain area more in depth than any other. At Anthology the direction became more academically avant-garde because we felt that that part was neglected. We felt that once a film is shown—at any of the showcases—no matter now good the film was, it had no chance of being reseen. Until just a few years ago it was mainly just new work that the showcases were interested in.

There are certain historical necessities that determine these developments: the volume of the production, the number of different directions in cinema, the size of audiences. Before, the audiences could all fit into one theater; now, if you put all the audiences together, they make big numbers, even for the independent films.

JR: What I find disturbing about this is how everything has become consumer-oriented and service-oriented. Consequently, there isn't much of a sense of mystery about the avant-garde anymore: people aren't curious about what they can't see the way that they used to be.

JM: I wouldn't say consumer-oriented. Millennium, for example, in the first place serves its own members, then serves all the others, so that it's a semi-closed group. What do you mean by consumer-oriented—that it brings money? Millennium programs don't make money.

JR: I mean much more the kind of money and attitudes that come from outside funding. I'm thinking that the success of certain points of view become institutionalized, that certain categories of films now pre-exist in people's minds.

I'm also thinking of the differences between film magazines now and then. In *Film Culture* in the Sixties—compared to what you'd find in *Millennium Film Journal* or *October* now—there's an amazing range of people coexisting, a real pluralism. In one issue—Winter 1962/63—it's actually possible to see Sarris, Farber, Kael, Markopoulos, Weinberg, Smith, and Stern, all cheek by jowl.

JM: Yes, that was a classical period.

JR: What seems so depressing is how relatively little opportunity there is now for exchange and cross-fertilization and people listening to other ideas.

JM: No, each one is interested only in their own thing and there isn't much variety, no.

JR: So if this same filmmaker from Kansas had to go to a film magazine today, he or she might have to choose one at the exclusion of another. It's all feudal strongholds now; one can no longer introduce a film into a single community.

JM: The only thing is, I don't know whether this is a negative or positive thing. What *has* developed is the phenomenon of the regional art centers. There are one or two hundred of these. And they very often try to show examples of all the varieties of film—some very new and "emerging" filmmakers, some classical avant-garde, some old Hollywood and some new European work. Some of them import films directly from Germany, or France, and other countries. You can see European and South American films in Houston at the Fine Arts Museum today that you can't see in New York, for instance. Without these regional art centers, we would miss a lot of the European avant-garde. They come only because they have engagements at six or eight places and travel from one to the other. So while the New York and San Francisco showcases may be restricted to single directions, across the country that is not true—unless some center is run by some kind of fanatic of one kind of film.

JR: Well, you would certainly have a better notion than me of how much Americans are exposed on a national level to European avant-garde. But it seems to me that in a New York context, the situation of the European avant-garde is vastly inferior to what it once was.

JM: For the last five or six years there's been a drop, that is true. Not that the European avant-garde is necessarily all that active. The Italian avant-garde died out. The British and German avant-gardes slowed down, relaxed. Only the French avant-garde is still active. But we don't see any of it.

JR: One thing I want to do in my book is include certain films that, in one sense, are avant-garde precisely because they're overlooked and ignored. For instance, I know of very few Americans who know about even the *existence* of Jacques Tati's last feature, **Parade,** a circus film made in video.

JM: I didn't know he made a film in video! But not knowing that a certain film exists doesn't necessarily make that film avant-garde . . .

JR: True enough. Although sometimes it's tempting to give preference to actual films over categories, regardless of the academic havoc this might create—there are so many homeless films of interest floating around, and so many standard avant-garde films of no interest whatsoever. I've seen **Parade** in both Paris and London; Tati made it in 1973. It's shot in video and transferred to 35mm film—an earlier version of the technique used on the Richard Pryor concert films. It's an experimental film not only in that respect, but also in its attitude towards the spectator. A lot of the film consists of a circus show that includes many of Tati's famous mime routines from his music hall days, but the audience consists of both real *and* artificial (i.e., flat and painted) spectators, and the camera is often positioned in such a way that this audience becomes just as prominent as the performers. Then there's an epilogue when a little girl steps down onto the stage after all the performers have left and plays with all the props that are left behind. Jean-Marie Straub has said that what's exciting about the film is that it's about all the degrees of "nervous flux—beginning with the child which cannot yet make a gesture, who cannot yet coordinate her hand with her brain, and going up to the most accomplished acrobats."

Parade, of course, represents only one example of an important work that is almost totally unknown in this country. Even when certain things get shown here, they often remain unknown. For instance, I just spoke to a graduate student who's taking a summer course in Rivette, Rohmer, and Chabrol and asked his teacher about Rivette's 1980 feature **Merry-Go-Round**—which he'd seen at the Museum of Modern Art in February 1980—only to discover that his teacher knew nothing about the film's existence!

JM: One of the reasons, maybe, for the new situation is that for the last five or seven years, the political avant-garde—or at least the avant-garde that calls itself political—has dominated: the *Screen* group, *Jump Cut*, *Cineaste*, *Camera Obscura*. To tell you the truth, the way I really feel about these films, they are neither political nor avant-garde. Only the talking and writing about these films, in *Screen, Jump Cut,* etc., has a political tint or style. It's not politics—it's, rather, politics as a fashion, or style. It has nothing to do with changing the status quo of society.

Nobody writes about Klaus Wyborny in those places, although Wyborny is more interesting and more political. Chris Welby is mentioned, but he's not given the credit he deserves because all these politically minded writers like Peter Wollen* are wallowing in certain semi-political and semi-feminist ideas. And semiotics is part of it. Fashionable politics. They can really make a film sound very interesting. They are all writers. They say, "A man is crossing the street," and you think, "That sounds very interesting," but you look at the film and it's got nothing, it's just a man crossing a street—you could get a child to do it. There is no more qualitative, historical, comparative criticism. From the standpoint of semiotics and structuralism, you can analyze *any* image; any and every image is illuminating. You can talk about any frame for hours: it has nothing to do with cinema and nothing to do with anything. But it has to do with semiotics and analyzing of lines and shapes and light and how they all relate to history and masculine and feminine. We had a lot of that kind of writing here. Daryl Chin's† writing, for instance, started out as perceptive and

---

*Author of *Signs and Meaning in the Cinema.* (J.R.)

†New York-based critic and performance artist. (J.R.)

sensitive. But no matter what he sees, he can write three or four or five single-spaced pages about it, and if one asks, "Should I go to see this film?" one gets only a description. You wind up knowing nothing. Everyone gets a lot of space, and that's it.

JR: One problem is, when critics *do* tell you what films to go to, they generally aren't writing about the avant-garde. Whereas people who *do* write about avant-garde often argue that there's something outdated about assigning grades to works. What bothers me even more is that critics in this country who are widely thought to be intellectuals of some sort—I'm thinking of people like Kael, Sarris, Simon, and Kauffmann—don't deal with intellectual films or subjects at all, as a rule.

JM: Yes, but I cannot reproach them for not treating avant-garde films anymore than I can reproach certain musicians for preferring certain instruments, or certain painters for preferring certain subjects or techniques. I mean, they are very deep in their own areas and doing well, and I think we have that in independent cinema as well, and in art criticism. There are no universal minds who can cover all the periods and styles. I think Andrew [Sarris] is doing very well in illuminating a certain type of film, and that's it.

JR: Sure. But in the public mind, he and the others are perceived somehow as writing about and representing the whole of cinema. That isn't entirely their fault, of course—but it does lead to an enormous amount of omission and even repression. Five years ago, in London, Andrew was insisting to me that nobody but nobody was interested in Godard any-more—but, of course, his idea of "somebody" now excludes the avant-garde. It's a vicious circle that becomes all the more exclusive when avant-garde critics ignore many of Godard's works as well.

JM: I don't think Sarris was so wrong about that. The avant-garde, especially the American avant-garde, was never really interested in God-ard. There was nothing in Godard for the American avant-garde, politically or formally. The only thing about Andrew is that he should just keep his mouth shut when it comes to avant-garde films in general. But he feels some time he has to open his mouth and say "Maya Deren stinks" or "Stan Brakhage stinks." By the same token, I wouldn't presume to pass judgment on Hollywood films anymore.

JR: But you used to, and I found it very interesting when you did.

JM: Well, I saw absolutely every film that opened until maybe 1970. Now my work doesn't permit me to catch up with everything, so I feel I have no right to speak about it. I cannot compare.

JR: This may be because of all my years in Europe, but it seems to me that a lot of my European friends tend to see all kinds of films, and see them in relation to each other.

JM: I don't know who your friends are, but some of them are publishing film magazines, and if you look at the magazines like Cahiers du Cinéma or Chaplin, none of them write about the avant-garde except for Cahiers, once in a blue moon. You need to have a blockbuster like Michael Snow or Nam June Paik in order to get attention. These magazines are not balanced.

JR: What about the Monthly Film Bulletin in England?

JM: I'll have to look at that one. For the others, I don't think those writers or magazines see all films. They do not see the avant-garde. I have been there with shows of American avant-garde, and they never came to see the films.

ROBERT HALLER: Lucy Fischer* is someone who writes about both commercial and avant-garde film.

JR: Sure, and there are others. I find, as a freelancer, that the most interesting films nowadays are quite often the ones that I can't write about, because they're not available or prominent enough. This is part of what I meant earlier about service- and consumer-oriented criticism.

JM: Dreyer's **Gertrud** has no distributor in the U.S.!

RH: There's been a collapse of the 16mm distributors in this country. Films, Inc. have bought out virtually everybody. It's a giant, and there are a couple of pygmies, and that's it.

JR: What makes me angry is that people keep saying that everything will become available on cassette soon—all of Brakhage, for example. It's not true.

JM: At the Film-makers' Cooperative in 1962 or '63 we discussed that—almost 20 years ago. Now it seems like it's already here. I don't know if it's really here. All I see is past enthusiasms and hopes. We get all these schedules from across the country of what gets shown—and there are certain constants, like Brakhage and Snow and local people. What understanding there is about what's shown, I don't know. Some aspects are rather bothersome. They rent only certain works—you begin to see the same titles over and over. Take Ernie Gehr. You will see **Serene Velocity** again and again, while a major film like **Still** rents once every two years. And others aren't seen at all.

JR: Is this because of what's written?

JM: It's partly that. Another thing is they feel they can't devote more to Ernie Gehr than one program every two years or so, so they tend to choose what's shown the most often. It *is* a problem.

---

*Contributor to Film Quarterly, Sight and Sound, Soho News, and other publications. (J.R.)

RH: The situation isn't the same as it was 20 years ago, in those places where museums and universities had bought collections and show their films on a regular basis. Apart from that, it *is* like it was 20 years ago.

JM: We were talking about places like New York, Chicago, and San Francisco, where people who were interested in the avant-garde film saw all of it, whatever was shown, so they had a wider understanding or knowledge. Now, if you are in Kansas and the regional art center will have, let's say, 20 film programs a year, maybe 16 of these will be devoted to Hollywood and European art films. And of the remaining four, two will be local works and maybe one or two will be classic avant-garde films. . . . I don't know how much knowledge there is now. I know that we show Sidney Peterson's films every four months at Anthology, and we always have three or four people.

II.

JM: It has to do with terminology a lot, because terminology can sometimes turn people off from a whole segment of cinema. Like if we say, "These are experimental films" or "These are avant-garde films." This has never been discussed very much in the open, but maybe it's time to look into this matter of categories. I tend lately in my own thinking to come to an approach that's very similar to that of the Metropolitan Museum. That is, I don't see how we can discuss all the varieties of cinema without setting one group of people against another, unless we take it as a whole. The Metropolitan Museum may not be up to date with the latest trend or vogue in art, but there are rooms for Egyptian art, for Greek art, for Impressionist art. There are different rooms for different styles and periods, and one building houses them all.

So one has to recognize that certain styles and forms are related to a place or time, they may not be repeated later, and you have to take and respect them for what they are. Certain historians gravitate only to one style or school or period. That period could be very brief—10 years or 15. But in cinema we have the situation that either we have writers or historians who are interested only in commercial film—all the Hollywoods of the world— or else just the avant-garde or experimental film, or else some in-between area, like the European independents. Now we have already another group, the American independents, who are neither avant-garde nor Hollywood. And usually those who write about one group exclude the others. So books and histories keep coming out that present very, very distorted views of film history. With me, this has become a standard practice, as far as the new books on film history go: the first thing I do, I look through the name index. If the names of Kenneth Anger, Stan Brakhage, and Bruce Baillie are missing, I throw the book out as amateurish and not serious.

JR: So what you're saying, in effect, is that we have no film culture—only film cultures.

JM: There is still this division according to how much it cost to make the film, is it done with amateurs or professionals, is there a union involved, is the government sponsoring it, or a bank, or am I sponsoring it out of my own pocket? That has to go out the window. What has to be stressed are the different varieties of forms, styles, and content areas, such as autobiography, for example. It's very possible that when we all look back at the history of cinema 20 years from now, we may find that autobiographical film blossomed between 1965 and 1975 or 1980. Then there's a whole period like direct cinema or *cinéma-verité* which left its mark and is gone now. The British documentary is another room in itself, just like the social documentaries of a certain period made in this country—or the wartime documentary, which is something else. But when one begins to create one collection of cinema, and that collection is selected by people who are uninterested in so-called "movies" or the avant-garde or the social documentary, of course all other areas will be excluded.

JR: But you're talking about taxonomy and preservation, which is what a museum does. How does one discover or create the necessity of including a new room? Furthermore, given the existing turf consciousness that seems to rule discourse among many prominent New York film critics—the notion that certain areas and subjects are staked-out property belonging to a few appointed or self-appointed individuals—how can new ideas or approaches manifest themselves? Where can they go? Is there a way of creating *or* addressing a broad community, or does one have to build another fortress, like Anthology Film Archives, to protect one's own critical investments?

JM: When we have a film selection committee meeting for Anthology, the films that we review and discuss are those which one of us very passionately stands for and suggests we should see. Therefore, unless there are one or two people who feel very passionately about the film, nothing will work. So that I don't see "turf" division as you say. Like you just came out recently very passionately for Straub. That is the only way Straub will get roots in this country among the audience and critics—if somebody such as you or Susan Sontag, as she has done, stands very passionately for him. The movement of avant-garde film is where it is today because some of us in the Sixties believed very strongly, and we screened those films and we screened and we screened. And now they are recognized. We managed to put them into the sensibilities and minds and eyes of the people. So if Amy Taubin* doesn't stand for anybody passionately, nobody is to blame.

---

*Journalist and critic specializing in the avant-garde, contributor to *October, Soho News, The Village Voice,* etc. (J.R.)

Or maybe she does—she stands very passionately for Marjorie Keller's **Misconception**. I happened to hate that film with as much passion.

I don't think one passionate supporter is enough to establish a filmmaker. Maybe there *are* others. That's how the turf develops: there must be passionate people defending certain films very passionately. Maybe the problem we have today is that nobody feels very passionately about *any* film.

JR: I don't know about that. I've been reflecting just recently on Straub and Huillet's last feature, **Too Early, Too Late**, which I regard as one of the most ethical and beautiful documentaries ever made—although it shares the problem of the Tati film in being truly homeless, rejected or ignored locally by documentary and avant-garde filmmakers alike. On the level of its composition, it's a film in which the customary relationship for Straub and Huillet between a physical setting and a written text becomes inverted. Here the landscapes are the "body of the text," while the text becomes the "setting" for those places in France and Egypt—a bit like jazz, where the passing human and animal traffic functions like improvisations on a fixed, given terrain. It's a film of endless activity supported by a sustained distance, a complete absence of characters, and a continual human presence.

I can understand many of the reasons for Anthology's selection and fortress strategy—especially now, when we're entering a time like the early Sixties when people think about living in bomb shelters. But what happens to the avant-garde as a social force, the way it was when you were defending Genet's **Un Chant d'Amour** and Smith's **Flaming Creatures**? How do the policies of *October* or *Film Culture* or *Millennium Film Journal* encourage young filmmakers or critics to think new thoughts? If *October* is following the lead of Vincent Canby* now in putting Fassbinder at the head of the class, what do we do about people like Straub-Huillet or Wyborny or Ulrike Ottinger? Do we bury them, too, in order to protect our own safety? Finally, if safety and self-preservation become the primary factors in aesthetic decision-making, how does our work differ from that of bankers?

JM: There are many things in your question that I'm not sure are being stated correctly. "Social force," for instance: was the avant-garde a social force at *any* time? And "encourage young filmmakers or critics": *Film Culture* was never too encouraging. How do you encourage anybody? I have always argued against film schools and "encouragement"—there is no such thing. From the very beginning, Arlene Croce[†] came on her own to *Film Culture*; so did Andrew Sarris and Eugene Archer.[‡]

---

*First-string film critic for *The New York Times*. (J.R.)

[†]Film and dance critic, founder of *The Ballet Review*, and presently dance critic for *The New Yorker*. (J.R.)

[‡]The late film reviewer and journalist for *The New York Times*, an early colleague and friend of Andrew Sarris. (J.R.)

JR: Because there was a place they could go to.

JM: They had passion and something to say. It wasn't because I was encouraging them. How do you encourage a writer?

JR: By allowing people with passions to exist there. By printing them. Where can we go to find that kind of passion today? That's what I mean by encouragement. It wasn't simply an old boy network.

JM: I see—a forum to express their ideas. Well, it was much easier at that time, maybe, because there were very few publications. Do we have many today? I don't know. (*Laughs.*)

JR: (*Laughs.*) I just named three.

JM: Not that many today. . . . "Social force"? Those were different times. The pressures, censorship, was much stronger then; it was imposed on us, and we had to defend ourselves—a clash was inevitable. But today that problem has been removed. It's more permissive now.

JR: Maybe so. But there's a way in which institutional acceptance and promotion can take the teeth out of certain kinds of art that have something to do with protest.

JM: What art do you have in mind? The avant-garde of the Forties, Fifties, and Sixties had nothing to do with protest.

JR: You don't think **Flaming Creatures** had anything to do with protest—

JM: No, absolutely no. He [Jack Smith] was floating around in that kind of reality. He was obsessed with that reality; he had to do it, and he did it with his friends. It had nothing to do with any politics; it was his world, the life that he lived.

JR: Don't you think that world and life was formed in relation to something else?

JM: Later, once it was shown, it *became* political. But the creation of it did not come from any political necessity. On the other hand, if you listen to Jack's soundtrack in **Blonde Cobra**, you can see that he himself, as a human being, did not like the type of civilization he saw around him when he walked down the street, obviously. So he created his own world that had nothing to do with what was going on around him in the offices or stores or Park Avenues.

JR: Your own films are full of things about politics.

JM: Indirectly, everything is political; everything under the sun can be interpreted politically. But the motivations for making it are not political in that sense; they're personal.

JR: But don't you think that whatever uses art is put to have political consequences?

JM: Consequences, sure. With a knife you can cut bread or stab somebody in the heart.

JR: I'm disturbed about the way that an extreme right-winger like Paul Schrader can accommodate Michael Snow's films to his own social philosophy.

JM: Do you think you can make a film that can appeal only to Democrats or Republicans?

JR: Well, no. But I *am* saying that art conceived of as social and political protest is received less warmly here than it might have been at another time.

JM: That's because in this country, it is very difficult for us to understand what's going on in another country, oppressed by dictatorships or devastated by political confusions. It's very difficult to identify with and really have some feeling for it. It has nothing to do with this time; it's any time.

JR: And yet if you think of the Sixties and the impact a film like **La Chinoise** had.... I remember Columbia students who saw it over and over again in New York at the Kips Bay only a few weeks before they helped to take over the Columbia campus—which happened, in turn, right before the May Events in Paris, which were inspired in part by what happened at Columbia. There was a way in which both news and certain feelings about things were able to travel very quickly.

JM: There was something very similar in the air then in Paris and New York. But if you bring in a film from some South American country today, you won't get the same response.

JR: I'm both intrigued and a little appalled by the local responses to Tarkovsky's **The Stalker**, which opened recently at Film Forum. Everyone who deals with the film, including everyone who likes it, says it's a film about the Soviet Union, and I certainly wouldn't quarrel with that. But nobody is saying or apparently even conceiving of the possibility that the film could be addressing what's happening now in America as well, the way that people are living and thinking at this moment. Nobody seems to want to make that connection, which is precisely what makes the film vital and meaningful. People assume it's "political" because it describes repression and cowardice elsewhere, not because it relates to their own lives. This is what I see as the problem: European work which could actually address the conditions of people's lives—and here again I include Straub-Huillet—is never being read as such; it's invariably translated into something else.

JM: Maybe it's the style and the sensibility of the Tarkovsky film. Godard had a style and sensibility that appealed to certain anarchistic and youthful minds here. He didn't appeal to the masses—let's face it. Masses do not know Godard's name. His form did it. It was his form, his style, his temperament—not the content of his films—that inspired the students of Columbia. But I don't think Tarkovsky has that kind of electricity that Godard has. No one has; Godard is unique. Tarkovsky's content is very noble—but it remains only content.

JR: Not for me. The really interesting aspect of **The Stalker** is how much it resembles a structural film—almost any random five minutes has the shape and structure of the whole—while describing the way that we all live and think and lie to ourselves. These two qualities actually support one another—one could even say that they make the film equally unbearable to confront, in a way.

What I'm basically objecting to is critics who write about both film and politics, but who avoid connecting them in any way that might be challenging—such as linking them up with their own lives, for example.

JM: When Amy Taubin writes about a film and interprets it politically, there is nothing sillier.

JR: Even when Peter Biskind* or J. Hoberman† or Annette Michelson‡ write about film or politics, they often tend to keep each category squeaky-clean, without any serious threat of mutual embrace. My criticism of *Millennium Film Journal* is that it's not a magazine that wants to change the world; it wants to keep the world exactly the way that it is.

JM: *My* objection is that it's not readable! Actually, I have two objections. The main one is, if you haven't seen the film about which someone in *Millennium* is writing, there is no way of knowing what it is—there is no perspective, no judgment, no comparison; it's all descriptive. Equal space and treatment is given to everything there. It's academic, but not on a high level—it's like a student's class assignment.

JR: How would you compare its film coverage to that of *October?*

---

*Editor of *American Film,* contributor to *Jump Cut, Film Quarterly, Seven Days,* etc. (J.R.)

†Contributor to *The Village Voice, American Film, Film Comment,* etc. (J.R.)

‡Film and art critic, teacher, editor of *October,* and former contributor to *Artforum.* (J.R.)

JM: *October* is in a different class. It's one of the most important magazines that we have, because it brings the best in its own area of interest. You may reject the whole direction, but at least it *is* a direction. And the pieces are always of a high quality. When it devotes a special issue to Fassbinder after 20 issues, then it's strayed from that direction—but that's a real anomaly. And I hope that it won't happen again, because it destroys what that magazine has achieved.

JR: I couldn't agree more.

RH: May I ask a question? I wonder what the two of you think about why institutions and artists do things. Very specifically, Emile d'Antonio is someone you probably think is a political filmmaker, and someone who's even interested in social change. But I don't think Emile is interested in social change. I think he's interested in articulating his feelings and ideas about what is happening in society. But I don't think he's under any illusion that he's going to change society.

JR: Well, one criticism that's been made of a lot of New York work generally—including, say, Yvonne Rainer's as well as Emile d'Antonio's—is that it's about politics without being political. And this differentiates it from some European work. One argument I make about Straub and Huillet is that they really want to change the world. Now you can say that's utopian, and maybe the only way they might change the world at all is if one person's consciousness gets changed in a certain direction, then that could lead to other changes. So it's not a plan for a whole social revolution. But it's a beginning.

JM: Do you really think that they want to change the world more than Brakhage or [Peter] Kubelka? Do you really believe so?

JR: I don't know. Maybe they want to change the world in reverse directions.

JM: Certainly Brakhage has affected things politically more through changing the vision of what and how one sees things.

JR: That's what Straub and Huillet do as well. But what kind of implications do you see in Brakhage's work and the effect it has on people?

JM: It's obvious that some believe at this point it's more important to restructure the government, the social system, and for them that's the political action. And there are others who feel that's very superficial, that won't work unless you change human beings some other ways—and that's their action, that we have to work on sensibilities and certain feelings and emotions, and that's a deeper change than just the system. Of course, if you change the system, you try to impose something—I think the Soviets are doing that from the other end. The Poland of politics. Disaster. And the other way, which Brakhage wants and many others, what some religious leaders try—*that* doesn't work so easily either.

But these are only two attitudes, and they're both political actions coming from a very deep engagement in how one sees the world, how one judges where things are weakest and how they should be strengthened. At this point, I support more Brakhage's direction than those who think of changing the system. From my observation of my short life, I think that Brakhage's direction at this point is more correct. Therefore, his politics are for me more vital to humanity than those of. . .I don't want to mention who.

JR: Where my formulation of the problem differs from yours is that I don't see it as an either/or proposition at all. To me, there's no way one can change a political structure without changing your own consciousness. Although I *do* understand that there's a way in which developing the self in a certain direction *can* be a movement away from trying to change social and political structures.

JM: I have no doubt that Straub and Brakhage would agree that the most important change is the inner change. From what I heard Straub say at the Collective last spring, I didn't hear anything which would imply that he's a political filmmaker in any other, different way. I think he just wants the same thing Brakhage wants.

JR: Let me approach this from a somewhat different angle. It's often been said that there's a certain religious atmosphere that's been created around the American avant-garde, particularly in New York. A friend of mine recently said that going to the Collective or Anthology is a little bit like going to church.

JM: You see the same 100 or 150 people, the same tiny island or group surrounded by 10 million people who are totally disinterested in what's going on there. So of course you get that impression—

JR: But why is the impression religious rather than political— transcendental rather than materialist? Why does it resemble a sect, and not a cell group?

JM: I don't see it as religion, I see only the limitation—the small audience, the small interest. When you go to see a commercial film, you know that there will be millions paying money. So you don't have to feel anything about it; you go home and forget. But here you sit there and know that only 50 or 60 people came to this film, so you feel a little bit friendly, almost, to all the other people who are there. It's not so much religion; you feel like it's a community. But that's natural. There is a certain beauty in it.

JR: It *is* natural. But I can remember, when I was in college in the mid-Sixties, I was a bit belated in getting interested in avant-garde film. And I can recall a certain attitude I encountered when I *did* go to see certain things in New York—that if one was serious, one went to everything, or most things; but if one was not serious, one only went to an isolated film here and there. The attitude was a bit like: Why weren't you in church last Sunday, the way you were supposed to be?

JM: Only Ken Jacobs* would say that. He said, "I never notice those who go to my films. I only notice those who *don't* come to see my films." And that is a religious attitude.

JR: It's understandable, in a way, because you and P. Adams Sitney† and Ken Kelman‡ were all going out on limbs—making a commitment which wasn't just a commitment of careers, but a social *and* aesthetic commitment. And there was a way of relating to that in a dilettantish manner, and a way of relating to it much more existentially. To me, that's what created an aura, which was not necessarily willed at all, that made it like a religion.

JM: Maybe it's impossible in 1982 because of the number of films and videotapes being made today. That's one of the reasons why I quit *Soho News*—a situation that was already coming while I was writing for *The Village Voice*. One of the reasons was that I wanted to do some work of my own, editing my own films. And I could still work on my films and see *all* of what was being done around me until some point in the Seventies. But it became more and more impossible as the Seventies progressed to see everything *and* do my own work. Before, one could spend two or three evenings a week and see everything, and still do one's work.

JR: How does being a filmmaker rather than a critic affect the way you look at films now?

JM: I don't think that I look at films differently. The difference is only that filmmakers aren't calling me that often to see their films. And I feel freer when I go to see their films, because I know I don't have to write about them.

JR: A big problem I'm having right now is with those packages of films by several different filmmakers at the Collective's retrospective. I nearly always find them indigestible—there are too many gear changes I have to make between each film. For the purposes of a survey on recent avant-garde film, you'd think these programs would be very helpful, but there's a phenomenological problem. I recently went to a whole program because I was especially interested in seeing a Wyborny film at the end; but by the time I got to it, I didn't feel that I was able to watch it.

---

*Avant-garde filmmaker whose best known film is *Tom Tom The Piper's Son*. (J.R.)

†Film critic and teacher, author of *Visionary Film*, editor of several collections of essays related to avant-garde film. (J.R.)

‡Playwright and film critic, contributor to *Film Culture*. (J.R.)

JM: I don't believe in potpourri programs. I am for one filmmaker in a program, so I'd never do what they're doing.

JR: Have you ever found that there's any way to make it work?

JM: It works with some of the classics which we have seen many, many times, but not with new and unfamiliar works. **Ballet Méchanique** wouldn't fall apart with **Étoile de Mer,** because we know them so well.

JR: Sometimes, though, certain odd pairings can work surprisingly well. Last night, for instance, at the Straub-Huillet season, **Othon** and **Every Revolution Is a Throw of the Dice** and Chaplin's **A King in New York** were shown in swift succession, and there were all sorts of beautiful and unexpected continuities—such as the fact that Chaplin begins his film with a revolution. Unfortunately, it's precisely this aspect of the series that was masked out in the service listings of The New Yorker and The Village Voice, both of which pretend it's only a straight Straub-Huillet retrospective because their formats apparently can't even contemplate anything that's slightly out of the ordinary. It's here again that the crushing inertia of institutions becomes relevant.

JM: In 1961, we wrote this manifesto of the New American Cinema. Eugene Archer was working for The New York Times then, and I showed it to him and asked him if they could print it. He said, "No, we couldn't—maybe The Village Voice could run it." Then I understood, of course, that the only kind of manifesto that The New York Times would print would be a press release, not a manifesto at all. In the same way, for an idea to get into The Village Voice today, it has to become not an idea, but something else.

RH (to JR): I think your notion that institutions are shelters and places of safety and protection is totally false. I don't think institutions do that; I think they try to fill voids and do what nobody else is doing.

JM: At some point Anthology came in to fill a demand and void, but it's conceivable that after it fulfills that function, then it becomes something else. This is new in my thinking. But I look back at certain people who were writing about experimental/avant-garde films like Parker Tyler* and Amos Vogel, who wasn't writing but was running the distribution and exhibition side. And the interest and passion of these people, on a very high level, lasted for about a decade, approximately. And then they more or less lost touch and lost interest. For years I would make snide remarks about that, because I thought I can bridge at least two or three generations. But on the other hand, I think now I was wrong to say that, because I think we should not ask from a critic, exhibitor, or disseminator to do anything for any other generation but his or her own.

_____
*The late, prolific critic, author of many books, most of them about film, including The Hollywood Hallucination, The Three Faces of Film, Underground Film, and Screening the Sexes. (J.R.)

There's a certain period when one really gets involved for 10 or 15 years. And if that is really done deeply, so much energy goes into it that later it takes another decade or two just to consummate it. The same applies to institutions. If Anthology Film Archives will serve any other generation of independent filmmakers but that of the Thirties to 1948, or even to 1968 or 1970, that would be perfect. It's a limited collection, it's there, you know what it is, it's no change, it's perfect. There is so much just to serve that period, to protect those works in the collection—we know now what it involves, to collect all the reference materials, etc., so you can really serve in depth university scholars on those 20 or 30 filmmakers. That's a big job, and it would be terrific just to do that and nothing else. But we've expanded, and I don't really know myself how wise it is to continue to expand and do more than that—to add new works, be in touch, make a video collection. Either it's a closed museum that represents a certain period or it's open. When it's closed, you can't accuse it of just protecting its own interests, because it has a definite, real function. But if it's open, then there are different requirements, and one has a right to ask and demand it to really do the job of an open museum—to represent contemporary work that's being done right now. So I see what you are saying.

So we're living in an era that's blasé and pathetic, where people aren't even worried (*laughs*)—and they *should* worry! One day they elect Reagan without thinking, and the next, a couple of years later, again without thinking, they begin to turn against him.

...the argument thus far

To bear witness to avant-garde film today, I have to assume first the existence of a primitive state of circulation that perpetually keeps important work beyond our reach. This means that I often have to depend on such practical, medieval tools as the library and hearsay as well as the movies I actually see—an elite list by necessity and by default, but certainly not by choice. Yet most of the time, we also (by necessity) adhere to the dubious yet expedient philosophy that whatever is most worthwhile in art will somehow magically wind its way towards us—as if we were magnets attracting brilliant works of art. This perpetuates the metaphysical myth that culture is a unified whole that is uniformly visible—a lie that leaps to our eyes every time we scan the small print listings in the front of *The New Yorker*.

Four years ago, when I programmed a cycle of films at the Bleecker Street Cinema called "Rivette in Context"—a series consisting of films by Rivette *and* films that contextualized his work (as critic and filmmaker)—I saw the very concepts that brought these films together "tastefully" elided by *The New Yorker*'s routine format, and each film returned to its status as pure commodity before anyone could suspect that it was being screened for any particular contextual or (heaven forbid) educational purpose. The emasculation of culture by good taste and talent which keeps *The New Yorker* alive and healthy—its inimitable combination of the iron fist with the velvet glove—is never more apparent than in its diced-out form of listings, "a *conscientious* calendar of events of interest" (my italics), which always makes art seem as easy to take and as easy to find as, say, groceries. "When I came to New York in September," English filmmaker Peter Gidal told me in 1980, "I noticed that almost every film review that I read used food metaphors and digestion metaphors to talk about art and cinema. Because consumption, digestion and predigestion is the dominant mode in this country. It's just one signifier of the attempt to break with materialism and process, and to anthropomorphize everything."

It would be wrong, of course, to single out *The New Yorker* too exclusively in this respect. As a New York institution which fosters the same illusion of inclusiveness in order to mask its own principles of exclusion and oversimplification, the New York Film Festival is no less insidious a means of pre-packaging film culture, and in such a way that even subversive ideological elements are often ironed out or rationalized into safe doses and unthinking formats. It was partially the major omissions of the New York Film Festival over the years, including the work of filmmakers as important as Stan Brakhage and Michael Snow, that led to the formulation of Anthology Film Archives, which opened in the early Seventies—an invaluable institution which is also somewhat handicapped (perhaps necessarily) by its own metaphysical conceits about what constitutes a full and adequate representation of film art. Like an assortment of petulant street gangs who all intermittently insist on their right to be King of the Mountain, New York's avant-garde intelligentsia continues to operate more in the spirit of divisiveness than in the interests of a single community; and certain major filmmakers have come close to being lost in the general ill-spirited shuffle. One of these is a filmmaker influenced by that intelligentsia, and who lived in New York for a spell, Chantal Akerman—who, as I write in late 1982, still has not had a single film to open commercially in this country. For the Kaels, Sarrises, and Denbys, it would obviously be a better world if such filmmakers didn't exist—which, of course, is one of the major reasons why we need Chantal Akerman more than we need Brian De Palma or Paul Mazursky.

CHANTAL ANNE AKERMAN.
Born in Brussels, 1950.*

1968—*Saute ma ville* (35mm, b&w, 13 min.)
1971—*L'Enfant Aimé* (16mm, b&w, 35 min.)
1972—*Hotel Monterey* (16mm, color, 65 min.)
    La Chambre (16mm, color, 11 min.)
1973—*Le 15/8* (16mm, b&w, 42 min.) (in collaboration with Samy Szlingerbaum)
1974—*Je Tu Il Elle* (16mm, b&w, 90 min.)
1975—*Jeanne Dielman, 23 'Quai de Commerce, 1080 Bruxelles* (35mm, color, 205 min.)
1977—*News from Home* (16mm, color, 90 min.)
1978—*Les Rendez-vous d'Anna* (35mm, color, 127 min.)
1980—*Dis-Moi* (16mm, color, 45 min.)
1982—*Toute Une Nuit* (35mm, color, 90 min.)

---

*Portions of this section appeared in *Artforum*, December 1982.

It's a sign of the times that **Jeanne Dielman, 23 Quai de Commerce, 1080 Bruxelles**—Chantal Akerman's major film to date—didn't open commercially in New York until 1983, eight years after it was made. At the same time, one should not overlook the fact that during this same period the film was widely discussed and debated outside mainstream channels.

In *Film Comment,* for instance, Patricia Patterson and Manny Farber published the last of their pieces to date on the film ("Kitchen without Kitsch," November-December 1977), and a little over two years later, Richard Corliss, in a summary piece about film in the Seventies, noted that "Godard's **Numero Deux** and Chantal Akerman's **Jeanne Dielman**. . .could be the two most influential French-language films of the decade; but to see them you practically had to join the SLA."

Although I was fortunate enough to see **Jeanne Dielman** at one of its first festival screenings in Europe, and wrote about it in detail at the time (see my "Edinburgh Encounters," *Sight and Sound,* Winter 1975/76), I cannot claim that Akerman's talent was immediately evident to me from the first reel—nor, indeed, that any of her films yields itself to the viewer *in toto* while it is being seen. In striking contrast to the (mainly gratuitous) rapid-fire pacing of most Hollywood films, designed for instant consumption and just as instant forgetfulness (to make way for more consumption), Akerman's relatively static and painterly images often take a day or more to seep into one's consciousness; but once this happens, one is not likely to forget them.

This is as true of Akerman's latest feature, **Toute Une Nuit**, as it is of **Jeanne Dielman** or **Hotel Monterey**, the earliest of her films that I've been able to see. (Due to the relative scarcity of her films in the U.S., keeping up with her work has not been easy. While I've managed to see all six of her features, I've had to do this in five separate countries.) As luck would have it, I also saw **Toute Une Nuit** at a film festival—Toronto, September 1982— and the audience response was, typically, somewhat fidgety. In Edinburgh in 1975, I recall, a few colleagues of mine who didn't feel up to over three hours of Delphine Seyrig doing housework (the film's principal subject and concentration) but who knew from diverse reports (e.g., the Edinburgh program booklet, people who'd seen the film in Cannes) that the film virtually ended with a murder, decided to leave for dinner and return in time for the "good stuff." (Unfortunately, this good-natured philistine approach backfired because they were given the wrong running time, and missed the ending entirely—which is perhaps just as well.)

But it stands to reason that what Akerman has to offer as a filmmaker would constitute a disruption to any normal film audience looking for instant gratification—in spite of the fact that her movies are all gorgeous to look at, particularly the 35mm films seen on large screens. This is not because Akerman herself is a theoretician or even especially intellectual— although there's no question that she's been influenced by intellectual filmmakers from Brakhage to Godard to Warhol to Snow. (In the course of an evening in Toronto, she admitted liking two other filmmakers; insofar as these radically different figures reflect different aspects of her own temperament and preoccupations, they make a fascinating duo—Werner Schroeter and Eric Rohmer. The non-narrative obsessiveness of the former and the fascination with the conventional and everyday of the latter seem equally important to her.) As French filmmaker Pierre Rissient has astutely pointed out to me, a certain amount of critical confusion exists regarding Akerman because she's basically a materialist who's treated as if she were a conceptualist. Yet perhaps more significant than either category is the fact that, as suggested above, she's an obsessive director, and one whose obsessions often carry more resonance than her putative plots or other quasi-narrative pretexts.

On a narrative level, the two most conventional Akerman features, **Je Tu Il Elle*** and **Les Rendez-vous d'Anna,** are the ones that have the most obvious autobiographical content—the former because Akerman herself plays the leading character, the later because the heroine of that film, Aurora Clément, is a Belgian filmmaker very much like Akerman, with ties in both Brussels and Paris. (Less conventionally, **News from Home** can be considered even more autobiographical, insofar as its off-screen commentary consists of Akerman's reading real letters she received from her mother while living in New York—a "narrative" base set against a relatively "non-narrative" flow of sounds and images from New York.)

Even while it displays a certain kinship with some of the German films of Wim Wenders and Peter Handke, and recalls some of the modernist practices of Bresson, Antonioni, and Straub-Huillet (such as the camera's lingering over rooms and other locations before characters enter them, or after they've left them), **Les Rendez-vous d'Anna** has a logical and intimate relationship to Akerman's previous work; it even recapitulates the structure of travel and meetings in **Je Tu Il Elle.** The film covers a three-day trip Anna takes by train back to Paris (where she currently lives) from Cologne, where she introduces a film (an event that we don't see) and picks up Heinrich (Helmut Griem), a schoolteacher whom she subsequently kicks out of her hotel bed with the unfashionable line *"On ne s'aime pas."* ("We don't love each other.")

On her arrival at the Cologne station, she is greeted by Ida (Magali Noël)—the mother of a former fiancé whom she has twice changed her mind about marrying. They converse briefly until Anna boards the Paris train, where she talks to a young German who's moving to Paris (Hans Zieschler)—one of the many lonely foreign exiles who crop up frequently in Akerman's work. She gets off the train in Brussels, her hometown, where she's met by her mother (Léa Massari). Instead of going home, where Anna's

---

*Which I regret not knowing better. Both critic Bérénice Reynaud and filmmaker Yvonne Rainer consider it one of Akerman's most important films.

ailing father is already asleep, they check into a hotel room where Anna, lying naked beside her mother in bed, calmly describes a lesbian affair she has recently become involved in and feels good about.

The next night, arriving in Paris, she's picked up by her regular boyfriend (Jean-Pierre Cassel), who takes her to still another hotel. Finding him feverish, she takes a cab to a late-night *pharmacie* to buy him some medicine. Finally returning home—it's still dark—Anna plays back the recorded messages that have come during her absence; one comes from her recent female lover ("Anna, where are you?"), whose voice belongs to Akerman herself.   •

As plot, this is obviously quite minimal. Each of the encounters described above consists mostly of a monologue delivered rather flatly—by Heinrich, Ida, the German on the train, Anna herself (to her mother), her French lover, Anna again (when she sings him a song—an old Edith Piaf hit, "Une Chambre à lover," recently revived by Mireille Mathieu), and the voices on her recording machine. In keeping with Akerman's usual respect for real time, large chunks of this mainly unacted material are simply set down like slabs in front of the viewer, without the usual punctuations of camera movements, fades, or dissolves. And, as noted above, the locations where these monologues are placed seem featured and lingered over— persisting before, during, after, and even in between the words that are spoken there, constantly threatening to swallow them up. These cramped, antiseptic, and anonymous spots take on a startling beauty and power in Akerman's chilly color images, shot by Jean Penzer. Curiously, the camera remains in total possession of these creepy places at the same time that Anna seems totally dislocated from them—perhaps conveying some of Akerman's own ambivalent relation to her heroine. The resulting claustrophobic strangeness of Anna's encounters often evokes Kafka's novels— and, beyond them, memories of the Diaspora and the legend of the Wandering Jew. (Akerman's own Jewishness is an important reference point for her. One of her most cherished projects—abandoned only due to a lack of funds—was to adapt an Isaac Singer novel.)

A film that assumes the ambition or pretension of taking the pulse of Western Europe while pursuing a narcissistic autobiographical meditation obviously isn't going to win everyone over—particularly when every shot has the visual weight of a battleship and nearly every facial expression has enough glumness to sink one. "*Take that,*" Akerman often seems to be saying, offering up yet another drab, neutral hotel room or train station at night, each one lit with precise, uncanny radiance, and hammering these cold, elegantly symmetrical compositions into our skulls with an obstinate will to power that makes John Milius and Sam Peckinpah seem like frolicking pussycats in comparison. Under the circumstances, whether we like this movie or not is almost irrelevant: it demands to be acknowledged and dealt with as a glittering, grating fact of life.

Toute une nuit

Toute une nuit

On the one hand, Akerman's approach reduces her story to a series of on-screen and off-screen meetings unified only by their common banality. ("If I have a reputation of being difficult," Akerman has said, "it's because I love the everyday and want to present it. In general people go to the movies precisely to escape the everyday.") On the other hand, without the compulsive mechanisms of naturalism and suspense operating at their usual levels, **Les Rendez-vous d'Anna** allows us to purify and examine our own responses, rather than simply remain at their mercy.

As B. Ruby Rich has suggested, Anna's spiritual malaise might be related to the existential "nausea" of Sartre, but probably has more to do with an illness associated with Akerman's generation: "anorexia nervosa, that favorite condition of young women without a center, the blockage of appetite, the malady that sends them back into their mother's arms." And in the most extraordinary sequence of this haunted film—the love scene between Anna and her mother—Akerman's pessimistic vision seems to admit a few rays of light.

Eavesdropping on Anna when she confesses her lesbian affair to her mother ("You wouldn't dare tell your father—"; "Don't tell him"), are we moved by identification, sympathy or voyeurism? What does it have to do with us, in a movie that, as J. Hoberman puts it, orchestrates its shots in a way that renders a musical score superfluous? Is **Les Rendez-vous d'Anna** a Buster Keaton film for the Seventies without laughs, complete with S-F gadgets, humanoid robots, and lonely self-containment, or an old-fashioned European art movie of the Eighties? Is it a movie about you (to paraphrase American structural filmmaker George Landow), or about its maker?

Toute Une Nuit is clearly about both. (I haven't seen the intervening Akerman film, the 16mm **Dis-Moi**—a film that Akerman herself told me is of little importance. She said she was given the chance to make a film about "somebody's grandmother"—not her own—and didn't want to pass it up, but apparently it's not a film she feels much affection for.) As reticent as **Les Rendez-vous d'Anna** is talkative, with dialogue so sparse and banal that it hardly needs subtitling, **Toute Une Nuit** was described by Akerman at the Toronto Festival as a film about gestures, working with "mythological representations of love and desire." It rings its mellow changes on romantic love in the form of overlapping vignettes—a compressed evening full of couples' meetings and individual forms of restlessness and solitude, comprising the same basic repertoire of images as **Les Rendez-vous d'Anna**, but more dispersed in narrative terms by being distributed to a much wider cast of characters.

The film was shot non-consecutively in Brussels (on high-sensitivity Fuji film by cinematographer Caroline Champetier) over five weeks (spread out over three different periods) with a cast more or less equally divided between professionals and non-professionals. Each scene took shape out of "three or four lines" in the script—not so surprising, given the film's construction of interlocking mini-plots that are simply stated, like musical themes, rather than developed in any detail. Wanting to make the film "intemporal" in relation to period, Akerman strove to make the characters' dress relatively neutral. In this respect, it's perhaps her most painterly film since the non-narrative **Hotel Monterey**, which similarly concentrates for long stretches on the discomfort of bodies in rooms, a preoccupation Akerman shares with Edward Hopper (a visible influence whom she admits to admiring enormously, insisting that his lighting is much more accomplished than hers.)

If Akerman's physical shortness makes her resemble an Ernie Bushmiller character, she may be not so much the Nancy as the two-fisted Sluggo of the comic strip. Her doggedly aggressive style—a spikey form of Belgian Jewish punk that remains trained on the utterly commonplace—almost seems to harden rather than develop from film to film. It's difficult to think of any other movie whose narrative is stretched over a single night in which the rhythm of sleep feels so absent: glowering cadaverous insomniacs and no less somber couples (apart from a couple of poker-faced comic duos seen in night-spots—both rather anomalous for an Akerman film) lurk in brooding pools of dark and semi-light while the Delvaux blue of the Belgian night outside seems to seep slowly into their very bones.

As noted earlier, the persistence and relative stasis of many of Akerman's images create a certain restlessness in terms of narrative expectations, but an unusual capacity to remain in the memory afterwards (a trait shared by Andrei Tarkovsky's no less gloomy **The Stalker**). **Toute Une Nuit** ultimately makes its impression more through its evocation of the night itself (and the subsequent dawn) than through any particular characters or events, all of which tend to flit through the film's texture like recurring details in a tapestry. An interim film, made while Akerman was trying to raise money for a more ambitious film (a "musical" set in a shopping mall), it may prove to be a sketch or study for that future project, much as **Hotel Monterey** can now be regarded in part as a preparation for **Jeanne Dielman**, and **News from Home** a sketch for **Les Rendez-vous d'Anna**. As in **News from Home**, the soundtrack (in this case, a combination of sync-sound and post-dubbing) is as aggressive in spots as the graphic boldness of the images, particularly after the sounds of early morning predominate, when they actually become hectoring, and almost brutal—the noises of outside traffic smothering an embracing couple on a low bed in the final shot, like an itchy woolen blanket.

. . . the argument thus far

If Chantal Akerman has been unusually slow in getting American distribution for her films, there are other, more local figures who have risen to prominence a lot more readily, in part through their precise, strategic, social and/or geographical placements and their stylish ways of presenting themselves to the world and the media, names and all. On crowded sites like Manhattan Island, where sheer physical space is always at a premium, the issue often becomes one of turf more than one of ideas, morals, politics, or aesthetics—regardless of whether one is speaking about cultural choices in the university or on the marketplace. In New York, English film theorist and *Screen* contributor Stephen Heath is "out" because it is felt that in London he is "in"; whether Heath is useful in relation to looking at or thinking about film is clearly felt to be a secondary issue. This helps to explain some of the crudeness and nihilism of New York in relation to non-turf considerations, in which the preoccupations and habits usually thought to dominate lower forms of animal life are made fashionably compatible with liberal-humanist (and even would-be socialist) and intellectual standards of behavior. The basic message: New York is in love with its own rudeness, and new ideas aren't wanted if the beat belongs to someone else.

Foremost in prominence among the new punk filmmakers are Scott B and Beth B, who, in the mere space of four years, have risen all the way from their initial Super-8 featurette **G-Man** to their first 16mm feature, **Vortex**, presented in 1982 at the New York Film Festival, an influential and powerful showcase that has not yet extended the same courtesy to avant-garde filmmakers James Benning, Jon Jost, Ulrike Ottinger, Yvonne Rainer, Mark Rappaport, or Michael Snow—to cite only the figures discussed at length in this book who have produced much more substantial bodies of work.

BETH B & SCOTT B.

Art school dropouts from the Midwest;
met and married in New York in 1977.

1978—*G-Man* (Super-8, color, 45 min.)
   Black Box (Super-8, color, 25 min.)
1979—*Letters to Dad* (Super-8, color, 15 min.)
   The Offenders (Super-8, color, 85 min.) (original 8-
   episode version, approximately 2 hours long, no
   longer available)
1980—*The Trap Door* (Super-8, color, 65 min.)
1982—*Vortex* (16mm, color, 90 min.)

While I haven't seen the early featurette **G-Man**, **Black Box** seems to set down the essential themes and approaches of Scott and Beth B with stark simplicity, condensed to a directness which almost seems to bypass the fussy details of ordinary plot; along with the subsequent **Letters to Dad**, it is their most conceptual film. The opening shot gives us a characteristically cramped "B-movie" interior: a blinking neon light outside a bedroom window reveals a large Warhol-like portrait poster just outside, in the background, while a woman lying on a bed in the foreground—the camera stationed behind her head—seems to command most of the rest of the space. A man enters, and a scene of lovemaking ensues until there's a jump cut to him turning on *Mission Impossible* on a TV set at the foot of the bed; she gradually seduces him away from the program.

The next shot, no less characteristic of the Bs—its precise equivalent appears in their latest film, **Vortex**—shows the young man being kidnapped in an overhead shot, framed through the opening in the ceiling of an elevator. (In **Vortex**, it is the leads, James Russo and Lydia Lunch, who are framed this way.) The remainder of the film simply presents us with the unmitigated and obscurely motivated torture of the nameless hero, administered first by a man and then by a woman (punk star Lydia Lunch). Harrassed first by a man who demands to be addressed as "doctor," the prisoner is informed that he was brought to this place for a "cure." ("We don't destroy our enemies—we modify them.")

Low camera angles seem to favor the prisoner's viewpoint, although J. Hoberman has implied in his review of the film in *The Village Voice* that the Bs' own identification is with the torturers, and argues that the "box of light and sound" in which the hapless hero is climactically confined by the woman, "based on an actual instrument of political torture,"* could be seen metaphorically as a camera or a film auditorium. By the same token, the film's political preoccupations could actually be translated in Hoberman's analysis without difficulty into the formal issues of modernism: "In a formal

---

*The Bs found a description of the "box" in an Amnesty International report.

sense, **Black Box** reflects on the mind control exerted by every 'thriller' from **The Cabinet of Dr. Caligari** to **Halloween**. The least that can be said for the Bs' blatant identification with their film's thought police is that, given their roles as directors, it's not hypocritical." "We were attempting to deal with the counterinsurgency techniques that many countries have been using," Scott B has said, and in fact, earlier versions of **Black Box** ended with one or more titles conveying some basic information about this subject—which were later cut because the Bs felt that the titles compromised the overall subjective effect on the specatator that they wanted to produce. "We wanted to confront people...not only in an intellectual way, but on a gut level."

The question that remains, however, is whether **Black Box** confronts people "in an intellectual way" very significantly in its present form—which indeed veers somewhat closer to pornography than to political analysis. The problem recalls the distinction that Jean-Marie Straub and Danièle Huillet have made between filmmakers who are "unsentimental about violence" (e.g., for them, Buñuel and the Hawks of **Scarface**) and those whose fascination with violence allows them to "slip on the side of the police" (e.g., for them, Nicholas Ray). The fascination with torture in **Black Box**, coupled with the casting of Lydia Lunch as the torturer and a bland nonentity as the victim, similarly allows the Bs to slip on the side of the torturers. It's a point of political crossover whose problematical side infects the whole school of punk filmmaking and its ideological innocence in relation to social protest. Hoberman's modernist defense of this strategy as "not hypocritical" can be taken only so far (real or hypothetical "snuff" films aren't necessarily hypocritical either). After that, the point at which a leftist critique becomes an authoritarian sado-masochistic fantasy—the same point around which the dubious success of R.W. Fassbinder as a "leftist" filmmaker gravitates—shouldn't be overlooked. It's a tradition that is traceable to a great deal of Sixties inconography: there's an interesting way in which the silvery walls and floor of the torture chamber of **Black Box** hark back directly to the sado-masochistic glitter of the Andy Warhol Factory in its heyday. And the image of the young man twisting in pain behind a cage-like mesh pattern evokes the brilliant opening of Peter Watkins's underrated and neglected **Privilege** (1967), which anticipates the entire punk movement (through the specter of Mick Jagger) with its notion of a lean rock star icon (Paul Jones) writhing theatrically in prison chains before an ecstatic concert audience—a succinct metaphor for the instant packaging and co-optability of protest in a pornographically inclined society.

The basic material used as a starting point in the Bs' subsequent film, **Letters to Dad**, is the letters that the Reverend Jim Jones persuaded his followers to write in tribute to him. According to David Ehrenstein, "The Bs had their actors excerpt particular phrases that interested them, and filmed them reading straight to the camera against a black background with a low electronic hum for accompaniment. This litany of mindless allegiance, self-recrimination and contemplations of suicide holds its inherent morbidity in check because of the actor's arm-length relation to the text. Just as in Godard's *Le Gai Savoir*, it's the distance *between* thought and its verbal expression that interests the Bs" (*Los Angeles Herald Examiner*, February 10, 1980). Here again, as with Hoberman on **Black Box**, modernism is invoked to present the Bs' viewpoint as distanciated and objectified—in this case, modernism with a Brechtian tinge.

Among the many actors who read excerpts from the letters—some of whom make a point of repeating their entire raps verbatim, once, twice, or even more—are John Ahearn, painter Ida Appelbroog (Beth B's mother), Vivienne Dick, Pat Place, Bill Rice, and both of the Bs themselves. Unfortunately (in one sense, at least), the printed title that explains what the actors are reciting from occurs only at the end of the film, so that, on first viewing, one's analysis of the social and historical meaning of these texts can only come retrospectively.

On the other hand, one could argue that the recurring references to "Dad" and the implicit responses and appeals to paternalism have their own stories to tell, even without any specific knowledge about the precise historical context. There are plenty of disturbing undertones (and over-tones) to these underlit faces speaking more or less directly to the camera—including one man in burntcork blackface, a woman prattling about sexual games ("I really like to play peek and see and not get caught"), Scott B declaring "I won't beg for mercy," a man speaking about wanting a "revolutionary death," an older woman talking about having had brain surgery at 41, a young man incongruously announcing "Ever since I was a young girl, I wanted to live right, I wanted to be perfect," Beth B speculating about how she'd react under torture, and Bill Rice announcing, "Dear Dad, I'm either going to leave or commit suicide; I'm going to leave you with the responsibility of changing the world."

While the Bs obviously belong to the political (and leftist) branch of punk filmmaking—along with, say, James Nares, and in direct opposition to, say, Eric Mitchell (whose characters are commonly more concerned with posing than with acting)—there's a somewhat monotonous reliance on the same kinds of subjects and treatments in their six films to date. Even **G-Man**, to judge from descriptions, swims in the same material, reportedly delving into "art trendies and terrorism" and concerning "the private and public life of Max Karl, the commanding officer of the arson explosive squad." (The echo of Karl Marx in Max Karl suggests yet another formaliza-tion of political content into artworld strategy.) Throughout all these films, the harsh, paranoid urban poetry of Fritz Lang—particularly in **Spione** and the Dr. Mabuse films—seems to hover as an almost constant inspiration and reference point.

Scott B has pointed out, though, that **Black Box** and **The Offenders** were both conceived for a rock-and-roll club audience, and his defense of working in Super-8 is essentially a populist rationale: "Part of our reason for dealing with Super-8 is that it's important that people who are not part of the industry, who are not part of the power structure or the economic elite in this country, can make films that do get out. . . ." Well over a decade earlier, in 1967, French filmmaker and former critic Luc Moullet was arguing in the pages of *Cahiers du Cinéma* that "we must democratize the cinema," citing 8mm even then as "a format sufficient for 200-seat theaters," and maintaining, more generally that, "Each person can realize a good film at least once in his life. Therefore, access to film-directing for 50 million Frenchmen must be facilitated, especially since there is room, each year in France, for thirty films costing one million dollars, but also for at least five hundred feature-length films costing $6000."

A pretty strong case could be made for the next two B features, **The Offenders** and **The Trap Door**, as their two best films to date, achievements representing an apotheosis of their work in Super-8. The former originally took the shape and form of an eight-part serial made specifically for weekly screenings at the famous one-time Warhol hangout, Max's Kansas City. Each successive episode, shot the preceding week, would be shown as part of a two-hour show also featuring live entertainment, which generally lasted from 11:30 P.M. to 1:30 A.M. (The usual order would be: an exposition of the serial's story so far, a live show, and then the new episode.) Later, the Bs edited out half an hour of footage (basically the repeated expositions of former plot) to produce an action-packed 85-minute feature version, which is the one described below.

After a somewhat metaphysical pre-credits prologue in which a shot of traffic at night is accompanied by a male voiceover, invoking a context "where green is the color of justice and change only comes from destruction," and credits that play against rock-and-roll, there's a very striking opening sequence that shows us Dr. David Moore (Bill Rice), a medical examiner, sitting at a lit desk some distance from the camera in the center of total darkness—a fancy expressionist effect similar to that used at the end of Katharine Hepburn's climactic soliloquy in Sidney Lumet's film version of **Long Day's Journey into Night**. Once Moore finally answers the phone that's ringing on his desk, he starts speaking to his runaway punk daughter Laura with frantic urgency while the camera zooms forward in successive lurches, as in Michael Snow's **Wavelength**. A very skillful dramatic monologue as scripted *and* acted, the scene provides an eco-nomical background for all the following action while a strange electronic hum gets progressively louder (another probable **Wavelength** influence, recalling the latter film's ascending sine wave).

Here and elsewhere in the Bs' work, the restricted visual field and narrow perspective—which tend to highlight stick-like figures against a blank background—recall the paintings of Ida Appelbroog, as well as some of the pared-down sets and compositions of the Bs' Crosby Street neighbor, filmmaker Mark Rappaport (whose preference for more rounded and less emaciated figures suggests a more classical temperament). Before long, Moore is being tormented by another phone call, this time from a man who repeats his name over and over again (and who later proves to be Laura's kidnapper).

Following a scene between two punk toughs on a sidewalk in lower Manhattan in front of a row of posters advertising **The Offenders** (a modernist touch that recurs elsewhere, incorporating the separate reality of the film as a continuing serial), a scene during which Laura (punk rocker Adele Bertei) contrives to knock her kidnapper unconscious with a liquor bottle and escape seems awkwardly contrived in comparison with Rice's former scene. (As a rule, actors in B films shine only in relatively autistic solo situations; scenes involving dialogue between two or more characters are generally more prone to collapse into playful camp.) When he drops to the floor, creating an empty frame, and rock promptly starts up on the soundtrack, one is once again struck by the Bs' stylish and mannerist flair for filling a frame sparely.

The episodic action that follows mainly oscillates between Laura's female punk gang (the fearsome title bunch, who seem hatched out of bad dreams caused by the Mercedes McCambridge-led motel brigade in Orson Welles' **Touch of Evil**) and the unhappy Dr. Moore, who seems to subsist in every scene on Pepto-Bismol. The latter is confronted by the kidnapper on an elevator and passes out, only to be revived by a friendly woman who feeds him various pills, in a cheerful scene whose behavioral comedy temporarily blots out the thriller atmosphere. Still later, the kidnapper is caught by Laura's gang, pinned down, and, after Laura gets the other gang members to leave, shot by her with a pistol at close range (another claustrophobic camera setup, lit almost like Jean-Pierre Léaud and Juliet Berto in the black studio of **Le Gai Savoir**).

The further adventures of The Offenders are announced and cele- brated in successive newspaper headlines screaming their exploits: *Rival Gang Suspected; Jewel Courier's Hand Chopped in Heist; Crime Wave Hits New York City; The Offenders Strike Again; Bandits Hit 4 More Banks.* An adroit use of split-screen shows Laura calling her father to arrange a meeting while Lydia Lunch gets picked up on the street by a guy who takes her to a supposedly vacant building to have sex, then handcuffs her to the bed and leaves. A father-and-daughter reunion between Moore and Laura develops, rather improbably, over take-home Chinese food (which Moore claims to have cooked himself) and champagne, capped by Laura's drunken admis- sion of her murder of the kidnapper, and her subsequent flight into Central Park after he calls the cops. By the time the film concludes with a car being pushed off a wharf, **The Offenders** has risen (or degenerated, if one prefers) to a state of almost pure action, where the usual narrative pretexts have become thin to the point of being perfunctory. (An off-screen male narrator is intermittently heard, awkwardly taking up the slack with occasional plot notations, such as one informing us that an eventually unhandcuffed "Lydia, the eye of the hurricane," arranges a meeting of The Offenders in a nightclub.)

The equally episodic plot of **The Trap Door**, a string of nightmarish sexual and/or professional encounters, concerns Jeremy Jones (John Ahearn), a young hero who's looking for a job. The closeted, layered sense of perspective created by the Bs with an ingenious studio approximation of a drive-in theater and a row of escalators is as elegantly claustrophobic as anything in their work. (The industry term "choker," for close-up, could have been invented for the Bs insofar as their tightly framed shots of talking heads literally seem to choke the owners of those heads, so minimal is the sense of surrounding air and space. In this respect, the quintessential old-fashioned "B" film that a "B-film" most resembles is Edgar G. Ulmer's minimalist **Detour**, which, writes critic Myron Meisel, "employs only three sets, plus a car driving interminably in front of an unceasing back-projection machine.") In one voluptuous two-shot near the end—Dr. Shrinkelstein (the legendary underground filmmaker, Jack Smith) in semidrag, fruitlessly trying to hypnotize the hapless hero with a Maria Montez medallion, before giving up in disgust and impatiently clubbing him unconscious, in order to go through his wallet ("Man is essentially brutal by nature—so is woman")—the thick, furry and fuzzy textures become practically Sternbergian.

Throughout **The Trap Door** are some very funny examples of how to slide (or slip) into paroxsymic excess without actually overdoing it—to essay the kind of paradox this film revels in. As the totally unreasonable Judge Wendell, Gary Indiana offers some of the finest maniacal cackling that I've heard since the salad days of Daffy Duck; Bill Rice performs something called the Duller Brush Dirge with similarly unlikely and welcome abandon (as well as big band accompaniment); and Robin Harvey, as the latter's sexy secretary, turns in a fair to middling Marilyn Monroe imitation. Dany Johnson, on the other hand, as the hero's momentary girlfriend, registers a bit self-consciously, although she does come across with one of the funniest lines, in response to Jeremy's marriage proposal: "Oh Jerry, that's icky!" Perhaps it might be correct to say that **The Trap Door** manages to be somewhat political as well as frivolous and silly simply by being about life. The very fact that its hero is concerned with something as practical and mundane as finding a job already gives it more clout than a reductive imitation of Fassbinder's **Katzelmacher** like Mitchell's **Underground U.S.A.**, which is more centrally concerned with standing around looking bored.

Bill Rice, James Russo, and Lydia Lunch in *Vortex,*
written, produced, and directed by Scott B & Beth B

Vortex represents an enormous escalation in budget and commercial
ambition for the Bs. Shot in 16mm on about a five-to-one ratio, over about
30 days (not continuous), and mainly in the Bs' Crosby Street loft in lower
Manhattan, it wound up with a budget of $80,000—well over 16 times as
much as any previous film of theirs. (As the Bs pointed out in their press
conference at the New York Film Festival, each of their earlier films cost
under $5,000, which took care of the lawyer's bill alone on **Vortex**.) After
distributing their own films in Super-8 for several years, they obviously
decided it was time to work their way up to the (relative) mainstream.

Once again, a very fancy pre-credits sequence and Bill Rice (this time
as Frederick Fields, a crazed Dr. Mabuse type in a wheelchair, watching
supposedly private encounters on TV monitors in a S-F nightmare about
corporations out of David Cronenberg) get the show rolling. Fields, a
reclusive Howard Hughes-like tycoon, phones Anthony Demmer (James
Russo), who's punching a bag in a gym, to ask for warm milk, donuts, and
"demonstration footage." A coded message instructs a midget bartender to
murder Congressman Theodore White (David Kennedy), which he
promptly does, shooting two electrode-type wires into his brain.

Lydia Lunch as female gumshoe Angel Powers is introduced in a
bubble-bath, listening to a report of the murder on the radio—a Langian
linking device, like the headlines in **The Offenders**. A bit later, she's briefed
by White's aide, who wants her to investigate the murder and hands her a
series of glossy photos that she pins to the wall behind her, in a fictional

collage/clutter effect somewhat analogous to that of the pictures tacked to the wall in **Kristina Talking Pictures** and the objects on the mantelpiece in **Journeys from Berlin**, the last two features of Yvonne Rainer (another close neighbor of the Bs and Rappaport in lower Manhattan).

Never before in a B film have star performances—Lunch's Mae West sneer and Bogart deadpan, Russo's Monty Clift mannerisms, both played to the hilt—commanded so much of the shrinking available space, so that the first big encounter between the two, when he approaches her in a bar, practically seems to take place in a phone booth. Unfortunately, all the multi-corporation detail is much too formulaic to come across as felt or convincing; it's merely iconographic. The direction of actors and the production values are both snazzier than what they've been in previous B films, but the basic formula of paranoid thriller politics plus giddy violence is only a further elaboration of moves we've seen many times before. (To impress Angel at one point, Anthony feeds a dead rat to a snake; to impress us, the Bs show us Anthony doing this.) An improved version of the split-screen technique in **The Offenders** has the upper-left corner of the screen lighting up to show us Fields phoning Anthony, in bed with Angel in the right foreground, thereby interrupting their sex. In a climactic struggle between the leads on top of a building (actually a dozen flights up, not a process shot), he unzips his fly, she scratches his face, he slaps her and then rapes her until she knocks him unconscious with a piece of lead pipe. When he recovers she electrocutes him with an exposed wire, so that he topples stylishly to his death. A typical B encounter, one might say.

...the argument thus far

At this point in our progression through the alphabet, it becomes necessary
to acknowledge that, according to Jonas Mekas's own rule of thumb, this
book should probably be thrown out as amateurish and not serious because
it lacks detailed discussion of Kenneth Anger, Bruce Baillie, and Stan
Brakhage. Why are they omitted? Less by design than by circumstance,
expediency, temperament, and bias. For one thing, I know that in the
relative scheme of things, these figures are not exactly neglected today (not
nearly so much, I would argue, as works that their champions often
neglect), and that future volumes in this series might well want to redress
the balance. That these filmmakers are all underappreciated in many
quarters is no doubt true. But the logistics of my own situation have
suggested that my time might be better spent on telling what little I can
about presently undistributed work by Akerman and Ottinger and Rivette
and Thornton than on work that already has the bank-vault protection,
custody, and support of institutions such as Anthology Film Archives. I have
gone on record elsewhere as believing that Brakhage's **Scenes from Under
Childhood**, the best of his films that I've seen, would make an excellent
midnight movie, but I haven't yet seen any of Brakhage's subsequent work,
and don't feel it would be especially benefical to a book of this kind to
attempt to cram (as if for an exam) when so many articulate critics and
chroniclers of these filmmakers, particularly of Anger and Brakhage, are
already out on the job.

I am still waiting, however, for a critique of Brakhage that begins to
deal critically with the familial, patriarchal, and phallocratic side of his
work and the reactionary political stance that inevitably derives from it. This
is an ideological aspect that, following the lead of Annette Michelson's
notorious essay on Brakhage and Eisenstein, "Camera Lucida/Camera
Obscura," in the January 1973 *Artforum,* has been made to seem almost
unproblematical—or, at the very least, marginal to a serious discussion of
Brakhage's work and importance. For Michelson, the matter is adequately
disposed of in a single sentence—well formulated and articulated, to be

sure—that can be read as virtually the only regretful backward glance at a
European Marxist sensibility that she surely must have shared at some point
during her long sojourn in Paris in the Fifties and early Sixties:

> It is a tragedy of our time (that tragedy is not, by any
> means, exclusively, but rather, like so much else, *hyper-*
> *bolically* American) that Brakhage should see his social
> function as defensive in the Self's last-ditch stand against the
> mass, against the claims of any possible class, political
> process, or structure, assuming its inevitable assault upon the
> sovereignty of the Self, positing the imaginative conscious-
> ness as inherently apolitical.

Having thus discharged her duty to the Left in one well-considered
sentence, Michelson happily abandons all pretense of squaring Brakhage's
ideology with any revolutionary consciousness, tacitly accepts the American argument that apoliticism is both possible and expedient (while
expediently forgetting the Marxist argument that such a position supports
the status quo and is hence right wing in effect), and, with an audible and
very academic sigh of relief, relegates the future of art and humanity to that
reliable banker T. S. Eliot, who always knows what's best for us.

In that single negative gesture, Michelson thereby capitulates to a
position that simplifies many subsequent academic careers and institutional
postures (her own included) by accepting "apoliticism" as a way of life,
even within the pages of a magazine that strategically calls itself *October,*
and rewriting her own history so adeptly that not many film students today
seem aware that, in the first (and arguably best) version of her 1966 essay
"Film and the Radical Aspiration," Brakhage was presented as a highly
problematical figure—less radical, in some respects, than the Alain Resnais
of **Last Year at Marienbad**, and himself a cautionary warning about some of
the limitations of the extreme consequences of Romanticism.

What follows that skeptical stance seems, perhaps, to belong chiefly to
a social history of the avant-garde—a social history of the kind that seldom
gets written, despite the fact that it tends to rule cultural change much more
than any conventional academic study of styles or forms will pretend to
admit. In Michelson's case and that of her many "apolitical" disciples, this
amounts in effect to a coalition between the right-wing forces associated
with the American avant-garde and various "apolitical" academics who
have similar formal interests—a coalition whose power remains fully in
force today, whatever social/personal complications have intervened to
make its inner workings more labyrinthine than ever. (As a parody-
summation of this psychosexual Romantic position expressed in filmic
terms, I can recommend Marjorie Keller's latest film, made in 1982, which I
am tempted to redub *Dog Star Sitney,* after P. Adams Sitney, its major
protagonist and Brakhage's principal critic.)

Having thus turned Brakhage into a meaty academic carcass capable of feeding and sustaining many generations of students to come, Michelson & Company have staked out a substantial claim, in more ways than one. To counter and refute it adequately here would be a major undertaking, requiring more research and screening time than I could afford to spend on any three or four other figures in this book and entailing a kind of dedication that would ultimately only strengthen the opposition by diverting attention from other filmmakers.

All this, one should add, is directly relevant to the case of James Benning, a very gifted Midwestern filmmaker, supported by Michelson, whose work exhibits a problematical relationship to politics—making for an explicit exposition of a contradiction that lies more hidden in the work of Michelson and most Michelsonian critics. In Benning's case, the fact that he used to be "politically active"—apparently chiefly in the civil rights movement—makes him feel guilty, by his own account, about his present "apoliticism." That he seemingly regards avant-garde filmmaking as an inherently apolitical activity, as an *alternative* to politics, can be attributed in part not only to his all-American background, but to the climate of approval for this attitude fostered by Michelson's criticism. (The degree to which Michelson has represented European intellectual tradition for Americans obviously lends additional authority and power to her sanctions.) A similar climate has informed and even dictated many of the terms of Michelson's support of such avant-garde filmmakers as Hollis Frampton, Paul Sharits, Michael Snow, and even Yvonne Rainer (whose absorption in politics—particularly anarchism and left-wing politics—makes her a much more complex and ambiguous case).

JAMES BENNING.
Born in Milwaukee, Wisconsin, 1942.

1972—*Time & A Half* (16mm, b&w, 17 min.)
   Art Hist. 101 (16mm, b&w & color, 17 min.)
1973—*Honeylane Road* (16mm, color, 6 min.)
   Michigan Avenue (16mm, color, 6 min.)*
1974—*8½ x 11* (16mm, color, 33 min.)
   i94 (16mm, color, 3 min.)*
1975—*The United States of America* (16mm, color, 25 min.)*
   9/1/75 (16mm, color, 22 min.)
1976—*Chicago Loop* (16mm, color, 9 min.)
   11 x 14 (16mm, color, 83 min.)

*(Made with Bette Gordon)

1977—*One Way Boogie Woogie* (16mm, color, 60 min.)
1979—*Grand Opera: An Historical Romance* (16mm, color,
   90 min.)
1982—*Him & Me* (16mm, color, 88 min.)

The first two things that are likely to impress you about a shot in a
James Benning film are the formal beauty and its capacity to evoke the most
passionate and trivial kind of nostalgia for industrial waste of one kind or
another. The fact that these two qualities tend to diverge more than mesh
produces a disquieting sense of absence common to Edward Hopper
paintings and Antonioni films, a sense of endless waiting and boundless
yearning that haunts his landscapes like a specter.

Sometimes one can puzzle over how lovely a frame Benning can
compose out of a patch of blue sky, a grassy hill, and a red billboard
advertising Winstons—a symmetrical, three-color triptych composition
that's quite characteristic of his work—without ever getting around to
considering in any detail what the narrative subject of the shot actually is. If
that makes Benning a formalist, there are other moments in his work when
one can see him trying to move in the opposite direction. For instance, in
portions of his latest feature, **Him & Me**, he is quite capable of deliberately
letting one lose all interest in the putative, minimal image and be taken over
by the soundtrack for minutes at a time, so that the subject annihilates the
form—as in the 11-minute shot of a 1954 wall calendar, radio, and window,
accompanied by a recording of lawyer Joseph Welch's celebrated repri-
mand of Senator Joseph McCarthy during the Army-McCarthy Hearings.
But even here, Benning's intentions are by his own account mainly formal,
so that even after one's concentration is taken over almost entirely by the
recording, the sight and sound of passing trucks as seen through the
window suffice to pull one back into the image.

As an undifferentiated slab of material—important in an environmental
way to Benning's youth, but not ostensibly relevant to either his life or the
film in any more specific way—these hearings are something that Benning
can play *against* but not *with,* which indicates one of the limitations of his
approach. On the other hand, considering the degree to which Benning is a
compulsive recycler of his own materials and those of others, there is a lot
of play with the different uses to which a shot can be put. **11 x 14**, for
example, takes 11 shots from the earlier **8½ x 11**—one-third of the 33 one-
minute shots—and uses them in a different order, "surrounded," as Benning
puts it, "by much more information, which makes it more confusing."

In the same film, an 11-minute take of two women lying on a bed and
making love is accompanied by Bob Dylan's "Black Diamond Bay," playing
on a nearby record player; later in the film, the same song, without a
narrative source, accompanies another 11-minute shot, this one of smoke
pouring out of a smokestack. Next, in **One Way Boogie Woogie**, Benning

uses an extended take of another smoking chimney, this time accompanied by Cab Calloway's "Calloway Boogie," to refer us back to **11 x 14**. Then, in **Grand Opera**, Benning re-edits ten shots from **One Way Boogie Woogie** in a different ordering system—cutting them according to the digits of pi, with each shot representing a separate digit.

In short, Benning's work tends to be highly self-referential, and he doesn't expect everyone in his audiences to keep up with all these references. Sometimes the most direct and personal of these references, like the poster for J&B whisky in **11 x 14**, are also the most arch. Some knowledge of these references obviously helps to clarify the meaning and/or function of certain shots: when I was finally able to see **8½ x 11**, the earliest Benning film that I'm familiar with, the 11 shots that are later reused in **11 x 14** immediately became much more legible.

Indeed, **8½ x 11** is the most easily read of Benning's films that I've seen in terms of narrative coherence. Two minimal "road" plots alternate, virtually on a shot-by-shot basis, until the last shot, when they briefly cross paths. In the first plot, much of which later turns up reshuffled in **11 x 14**, two women in a car pick up a couple of men who are hitchhiking and then eventually drop them off. In the second plot, we follow another male traveler, solitary, traveling on smaller roads and, as Benning puts it, "interacting more with the landscape"—working briefly on a farm, for

Him and Me

instance. In the final shot, the women drive over a bridge while the man is bathing in the river below. Their car slows down, almost as if to get a better look at him, before continuing out of the frame, and in a way this brief confrontation of narrative trajectories recalls the moment at the precise center of Jacques Rivette's **Out 1: Spectre** (a movie that appeared, interestingly, the same year), when Jean-Pierre Léaud and Juliet Berto—the two connecting links between all the other characters and plots in the film—briefly cross paths in a boutique where Bulle Ogier works, significantly called l'Angle du Hasard.

Another important European cross-reference seems worthy of citation here. Film scholar and historian David Bordwell has informed me that prior to making **8½ x 11** in 1974, Benning was working as Bordwell's teaching assistant at the University of Wisconsin's Madison campus (where he was pursuing an MFA) and became especially interested in Jacques Tati's **Playtime**, which Bordwell was teaching at the time. With the benefit of hindsight, it is indeed tempting to see some possible influence of the separate narrative trajectories of the major characters in that film—Hulot, Giffard, Barbara—over basically the same terrain (which in the case of **Playtime** is exclusively urban). The points at which these characters cross paths and eventually meet can be singled out as key privileged moments around which the entire *dispersed* narrative of **Playtime** is structured.

Regarding their respective titles, to cite Benning's own explanation, **8½ x 11** are the dimensions of a sheet of typing paper, **11 x 14** the dimensions of a sheet of photographic paper. **11 x 14** starts, in a way, where **8½ x 11** ends—with two characters who remain separate for the remainder of the film coexisting in the same shot, in this case with a stronger narrative connection: a man and woman saying goodbye in long shot, beside a wall and hill under railroad tracks, and walking off in opposite directions. They are never seen again within the same frame; in the last two shots of the film, each of them—first the woman, then the man—is made to seem to disappear into the image itself.

In the first case, featuring what may well be the most elaborate *mise en scène* and most melodramatic action in the film, the two women and two men on the road enter a corner tavern called Mickey's, and the camera waits patiently across the street. Eventually one woman runs out and looks around as the two men emerge as well; the latter two break into a fight and fall to the ground just as a truck rounds the corner near the camera and parks, blocking off a significant part of the action. Then the truck driver opens the back of his vehicle, totally ignoring the scuffle that is now occurring off-screen and thereby shutting out even more of the putative (if hyperbolic) story; the woman meanwhile runs off into the distance, down the sidewalk beside Mickey's. The film's final shot—less interesting and more prosaic—shows us the man on a golf course hitting his ball out of bounds and walking out of frame to retrieve it; the camera pans after him a little, but misses him. As Benning puts it, "My idea was to have the narrative itself being swallowed up by the form of the film, being consumed by it."

The first really long take in **11 x 14** is of the man in the opening shot riding on the Chicago El—a handsome, epical 11-minute shot framed by front and side windows on the train, the silhouetted figure of the man appearing over the front window. Once again, it is difficult not to think of a contemporaneous European counterpart to this sequence—namely, the lengthy car rides through Rome in Straub-Huillet's **History Lessons**, which are similarly built around a central anonymous male figure and front and side windows framing the surrounding scenery.

Throughout **11 x 14**, silhouettes and shadows seem emblematic of off-screen, *implied* narratives, elliptical plots (or allusions to same) that never quite assume a central emphasis or focus. A series of formal permutations are played with these teasing story fragments, including tricks with memory and camera placement. (A long episode with one of the women in a filling station concludes with a camera angle that relocates the setting in the realm of the familiar, a place we've been before.) Individual shots can come across as mainly enigmatic (a man leaning against a white wall, putting on lipstick), graphic (zebras in a zoo), poignant (the marquee of the Coronet, an old Balaban & Katz moviehouse, complete with missing letter: "*The Man Who Would Be Ki g*"), tricky (a woman in a chair reading beside a TV, also facing us, which shows Doris Day and Rock Hudson in split-screen—one of Benning's goofiest triptych notions), unreal (an enormous moon over a house whose enormous, upholstered front lawn dominates the shot), liquid (the protracted lesbian scene cited above, as gracefully slow as Dreyer or molasses), or simply evocative (the magisterial Winstons billboard). They are nearly always elegant.

One Way Boogie Woogie, Benning's masterpiece to date, is also probably the most structured of his films, as well as the purest, comprising 60 one-minute shots in which the camera remains motionless. Benning cites the film as one of his own favorites, but adds that "it's the most difficult to watch for general audiences, because it's the least narrative. It uses a lot of narrative devices, but at the same time doesn't pretend to be narrative like the other films." One should note, however, that even at their most difficult, Benning's films are the easiest to watch of any non-narrative films that come to mind.

The title refers to Piet Mondrian's painting "Broadway Boogie Woogie," the "One Way" deriving from the preponderance of one-way signs in the film—both suggesting together a certain formalist and minimalist rigor that the film certainly lives up to. But at the same time, Benning's aim has a personal and documentary aspect—specifically, the desire to document an industrial valley where he grew up and played as a child, an area comprising about two square miles. "In the late Sixties and early

Seventies, most of it was being ripped down and replaced by buildings that were fabricated out of metal, much cleaner and less interesting than those that were there before."

As elsewhere in Benning's work, the shots tend to be perpendicular to flat surfaces, with frequent use of a wide-angle lens enabling Benning to introduce sudden changes in depth cues by bringing people or objects into the foreground. Another characteristic Benning touch is a tendency to turn many of his one-minute "compositions"—each a separate mini-film in a way—into a kind of game or puzzle that has to be solved. One shot which features a man's large, protruding stomach has an off-sceen male voice reading a math problem invented by Benning (a former college math teacher) and translated into French—a problem about painting boxes red, yellow, and blue, which refers to the film's use of primary colors. A couple of other self-references in the film show the flat surface of the frame being measured by a ruler (it comes to 11" x 14"!), and a spool of red twine being unwound in a railroad yard by a woman and man to "measure" the z-axis, or the shot's depth.

Another example of Benning's obscure playfulness: a close-up of an American flag waving in the wind, accompanied by a male voice speaking in German. The solution to the puzzle? The flag is in Milwaukee's County Stadium; the voice is that of a sportscaster describing a baseball game in which the Brewers are playing. German is used because of Milwaukee's ethnic background, and the batter is named Johns—which for Benning makes reference to Jasper John's flag paintings. A very strange and striking shot which shows two women standing outside on opposite sides of a front door and leaning against the building, one drinking a can of Coke and the other taking puffs from a cigarette, both in precise synchronous relation to the sounds of an off-screen foghorn and ringing phone, has an auto-biographical/historical aspect for Benning that nicely balances the strictly formal side. It derives from his memories of junior high school: "There were a number of people at noon who wouldn't eat lunch but would go into a back alley and drink Cokes and smoke cigarettes. I always thought that was a strange way to take a lunch break."

Even without this information—or the supplementary fact that the two women used are twins—the shot remains a staggering achievement, an uncanny, rhythmic coupling of sound and image that never ceases to fascinate, even in its irrationality. Yet the combination of nostalgia with formalism undoubtedly leaves its mark regardless of whether or not one decodes the specific references. Elsewhere, the use of Johnny Mathis's record of "Chances Are" to accompany a chimney spouting smoke and flames contextualizes formal beauty with another specific Fifties reference. (For me, the only total embarrassment among the film's references is a feeble, jokey tribute to the Odessa steps sequence of **Potemkin** in which a baby carriage topples down a steep pavement while a political speech is heard—a trite in-joke that is decidedly a cut below the equivalent one offered in Woody Allen's **Bananas**.)

A good deal of **One Way Boogie Woogie** can be read as gambles that pay off, in which personal/historical signification and abstraction seem equally matched and poised in a precarious balance, each side preventing the other from overwhelming the affective power of the shot. At its best, this provides a kind of primeval tension and excitement often found in the pre-credits sequences of otherwise conventional Hollywood narrative films, moments of pure possibility in which fixed meanings and functions haven't yet been sorted out—"Eden before Adam got around to naming the animals," as Dwight Macdonald has aptly described the phenomenon. Certain aspects of Benning's formal vocabulary—such as the industrial ribbed patterns that crop up so frequently in his compositions—have historical as well as formal significance, so it would be misleading to claim that abstract and non-abstract qualities in his work are always easy to separate. But when his films are operating at maximal intensity—which happens more often in **One Way Boogie Woogie** than anywhere else in his work—Benning manages to construct a kind of double trajectory that, contrary to his title, suggests a two-way boogie woogie. Perhaps the real form of the mastery achieved here is the actual succession and order of the shots, which never seem arbitrary even though one is usually at a loss to explain what the reasons for the order are. Significantly, Benning prepared this film by taking color 35mm still photographs and slides of the locations used and spending a lot of time working out the order of the images on the basis of the slides he accumulated. Whatever the rules of arrangement, it is an exquisitely constructed visual music.

Regrettably, one can't say the same for either of Benning's two more recent features, despite their isolated moments of power. As Jonathan Buchsbaum notes in the conclusion of his useful study of Benning's features up through **Grand Opera** ("Canvassing the Midwest," in *Millennium Film Journal* Nos. 7/8/9, Fall/Winter 1980-81), "**One Way Boogie Woogie** may have represented a limit to a specific structure, but the relaxation of **Grand Opera** results in a rambling collage which fails to mine the formal accomplishments of the previous films." The results, while seldom boring, frequently verge on the trivial and often betray a kind of complacency that is seldom apparent in the earlier works (barring a few lapses, such as the **Potemkin** gag in **One Way Boogie Woogie**). As I had occasion to write of **Grand Opera** when I first saw it, at a film theory conference in Milwaukee I was covering for *American Film*, it "could conceivably go down in history as the first entirely non-threatening non-narrative film in the American avant-garde. Warm, loose, and expansive, in the manner of a Whitman or a Kerouac, this good-natured bundle of sketches—inspired by the blowing up of Oklahoma City's Biltmore Hotel—is a grandiloquent kitchen sink film,

like Louis Hock's **Pacific Time**, with a little bit of everything thrown in. . . . If
a lot of **Grand Opera** looks like déjà vu, this is part of the sloppy, semi-
likable point of it. Without succumbing to a single dull moment in ninety
minutes, it so thoroughly eliminates any spirit of threat or challenge from
the avant-garde tradition it invokes that one could safely confine most of its
nostalgic pleasures to a dentist's waiting room."

A grandiose stew of aspirations and accomplishments, **Grand Opera:
An Historical Romance** uses a wider range of material than any other
Benning film, belying an ambitiousness that often seems to verge on
blockbuster proportions. Over 70 distinct sections—which are usefully
described, labeled, and/or illustrated as "Sounds and Stills from **Grand
Opera**" in October No. 12, Spring 1980—Benning runs through a repertoire
so flaky and varied that Vaudeville might actually be a more accurate
descriptive title. A recording of Amy Taubin's voice on the phone over black
leader at the beginning offers a variation of her visible phone call to
"Richard" [Foreman] near the end of Snow's **Wavelength**. ("Hello, Richard,
this is Amy. I just got here and there's been an explosion and a man's lying
on the floor and I think he's dead. Well, what should I do? I'm frightened.
No, I can't do that. Could you come over? Please.") The only change from
the original dialogue is, of course, the reference to "an explosion"—an
event which according to Benning inspired the whole film, and which is
finally depicted in the sixty-ninth and penultimate sequence: the blowing
up of the Biltmore Hotel in Oklahoma City. Like the explosion of a chimney
during which the entire action of Cocteau's **The Blood of a Poet** is
supposed to take place, this explosion is meant to reverberate throughout
the film.

Whether or not Benning's explosion can be traced back to Cocteau's,
the multiple allusions to—and direct uses of—other avant-garde filmmakers
remain one of the more problematical aspects of the film. Superficially
similar to Godard's homages to other directors (which crop up most
frequently in his Sixties films), Benning's tributes actually register quite
differently because of his relative remoteness from film history and film
culture. (In this respect, it is important to note that Benning didn't shoot his
first film until he was around 30. While Godard was nearly as old when he
made **Breathless**, his first feature, this was after nearly a decade of making
shorts and doing film-related work. Benning, by contrast, worked as a
college math teacher prior to his involvement with film.) All the filmmakers
he alludes to in **Grand Opera**, with the exception of Cocteau, are
contemporaries, and while it seems clear that Benning is using them in a
way to "measure" and "clarify" his own practice as a filmmaker, the
manner in which he pursues this is at once so jokey and so programmatic
that each filmmaker is effectively reduced to a cartoon silhouette of his or
her aesthetic identity—with the exception of Jean-Pierre Gorin, whose
aesthetic persona is already so cartoon-like that Benning can seemingly
only duplicate it.

Five shots after we hear Taubin's voice—following shots of a notebook, a folk singer, a five-minute slab of crawling autobiographical text about Benning's childhood, and the ruins of a building—Benning presents us with four filmmakers in turn: Hollis Frampton, George Landow, Michael Snow, and Yvonne Rainer. Each is facing the camera in front of a different backdrop, reciting the same statement about the same event: "Keep your eye on the brown structure. Two planes will pass overhead. It will explode. And a mushroom cloud will cover the city."

Then, after another four-shot interval—this time consisting of characteristic Benning-like industrial landscapes (portentously meant to represent "art," "war," "industry," and "religion," as we discover in the printed version of the film in *October*)—Benning completes his pantheon by returning to black leader and a recording of part of a lecture by Stan Brakhage (after a handwritten "By Brakhage" signature wiggles and flashes by) about his rationale for shooting silent rather than sound films. At the very end, Brakhage notes that "I'm not against sound films ... I rather think of it as grand opera," thus furnishing Benning with his title.

I think one could argue that this use of Brakhage—which wittily takes him at his own word while paradoxically reversing his practice—is a somewhat more defensible gag than the earlier and subsequent uses of Frampton, Landow, Snow, and Rainer, who are made to recur at intervals almost as if they were vaudeville performers. When Benning gets his young daughter to appear in the film for the second time, standing in front of an oil pump and reciting the alphabet, then saying, "This is for P. Adams Sitney," he is stooping to the level of a Bob Hope movie in-joke in, say, **Road to Bali** (although in all fairness to Benning, Snow's **"Rameau's Nephew" by Diderot** ... stoops just as low, and it's highly unlikely that Benning's gag would ever have been formulated without Snow's film, to which it appears to allude directly). Benning himself acknowledges, though, that such ploys often tend to divide his audiences between initiates—in this case, people who know who P. Adams Sitney is (and, one step up from that, those who catch the reference to the Snow film)—and outsiders, who are alienated only that much more by the sound of other people laughing. If there's any defensible merit in such procedures, this may be simply to expose and foreground the in-group chumminess that at once organizes, strengthens, and (at times) trivializes the avant-garde as a self-regarding, self-ingratiated social unit.

Grand Opera contains a little bit of everything: a cross-country car journey punctuated by jump cuts between all kinds of weather, terrain, and times of day, in which a windshield becomes a movie screen (as in the car rides through Rome in **History Lessons**, cited earlier); a man painting a wall behind a transparent, printed text while a soap opera soundtrack is heard; lovely greeting-card and postcard vistas; pixillated leaps in physical action synchronized to a pianist moving up a scale; 360° pans around various neighborhood streets (over which names of places and dates are superimposed, such as "Evanston, Illinois/1975") timed to nostalgic rock hits; oil pumps contrasted with one another via editing, as mechanically as Frampton, Landow, Snow, and Rainer are juxtaposed; a recorded patter about Mount Rushmore, distorted aurally and heard over a shot of the Statue of Liberty; a re-editing of ten shots from **One Way Boogie Woogie**, with each short reportedly representing a digit from 0 to 9 and re-edited "in 20 frame lengths to the first 527 digits of pi" to snatches of "Chances Are" by Johnny Mathis—all of which comes across as an interesting sequence of alternations done with a "...and a partridge in a pear tree" construction: overlong, perhaps, but fun for a spell.

If I seem to be highly equivocal about **Grand Opera**, I should confess that this has something to do with my own rather ambitious (and admittedly uneven) experiments with autobiography in my book *Moving Places: A Life at the Movies* (Harper Colophon, 1980), combined with the fact that I'm the same age as Benning—factors which undoubtedly complicate and perhaps even dictate part of my response. Although I believe that my own relationship to nostalgia, while equally passionate, is more ambivalent and critical than Benning's is—hence more political, I would say, at least from a leftist perspective—the limitations of self-exploration are apparent, I would argue, in both our works, and perhaps even for related reasons. Speaking for myself, the importance of establishing precise times, dates and places was a necessary part of my preparations for *Moving Places;* in jazz terms, they were the chordal structures that I felt I had to establish before I could feel free to improvise. But writing now from a distance of three years from the book's completion, I sincerely doubt that the issue of when and where I saw particular movies means any more to the detached reader than "Evanston, Illinois/1975" over a particular house and neighborhood does to the detached (i.e., unaffiliated) spectator of **Grand Opera**. In both cases, the information is too private and specific to contribute anything more than a screen or filter through which the reader/spectator has to perceive the more salient aspects of the work. By itself, it can perhaps serve as an "Open, Sesame" only if the spectator/reader uses it as a springboard into his or her own explorations; otherwise, it cannot be considered relevant or usable in its own right.

Him & Me, Benning's latest and to my mind weakest feature, is like **Grand Opera** with most of the juices removed. Opening with a 90° pan to the left, from a 1942 Hudson parked in front of an old factory (over which is superimposed the title "Milwaukee 1942") to the New York skyline seen from across the East River (under the title "New York 1980"), the film once again treats Benning's own life as the essential raw material, this time placing more emphasis on the American social and political history background than on the American artworld topography background. The problem is that, while Benning's relative distance from and even apparent naïveté regarding the avant-garde establishment lend portions of **Grand Opera** a certain embarrassing authenticity—a whiff of narcissistic complacency that indeed informs a world which, to all appearances, he seems to want only to celebrate—his relationship to American social history seems equally naïve, yet without the same capacity to reveal or illuminate anything about it. The fleeting appearance of Annette Michelson in **Him & Me** almost registers, in effect, like the unambiguous product plugs worked by Jerry Lewis into **Hardly Working**, but it has the similar disadvantage of revealing nothing about what's being promoted. *Mutatis mutandis*, the more substantial "appearances" in the film of Senator Joe McCarthy, Joseph Welch, and civil rights activist Father James Groppi are equally unrevealing—unrevealing, that is, in relation to any analytical context established by Benning.

Too much of the film, in short, winds up as an unmediated scrapbook. The polytextual surface of **Him & Me** suggests the collage techniques of Godard as well as Yvonne Rainer, but what it seems fatally to lack are a rigorous principle of selection of texts and an overall formal strategy that could transform or at least contextualize this raw material beyond its more literal and trivial signifiers. Benning has explained that the film grew out of "a really tragic experience," which occurred on November 4, 1979—one that is described at some length by a woman in a phone conversation towards the end of the film, in the thirty-seventh and penultimate sequence (two 11-minute takes that were pared down with jump cuts)—of waking up and discovering that the person beside him was dead. Significantly, this basic kernel of meaning occupies the same position in relation to **Him & Me** that the explosion of the Oklahoma City Biltmore occupies in relation to **Grand Opera**. The fact that it is so comparatively private an experience, at least in the terms that Benning formulates it, undoubtedly helps to explain what makes **Him & Me** a less accessible and interesting film—more autobiographical in its use of politics, yet less critical or dialectical in relation to any visible grasp of those politics.

The fact that Benning moved to New York in 1980 is clearly an important aspect of the autobiographical context, as is indicated in the opening shot and all the subsequent footage which intriguingly treats New York as just another Midwestern city. The fact that he painted his loft walls salmon-pink and pea-green while making the film—colors that reminded him of his Fifties youth—and then incorporated this into the film already begins to indicate some of the ambitions as well as the limitations of his approach. But the fact that Benning woke up next to a dead person on the same day that the Iranian hostages were taken is so specialized and personal that one would not expect it to be meaningful to anyone else. Yet even though Benning, by his own account, places this incident at a later date in the film, he still insists on using the Iranian hostages as yet another leitmotif, with "day 200," "day 206," "day 209," "day 212," "day 217," and "day 220" flashed at different points on the screen—a theme that remains obstinately irrelevant to everything else outside Benning's very specialized context.

The question raised by this is whether Benning's attitude towards this phenomenon is as doggedly apolitical and circumstantial as that of Michael Snow towards El Salvador in **So Is This** (see the section on Snow). If so, one wonders why Benning chooses to juxtapose this attitude uncritically next to a seven-minute sequence of re-edited TV footage about Father James Groppi's civil rights work in Milwaukee—which, according to information Benning imparts only when speaking *about* the film, he was personally involved in as an activist. Do commitment and lack of commitment become formal equivalents on an editing table? Finally, Benning's attempt to split himself into two characters, one of whom is female—an effort that is reflected in the film's title—seems more willed than functional in establishing a critically useful vantage point from which to perceive the varied material. (Benning's own description of the strategy involved is not very helpful or encouraging: "I'm really just presenting a man's view of the last 30 years. The women don't represent a woman's viewpoint so much as the viewpoint of a man my age towards a woman—how the sexual politics have changed.")

Him and Me

It is difficult to "bare the device" without an adequate grasp of or interest in determining what the device is, and Benning's apparent interest in bearing passive witness to his own ideology makes no sense without an adequate sense of what that ideology is. Highly symptomatic to me of what's wrong with **Him & Me** is the twelfth sequence, an 11-minute shot of a 1954 wall calendar and radio beside an open window, accompanied on the soundtrack by the sounds of passing traffic and a climactic episode in the Army-McCarthy Hearings—a sequence described at the beginning of this discussion. Benning admitted to me that his interest in these hearings is mainly "environmental"—as something that formed part of the background of his youth, although he didn't understand much about it at the time—while his relation to the civil rights movement in the Sixties, represented in the twenty-fourth sequence of **Him & Me** (a "seven-minute condensation of a year's worth of television" on Milwaukee's Channel 12, shown on an actual TV set), was more direct and engaged. Yet the fact that he fails to make this distinction intelligible or useful to the spectator has the consequence of making both blocks of material—radio and TV broadcasts, respectively—equivalents of one another in much too facile and unconsidered a fashion, both reduced to the status of plugs rather than phenomena meant to be analyzed or reflected upon.

Much the same can be said, alas, of the use of the title "Vietnam" over one shot of New York and "Phnom Penh 1970" over another. Admittedly, both shots represent the same point expressed in the title and approach of the collective French film **Far from Vietnam**; where I believe they crucially differ is in the depths of their articulations and what these imply. The statements of **Far from Vietnam** were all forms of work and engagement with a problem; Benning reaches for a gag or gag equivalent whose usefulness evaporates as soon as the punchline registers—it is as fundamentally cynical, in this respect, as a Woody Allen gag, a glib admission of spinelessness that congratulates itself on the correctness of its stance.

For this reason, I strongly differ with J. Hoberman when he praises Benning's uses of the Iranian hostages, "Vietnam" and "Phnom Penh 1970" for their "economy and resonance." But I couldn't agree more with his conclusion that if Benning "wants to move beyond formalism"—as the muddle of **Him & Me** seems to indicate—"he'll have to find a subject." The problem seems to be that Benning is interested, as often as not, in exhausting and draining an image of possible meanings—a basic strategy in his long takes—which obviously can't sit well with a desire to bear political witness to a time and place. Thus, the extended truck ride from Manhattan to Brooklyn in **Him & Me**, which according to Benning "begins as narrative and ends as formal experiment," moves in the opposite direction of the car rides through Rome in Straub-Huillet's **History Lessons**, at least for any attentive and serious spectator who uses the ride as a mechanism for looking. Benning uses it as a mechanism for making a film sequence.

Poised between narrative and non-narrative, Benning's four features to date represent four separate attempts to justify a capacity for producing uncannily evocative and "incomplete" images that hover vibrantly over narrative possibilities without ever entirely succumbing to them. But **11 x 14** and **One Way Boogie Woogie** are each wise about where to stay reticent and objective about its procedures. **Grand Opera** and **Him & Me**, by contrast, embark on the more dangerous project of intertwining overt autobiography and social history, courting all the excesses of personal subjectivity, which puts Benning's compositional flair with sound and image to very different purposes—into areas of action where people live and Benning's films, from his own viewpoint, are ineffectual by definition. This places his recent work in a political and existential impasse: one feels him poised uneasily on the edge of a cliff, temperamentally unable to step backward into the comfort and security of narrative fiction (although he confessed to me that if he *did* make "more narrative" films, these would probably be influenced by Chantal Akerman), and just as unable to step forward into the risky vertigo of political commitment.

Clearly, he has to move somewhere. On the other hand, the conveyed sense of paralysis—epitomized to an embarrassing degree by the sheer diagrammatic facility and inadequacy of the "Vietnam" and "Phnom Penh 1970" titles—has an integrity and honesty that is noticeably lacking in, say, the snobbish upper-class "radicalism" of an "avant-garde" that aims for social approval and acceptance above all else—the epitome of that congealed, safe academicism that resolutely strives to keep all social confrontations rigorously restricted to dark auditoriums, so that one is free to get down to serious, urbane partying as soon as one emerges. Less of a smoothie in keeping his political contradictions so firmly under wraps, Benning has more to offer in his failures than all his star-struck contemporaries who hanker after Hollywood or its equivalents do in their "successes." For all the inadequacies of Thomas Wolfe as a role model in today's avant-garde, he is nevertheless vastly to be preferred to a Tom Wolfe.

 ROBERT BREER.
Born in Detroit, Michigan, 1926.

1952—*Form Phases I* (16mm, color, 2 min., silent)
1953—*Form Phases II & III* (16mm, color, 7 min., silent)
1954—*Form Phases IV* (16mm, color, 4 min., silent)
        Untitled (16mm, color, loop, silent)
        Un Miracle (16mm, color, 30 seconds, silent)
1955—*Untitled* (16mm, b&w, 3 min., silent)
1956—*Image by Images* (16mm, color, 2½ min.)
        (unavailable)
        Cats (16mm, color, 1½ min.)
        Recreation (16mm, color, 2 min.)
        Recreation II (16mm, color, 2 min.)

1957—*Jamestown Balloons* (16mm, color, 5 min.)
    A Man and His Dog Out for Air (16mm, b&w, 2 min.)
1958—*Par Avion* (16mm, color, 3 min., silent)
    (unavailable)
    Chutes de Pierre, Danger du Mort (16mm, color, 4
    min.) (animation sequence by Michel Fano;
    unavailable)
1959—*Eyewash* (16mm, color, 5 min., silent)
    Trailer (16mm, b&w, 1 min., silent) (unavailable)
1960—*Inner and Outer Space* (16mm, color, 5½ min.)
    Homage to Jean Tinguely's Homage to New York
    (16mm, b&w, 9½ min.)
1961—*Blazes* (16mm, color, 3 min.)
    Kinetic Art Show Stockholm (16mm, color, 15 min.)
    (unavailable)
1962—*Horse over Tea Kettle* (16mm, color, 8 min.)
1963—*Breathing* (16mm, b&w, 6 min.)
1964—*Fist Fight* (16mm, color, 11 min.)
1966—*66* (16mm, color, 5 min.)
1968—*69* (16mm, color, 5 min.)
    PBL 2 (16mm, color, 1 min.) (produced for PBL TV)
    PBL 3 (16mm, color, 1 min.) (produced for PBL TV;
    unavailable)
1970—*70* (16mm, color, 5 min., silent)
1971—*Elevator* (16mm, color, 1 min.) (produced for CTW
    TV; unavailable)
    What? (16mm, color, 1 min.) (produced for CTW
    TV; unavailable)
1972—*Gulls and Buoys* (16mm, color, 7½ min.)
1974—*Fuji* (16mm, color, 8½ min.)
1975—*Rubber Cement* (16mm, color, 10 min.)
1977—*77* (16mm, color, 7 min.)
1978—*LMNO* (16mm, color, 9½ min.)
1979—*TZ* (16mm, color, 8½ min.)
1980—*Swiss Army Knife with Rats and Pigeons* (16mm,
    color, 6 min.)
1983—*Trial Balloons* (16mm, color, 6 min.)

All the major recent films of Robert Breer, an American who spent a crucial decade in Paris (1949-1959), are available in this country. But considering the fact that they're independent animation, and that Breer is a one-man industry and not a Hollywood studio, they might as well be on the moon. They clearly inhabit a ghetto even more confining than that of the "foreign film," because most critics lack an apparatus for dealing with them;

hence, they find it easier to pretend that the works don't exist. As uncontroversial as it might appear to be in most contexts, it is probably not irrelevant to note that when one of Breer's most recent films, the characteristically brilliant **Swiss Army Knife with Rats and Pigeons**, was screened at a New York Film Festival press show in 1982, it was rudely and audibly (if inexplicably) hissed. And candor compels me to admit that although—perhaps even because—Robert Breer impresses me as *the* key figure in avant-garde animation, my task in this book would be a good deal simpler if I too could pretend that he doesn't exist, for the challenge of his work is precisely its capacity to reveal the inadequacy of any criticism that seeks to describe it—the challenge that can often keep the very best new avant-garde work either ignored (the standard journalistic ploy) or dealt with only circumspectly (the standard academic ploy).

To represent my own dilemma, let me reach for a device which seems somewhat compatible with Breer's own sketchbook methods—namely, transcribing my own disconnected notes on a screening of **Fuji** which I attended almost three months ago. The point of this exercise is not to show off my tentative scratchings as if they were intrinsically interesting, but rather to demonstrate the impossibility of notating a film in progress whose very shape and experience are predicated on nonstop transformations. Every italicized passage in parentheses, I should stress, represents an afterthought and addition made to correct or amplify a previous impression, usually a few seconds later. Each of these revisions, moreover, had to be made while still other transformations were occurring, making it literally impossible to write anything without missing something. Hence even the generalities that are set down here, modest as they are, were arrived at only through strenuous, uphill effort:

Sound of hammer on anvil *(train sounds)*.
Live-action is visible through train windows.
Changing colors, overlapping sketches *(of scenes and figures with shifting colors)*.
Sections of black leader between each section.
Fuji changing from shifting perspective of train windows.
Pixillated red blob *(different and changing shapes)* appears over Mt. Fuji, like red circle on the Japanese flag.
Three-dimensional spinning shapes that undergo continual metamorphoses.
Then: single frames *(flash-frames)* of objects and shapes coincide with a slower train rhythm *(that gradually accelerates)*.
Then still shots of Fuji *(animated)* with the same steady train noises *(which persist longer than the visuals, over black leader at the end)*.

At the very best, some of this may correspond to a rough form of rhythmical notation, but conceptually it tends to establish itself in quicksand. In a context so slippery that the sound of a hammer on an anvil can quickly "become" that of a train, when a moving blob becomes too amorphous to remain even a blob, and something can't get slower without getting faster again—and even a supposedly still shot becomes animated—what anchor of discernible meaning, content or formal pattern can possibly be established by the hapless journalist, notebook poised in hand?

Rather than attempt to answer such a rhetorical question abstractly, let me turn to the confident and accurate description of the same film by Lucy Fischer, evidently with a little more time, space, and information on her hands, writing for a Museum of Modern Art film catalog supplement:

> *Fuji* is a work that represents a further stage in the development of Breer's use of the rotoscope technique. The film constitutes an abstract recreation of the experience of a train ride past Mt. Fuji in Japan. Breer characteristically mixes modes of representation. In addition to rotoscope imagery he utilizes live-action footage and simple line drawing, and manages to shift between them with a fluidity that blurs perceptual distinctions. In abstracting the original photographic material, Breer emphasizes its compositional form. Mt. Fuji is a giant triangle and the passing landscape a series of rectangles punctuated by the vertical lines of electricity poles. *Fuji* transforms the visual imagery of a train ride into an experience of kinetic geometry.

The first Breer film I had the opportunity to become familiar with was **A Man and His Dog Out for Air** (1957), which was shown with **Last Year at Marienbad** during the latter's initial New York run at Carnegie Hall Cinema in 1962. Returning to **Marienbad** again and again, I inadvertently wound up seeing the two-minute Breer short just as many times over that nine-month period. I certainly didn't mind seeing it so often, but it never would have occurred to me, at age 18, that there was any discernible formal relationship between the dazzling spatio-temporal displacements and transitions being effected by Alain Resnais and Alain Robbe-Grillet and the constantly shifting line drawing of Breer, which oscillates at regular intervals between representation and abstraction. (If memory serves, the drawing resolves itself aurally *and* visually into the title subject only in the film's closing seconds.)

As a plastic artist, of course, Breer was better equipped to deal with abstraction in much more literal (i.e., non-representational) a fashion than Resnais and Robbe-Grillet could have possibly attempted (being obliged to work, in their case, with actors, sets, costumes, dialogue, plot, and other narrative trappings). Unfortunately or not, most of the arts haven't developed in any true parallel fashion, and for someone like myself whose background had more to do with literature than with painting or sculpture, Resnais and Robbe-Grillet were much more obviously innovators than Breer, a mere fancy cartoonist in my eyes. That same year, however, Breer published a statement in *Film Culture* (No. 26) which begins, "*Hurray for a formless film, a non-literary, non-musical, picture film that doesn't tell a story, become an abstract dance, or deliver a message. A film with no escape from the pictures. A film where words are pictures or sounds and skip around the way that thoughts do. An experience itself like eating, looking, running, like an object, a tree, buildings, drips, and crashes. A film that instead of making sense is sense. Because it's a picture film it might combine reason and kite flying and torpedoes and golf. People can talk in it. It can turn on and turn blue and turn off.*"

According to Sandy Moore's helpful monograph on Breer (Film in the Cities, 1980), the filmmaker "explains that he feels numbers correspond to abstraction, letters to figuration" in the titles of his films. I haven't seen **Rubber Cement**, Breer's 1975 film, which reportedly uses color xeroxing techniques, but **77**, made two years later, does seem in retrospect like a film where abstraction predominates, despite a few recurring objects (e.g., a briefcase, a circular electric fan, a tricycle, a desk lamp), most of which rotate 360° before collapsing back into abstract lines and shapes. The extraordinary maelstrom of movement and detail found in all of Breer's recent work gives one the impression that each short generates enough visual material to stock a narrative feature, pressed into a time frame that's roughly only one-twelfth as long—making one realize how much substance there may be behind Greg Ford's argument that there are more short masterpieces than ones of feature length. (The purist, aesthetic preference for the six-to-ten-minute animated film over the live-action feature is analogous in certain respects to Edgar Allan Poe's defense of the story and poem that are brief enough to be consumed in a single sitting, over the more variable vicissitudes of the book-length work.)

What seems most prodigious about Breer's recent work, making it far more than a self-reflexive version of (say) Norman McLaren, is the absolute economy of gesture, the evocative power of the sketch—comparable, all things considered, to aspects of *Finnegans Wake* and the late work of Samuel Beckett—and the profusion of content within a relatively small area that this makes possible. In **77**, all the fluttering fragments of line and design that rush past the consciousness, like the increasing vibrancy and brightness of the colors, point to a festival of ideas that are appropriately offset by the simplest of noises on the soundtrack, like the sound of wind. These ideas inhabit a field that might be regarded as philosophical as well as perceptual; as Fred Camper writes (in program notes for Millennium in 1979), "The animated abstract shapes have a vivid, suggestive, almost anthropomorphic life: they have many of the qualities of representational objects, while the drawn objects occur with a kind of irrelevant (in a narrative sense) randomness that makes them less narrative, more purely moving forms, than similar objects have been in earlier Breer films." This shifting, ambiguous relationship between the abstract and concrete lends an additional quirky life to Breer's perpetual transformations.

LMNO—conceivably the best of all of Breer's films to date—has more to do with figuration, according to Breer's formulation regarding titles with letters and numbers. (As he put it in his interview with Jim Trainor in the Spring 1980 Upstart, "Letters are more literary and therefore more representational.") This becomes clear right away as the title letters are intercut with a flurry of fish swimming past the frame lines, which are made all the more literal through the associative chain established by a snippet of Schubert's Trout Quintet heard on the soundtrack, along with footsteps—which continue over a profusion of other shapes, colors, and objects, including the title letters again.

Indeed, as Elena Pinto Simon has pointed out in a review of the film (Millennium Film Journal, Nos. 4/5, Summer/Fall 1979), LMNO extends representation to the point of becoming "a play on the idea of narrativity— the film abounds in anecdotes and small stories that erupt, dance brilliantly and briefly before our eyes, and disappear only to evolve into another brief narrative passage." Consequently, certain objects that recur in the film—a biplane traversing the frame, a hammer, an aerosol spray can, a faucet, a milk carton—take on the status of narrative characters in certain respects (along with a jogger who keeps coming back, almost as regularly as the jogger in Resnais and Mercer's **Providence**—a literal character). And the dazzling sweep of Breer's rich, orchestral visual music here becomes expanded from mere shapes and objects into small dramatic situations and mini-plots: a croquet game, which follows the progress of a croquet ball through a wicket while it changes color, proceeds in separate shots from different angles like a classically edited découpage; a subsequent sequence of events recreates a pratfall out of silent slapstick with a banana peel, a knife, a milk carton, and a man who slips on the banana peel before splitting in half (which, incidentally, is what happens to the croquet ball at the conclusion of the previous sequence).

While it is usually standard operating procedure to oppose Breer's sort of animated work with Hollywood's, the fact remains that the rapid flood of images succeeding one another towards the beginning of LMNO—a snapshot of a building, a bathtub, a tennis racket, a boat, a plane, a target, several trees—is not all that different in effect from the surrealist array of successive objects which drop from the sky and crush a crazed alley cat in Tex Avery's **Bad Luck Blackie**. Both parody the accumulative processes of narrative itself; the fact that Avery does this in a context that veers more

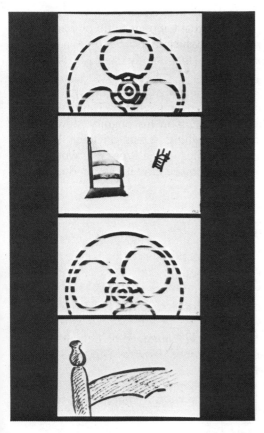

TZ

conventionally towards narrative makes the slam-bang approach seem only slightly more hyperbolic. No less Averylike, one should add, is the self-referentiality of a sequence involving a rotating 16mm movie projector and a filmstrip full of moving images that exposes the film process on several interlocking levels of paradox at once.

That Breer himself is highly conscious of working within an established tradition of animation is made clear in many of his statements. Sandy Moore's monograph, for instance, points out that "the little blue self-pitying figure" who "suffers several deaths" in **LMNO** is a reference to the figure of the policeman in Emile Cohl's films, while an abstract sequence towards the end of **TZ**, Breer's subsequent film, actually has its origins in the cartoon insects on bicycles in Windsor McKay's **Bug Vaudeville**. And yet the fleeting quality of all his inventions is such that one begins to see such references existing on the same plane as the photographed and drawn images of the Tappen Zee Bridge (visible from Breer's apartment in Nyack,

New York) at the beginning of **TZ**—material that exists mainly to be transformed, that is, banal, everyday material that happens to be on hand. (Within the same film, a phone becomes a car, which in turn becomes a cat in a car—an almost rebus-like progression that faintly suggests Saul Steinberg's conceptual conceits.)

The artisanal integrity of Breer's technique mainly involves drawing on thousands of unruled white 2" x 5" index cards over a lightbox. This makes it possible for him to include anything he wants in his ongoing stew— although how and when he includes something seems anything but arbitrary. Working out what formal necessity means in a Breer film would be a useful activity—like taking apart a clock to see how it ticks, and one would like to see it done.

MANUEL DE LANDA.
Born in Mexico City, 1952.

1975—*Shit* (Super-8, b&w, 30 min.)
    (unavailable)
1976—*Song of a Bitch* (Super-8, color, 30 min.)
    (unavailable)
1977—*The Itch Scratch Itch Cycle* (16mm, color, 8 min.)
1978—*Incontinence: A Diarrhetic Flow of Mismatches*
    (16mm, color, 18 min.)
1979—*Ismism* (Super-8, color, 8 min., silent)
1980—*Raw Nerves: A Lacanian Thriller* (16mm, color, 30
    min.)
1981—*Magic Mushroom Mountain Movie* (Super-8, color, 8
    min., silent)
1982—*Massive Annihilation of Fetuses* (former title: *Micro
    Drama*) (Super-8, color, 7 min.)
    Harmful or Fatal If Swallowed (Super-8 blown up to
    16mm, color & b&w, 12 min.) (incorporates footage
    from *Shit* and *Song of a Bitch;* original 8-minute,
    Super-8 version, also 1982, unavailable)

An anarchist who studies analytical philosophy, Manuel De Landa makes aggressive, wild movies that simultaneously leap all over the place and stand absolutely still. His punchy Dada-like stances have a certain built-in versatility insofar as they manage to defy The System while both embodying and benefiting from it. As a charming middle-class Mexican in his early thirties who works on computer animation for TV commercials, and who recalls growing up in the most Americanized suburb of Mexico City, De Landa brings a certain Latin camp wit to his European theoretical models, from Wittgenstein to Deleuze and Guattari. A touch of the happy charlatan is similarly brought to his glitter punk credentials that hark back to such diverse Spanish-speaking surrealists as Arrabal, Buñuel, Dali, and Jodorowsky—although, unlike most of his predecessors, De Landa prefers LSD and computers to the sacraments and anti-Christs of Catholicism in establishing the terms of his shock (and semi-mock) rebellion.

The spiritual son of Frank Zappa in more ways than one (who counts the early Mothers of Invention album *We're Only in It for the Money* as a seminal influence), De Landa is up to his old demonic tricks even in his earliest films. The scatological frenzies of the street scenes in **Harmful or Fatal If Swallowed**—a film that neatly encapsulates his seven-year ouevre to date by recycling material from his two earliest works, which he made just after he came to New York from Mexico as a filmmaking student at the School of Visual Arts—are as riddled with fancy optical transitions as **The Itch Scratch Itch Cycle**, a "study" for the much more ambitious look at bickering couples in **Incontinence: A Diarrhetic Flow of Mismatches**.

De Landa's own theorization and description of the last two films is worth quoting in detail:

> Part of the process of transplanting the narrative space of bourgeois theatre and novels to film involved learning to use off-screen space meaningfully. The main function assigned to it was the *homogenization* of the space of action. This is the subject matter of my first two films. In *The Itch Scratch Itch Cycle* the editing technique called "shot-countershot" is explored. This rhetorical figure is very important because it *sutures* the body of film. The film consists of five different versions of the same scene. The "real space" of a four-wall set is actually traversed by the camera in a figure-eight dolly movement around both characters in the first variation. The space thus produced is then subjected to extreme optical violence in each of the following variations which alter, one at a time, some of the principles on which the editing technique in question works (e.g., unity of point of view, unity of the scene depicted, relative plausibility of the angles of framing, etc.)
>
> My second film, *Incontinence*, explores other rhetorical uses of editing which homogenizes film's body, manipulating off-screen space. The use of matching techniques, particularly the so-called "sight-line matching," makes heterogeneous and distant spaces look contiguous and as part of one unitary space.
>
> In *Incontinence*, optical violence is done to matching techniques by forcing them to operate in extreme situations, but also to one of the main elements of their mechanism: the image of the body. Each one of the coordinates that guaran-

tee the unity of a character's body image is systematically altered. Thus the integrity of the image is destroyed by making it lose its size, change its relative position, vary in its permanence in time or space, switch identity, etc. This concerted destruction reaches its peak when one of the characters actually blows up.

In both **The Itch Scratch Itch Cycle** and **Incontinence**, the editing strategies parallel the depicted personal relationships every step of the way, and a mismatched cut is literally only the other side of a mismatched couple. (Hollis Frampton's 1971 **Critical Mass** almost certainly exerted a strong influence, as it did on Yvonne Rainer's latest features as well.) The willed perversity of the structures created defines the properties of De Landa's jazzy style. The tacky settings and ugly male-female quarrels of both films are redolent of the campy Mexican effect, which is also underlined by the deliberately strident acting. (Among other aspects tying these two films together, both actors in the former, Susan Schneider and Rory Gerstle, appear in the latter, and the soundtracks for both films make prominent use of swing violinists.)

Incontinence, directed, edited, and special effects by Manuel De Landa

The crazy wipes that oscillate back and forth between separate shots—as prominent here as they are in **Raw Nerves: A Lacanian Thriller** and **Harmful or Fatal If Swallowed**—deserve to be considered in some detail, for they all but constitute De Landa's signature. ("Before coming to New York," he has said, "I had developed a technique for hand-drawing wipes and other effects directly on the film, and I've used that technique in all my Super-8 and my 16mm films.") One of his most original, striking, and seemingly radical devices—which at once foregrounds and undermines the very notion of transition by bobbing back and forth between shots like a needle stuck on a record, or a rat trapped on an endless treadmill—it is, interestingly, one of the facets of his work that most suggests circularity and stasis, insofar as its violence against convention quickly becomes mechanistic, contained, and directionless, a sort of loop (or at best Möbius strip) of controlled aggression.

Incontinence was the first De Landa film I encountered—as part of the Whitney Biennial's first film program, in 1979—and in some respects it remains the most impressive, bursting with inventiveness and energy. (J. Hoberman and I each nominated the film for a *Soho News* award that year as the best film by an emerging filmmaker, although the prize went to **Grand Opera** by James Benning—who later complained about still being regarded by New Yorkers as "emerging.") In place of the preceding film's single couple are several couples whose quarrelsome dialogues are direct steals from the Edward Albee play *Who's Afraid of Virginia Woolf?* The film also appropriates as soundtrack more modest chunks of Zappa's *We're Only in It for the Money*—notably a brief composition consisting of overlapping peals of hysterical male laughter recorded at different speeds—and one might say that the spirit of Zappa is invoked throughout, particularly in the use of zany sound effects as interruptions to punctuate quick cuts.

Rarely have sound, image, and the spatio-temporal coordinates of narrative illusion been buffeted about as vigorously as in **Incontinence**, although the net effect of this violence may ultimately be no less circumscribed than the maelstrom inside a washing machine. Ordinary rules of spatio-temporal logic are repeatedly flaunted through the seesawing wipes and the uncanny transitions between scenes, so that, for instance, after an opening quarrel between a middle-aged couple, Rory Gerstle and Susan Schneider make their entrances by dropping successively from nowhere into a room. The latter significantly wears the same blue-green-purple blouse knotted at the midriff that she had on in **The Itch Scratch Itch Cycle**; the former turns up next in a restaurant scene, under characteristically chintzy lighting.

In the restaurant, the woman is called George, the man Martha, after Albee's couple; the image splits in two, and a modern jazz number with vibes accompanies a slow dolly up to the table, turning romantic Hollywood "expressiveness" into a kind of delirium that's as irrationally repetitive as the wipes between shots. Then the scene undergoes another dreamlike spatial transition when the camera follows a character into a park—without a clear division between interior and exterior—where another Albee dialogue ensues between "George" and "Martha" (this time embodied by two men) on a park bench. One of the men is a grotesquely misshapen figure with a switchblade who suggests the psychotic hipster in Albee's *The Zoo Story*, while a red light winks on and off in the background. Then Schneider drunkenly staggers past the men and the camera moves with her, leading back just as irrationally into a domestic interior—the same ghastly room with yellow walls, it seems, that we saw in **The Itch Scratch Itch Cycle**—where she keeps popping in and out of the image while objects like a chair and cushion jiggle about in a pixillated frenzy.

Around this time, a suitcase is lowered into the room by rope, and out of it, thanks to camera magic, leaps a veritable Wild Man from Borneo—the infamous Professor Mamboozoo, an important De Landa collaborator whom we will encounter again. Mamboozoo promptly lights a fuse inside his shirt, which sets off a long string of firecrackers and seems to blow him up—achieving the apotheosis described above by De Landa—after which he leaps about making diverse wild-man noises, mooning, etc. . . . Later, there's more or less more of the same, with Gerstle appearing in double exposure on a bike, and the percussively staccato, vamp-like intro to Zappa's tune "Flower Punk" used to punctuate some more zany wipe effects.

The same year, De Landa completed the Super-8 **Ismism** he had started and worked on much earlier (between 1975 and 1978), a silent film that documents his own street graffiti in New York. Made originally for a course in language and film taught in 1976 by P. Adams Sitney, De Landa conceived of **Ismism** having "the form of a manifesto against the orthopedic power of language." This manifesto essentially takes two forms: monstrously gaping lips, teeth, and eyes transplanted or transferred by De Landa from and to several commercial street posters, often framed in repeated zooms, and individual words painted on diverse street locations which are framed in static shots (like the individual letters in Hollis Frampton's **Zorns Lemma**) and then strung together by the editing to spell out secret messages—secret, that is, from the casual pedestrians who pass by the single words. These are messages, in short, that the filmmaker and film alone can articulate, in successive shots: "Unconscious/desire/expresses/itself/through/gaps/in/language,/slips/of/the/tongue. . ."; "Use/illegal/surfaces/for/your/art"; "Let/the/slang/of/your /desires/drive/ language/ crazy"—the latter of which could practically stand as De Landa's motto. (Shortly before his twenty-third birthday, while spreading his graffiti around town, he was arrested for both defacement of public property and possession of marihuana, but released a few hours later, reportedly after De Landa insisted he was Puerto Rican. Almost six years later, at a nearly

Ismism, graffiti produced and filmed by Manuel De Landa

complete retrospective of his work at Millennium Film Workshop, he distributed xeroxed copies of the police report as partial program notes.)

Raw Nerves: A Lacanian Thriller is De Landa's most ambitious film to date; along with **Incontinence**, it also represents his best work. Conceptually, it has been described by its maker as "my personal testament against psychoanalysis," and, in fact, though few unalerted spectators would be likely to guess it without prompting, a polemical rethinking of the Oedipus complex *does* lie behind the film's parodic *noir* structure and private-eye plot. But once again, we should give De Landa the microphone regarding the film's intentions:

> The film is an allegorical mise-en-scène of certain key concepts in contemporary psychoanalysis. It does not interpret or explicate those concepts; rather it enacts them. Whereas critical discourses often attempt to elucidate the structure of films by describing them in terms of some theoretical system, here the film operates as a dramatization of a part of one of those systems. The result is not didactic. It does not add to the understanding of those concepts. It displaces them from the context where they are operative and inserts them in a narrative space where they can be properly *misused.*

Raw Nerves is the noir version of the Oedipus complex. The private eye personifies the Ego who narrates the story of how he learned language. Only in the film, instead of the traditional image of the castrated mother which is supposed to mediate the encounter with the Signifier (the Law), we have a secret message written on a public bathroom wall. Our hero is there, just taking a shit, when he suddenly sees it—he doesn't know what it means but he knows he knows too much. So instead of having a private encounter with language in the coziness of the family, here it is the secret message which inserts the subject directly into a social project which preexists him and swallows him up without mercy.

Of course, throughout the movie the naive Ego believes that he is telling us his story, that his speech merely expresses his intentions to communicate.

He will find at the end that the "secret meaning" was precisely that he has never spoken but that he was spoken by a strange object, decentered with respect to itself, which kills him after revealing him its truth.

Desire is made to circulate through six series of parallel actions which function mainly metonymically, since the metaphorical point of convergence of the series, the point at which meaning arises, is indefinitely delayed.

Raw Nerves

It is interesting to find the secret messages of **Ismism** intersecting here with a (symbolic) infant's first encounter with language. (An obsession with "codes" of all kinds runs through his work.) And De Landa's insistence on the public over the private does indeed "interpret" and "explicate" certain psychoanalytical concepts, despite De Landa's disclaimer (which characteristically allows him to work both sides of the street at once—that is, work both with and without the Lacanian paradigm). As De Landa said to me by way of further elaboration: "It's just the situation of the baby when he sees a little girl or his mother walking around naked, and is going to try to deny and explain or rationalize the image of castration. Displacing the primal Oedipal scene from a private, middle-class warm space to a public, cold, wet public bathroom is a way of saying that your encounter with the symbolic, your access to language, is never a private little cozy event. Not even if you say first the family, then society—not even that. Your father is always somebody else's boss and servant—there's always the social field present."

On a visceral level, **Raw Nerves** is almost as much of an assault as **Incontinence**, starting with the lurid, almost Day-Glo pinks, yellows, and slimey greens of the opening images, the brassy noirish music, and the customary abrasive wipes between alternating shots, which ultimately dissolve the distinctions between past, present, future, and subjunctive (as in **Last Year at Marienbad**) by placing everything on the same dubious, campy, and melodramatic level. A flashback via a snazzy spiral-shaped wipe (the first of many such cookie-cutter effects) leads to an overhead shot of the hero reading the coded message—obscene-looking hieroglyphics— on a roll of toilet paper in front of him, which alternates with a frontal view of the same "primal scene." ("The main point of the movie," De Landa told me, "is that I'm defining the first signifier as the final scribble of a man who has just taken his last shit in this world.") All this is set in hallucinogenic relief by greenish lighting and pink graffiti.

The ensuing paranoid plot owes a lot to both **Kiss Me Deadly** and the Mickey Spillane novel it's based on (which furnishes part of the dialogue— although the script is credited to Joan Braderman, Paul Arthur, and De Landa, among others), with iconographic (and graphic) lifts from Forties and Fifties noir as well: shadowy grill patterns on walls, colors like the inside of a fruity Fifties jukebox. In a surprise ending, the off-screen narrating voice of the hero proves to belong to a woman, who declares, "Never trust a first person pronoun" before shooting him dead.

Shot at the School of Visual Arts (like **The Itch Scratch Itch Cycle** and much of **Incontinence**), De Landa's private eye saga is enhanced by its technical polish, ascribable in part to the excellence of Bill Brand's optical printing. That one of De Landa's ambitions is to crack Hollywood can easily be deduced from the film—not only because of its technique, but also because of the *noir* trappings, the most conventional aspect of the film. (The confrontation of Freud with Sherlock Holmes, imagined in mainstream terms in **The 7½% Solution** and in arthouse terms in **Bad Timing**, is also one of *the* most popular idioms to hit the American avant-garde and independent film in the Seventies—as trendy as political/avant-garde films about vampires were in the Sixties, especially in Europe and Latin America. By the early Eighties, the confluence of psychoanalysis and detection can be said to have formed a genre in its own right, thereby shrewdly tempering De Landa's originality with something more familiar and less threatening to resonate against.)

1981 saw the completion of only one De Landa film—the uncharacteristic, quasi-ethnographic **Magic Mushroom Mountain Movie**, an eight-minute, Super-8 digest of De Landa's annual visits to a peyote cult family in Huautla, "a tiny little town in the middle of La Sierra Mazateca in Mexico." This color, sound film lodges itself in the memory as a kind of documentary impressionism, meditative and suggestive in its hallucinatory moods rather than hyperventilated in the usual De Landa manner.

On April 30 of the same year, De Landa put on a notorious live performance at The Kitchen in lower Manhattan which deserves some mention here. Appearing in a program held under the auspices of *Semiotext(e)* magazine, in conjunction with a recent issue on polysexuality, De Landa hired Professor Mamboozoo to join him and contribute his own forms of dada assault. After lying to the show's organizers (De Landa said he would appear with paper-maché sex organs), the two concocted a sort of voodoo ceremony under Mamboozoo's guidance that involved a double-barrel shotgun loaded with blanks, the freshly decapitated heads of a cow and pig (purchased in a New Jersey slaughterhouse), and large quantities of snakes, frogs, mice, and crickets in boxes that were released in (or thrown at) the audience after the shotgun was fired.

"Now that's all that was in the script," De Landa recalls. "But of course Professor Mamboozoo had to do something that would shock me, his assistant, too. So at this point I had the snakes and frogs, and he had the mice. They started to crawl on him and bite him—we had to give him some rabies shots afterwards—so he starts biting back, and biting their heads off." By this time, needless to say, most of the audience had fled the premises. "It *is* fascism in a way," De Landa admits now of the performance, "in the sense that you're attacking people. Someone could have died that night." Despite this (once again) characteristic disclaimer, De Landa got all the publicity and notoriety he wanted from the event, which continues to fuel his legend.

The seven-minute **Massive Annihilation of Fetuses**—originally entitled **Micro Drama**, more recently announced as the first part of The Jerry Falwell Series (with a title deriving from Falwell)—is almost as grungy in a way, and easily just as apocalyptic. "This film is my tribute to the real master race that will soon inherit the planet," De Landa has explained. "Cock-roaches have not only invaded the flip side of my house (i.e., the back of my kitchen, the other side of my walls, etc.) but they have also taken over some areas of my unconscious.... Since I started the film the structure of my nightmares has changed, almost as if I had violated their laws and they were getting ready for revenge."

Sounds of eerie yells and screams on the soundtrack (electronically developed out of De Landa and Joan Braderman's voices) accompany shots of cockroaches in close-up as well as in long shot, skittering about. Eventually, afflictions of an almost biblical nature are visited upon them by an off-screen De Landa playing God (revealing that his "tribute" is actually a form of revenge in advance for a species that, unlike mankind, might survive a nuclear holocaust): a slab of striped toothpaste falls on one, a fork prong and a screw successively crush two more; others are drowned in honey, sliced by a razor, and lit by a match.

Harmful or Fatal If Swallowed—reportedly screened to loud boos at the New York Film Festival, where it was shown with the more hospitably received **Vortex** (by Beth B and Scott B)—is in a way just as conventional a film, a kind of compendium of scatological street humor that has been a staple of the more commercial New York independents (from Robert Downey to John Waters) for at least two decades. With its **Ballet Méchanique** tropes (e.g., two businessmen walking forward and backward to a Strauss waltz), customary zany wipes, defecating dogs, fish-eye-lens-views of pedestrians, electronic bleeps and heavy percussion on the soundtrack, edited alternations between consumptions of hot dogs and excretions of dog turds, it encapsulates an entire history of flaky adolescent city humor with a great deal of facility, but much less inventiveness than one would be apt to find in any of De Landa's other films. Intercutting several pedestrians looking in a shop window with snippets of hardcore porn footage is one of the more hackneyed devices, but there are others just as conventional.

According to De Landa, there is an "extra-strength Tylenol version" of the film, slightly longer and seldom shown, which presents Professor Mamboozoo improvising a racist and sexist rap—a sequence that a member of the New York Film Festival's selection committee persuaded him to cut from the film before it was shown publicly, in the fear that it would wind up alienating everyone (as it was no doubt meant to do). The paradox in the act of self-censorship—which De Landa himself seems less than perturbed about—seems entirely fitting, in a way, for a brilliant and talented filmmaker with an asocial image to sell and a highly social way of putting it across, a theorist who could write a careful academic paper about "Wittgenstein at the Movies" at the same time that he encourages us all to dream of destruction. Working both sides of the traffic with a gleam in his eye, De Landa knows how to play it hard and easy with alternating pedals, carrying us everywhere and nowhere at once in an awful hurry.

SARA MILLER DRIVER.
Born in New York, 1955.

1979—*Dream Gone Bad* (16mm, b&w, 2 min., silent)
(unavailable)
1980—*Death in Hoboken* (16mm, b&w, 3 min.)
(unavailable)
Sir Orpheo (16mm, b&w, 18 min.) (unavailable)
1982—*You Are Not I* (16mm, b&w, 50 min.)

If Sara Driver is the youngest filmmaker included in this survey, **You Are Not I** does not convey that impression. In this respect, it represents a quantum leap from a student exercise like **Death in Hoboken**, which is the only previous film by Driver that she's been willing to show me.

A sketchy thriller chase ending in a murder, staged in and around the decrepit atmospherics of Hoboken's Erie-Lackawanna Railway Terminal, the earlier effort, shot in high-contrast photography, resembles an arty fragment of something like Orson Welles's **The Trial**, or perhaps closer to the mark, Arthur Penn's **Mickey One**. The only original touch in the film is the use on the soundtrack of a 1950s jazz album featuring added sound effects—a record whose odd percussive effects create a certain zone of narrative ambiguity about the possible proximity of the pursuing to the pursued inside the station. It's an interesting uncertainty, because given the film's stylistic aggressiveness and use of subjectivity (the viewpoint is basically that of the man being followed), there's no objective way of distinguishing narrative fact (the off-screen, approaching heavy) from expressive commentary (the threat or possibility of same). Significantly, it's the same sort of ambiguity in relation to the heroine's schizophrenia in **You Are Not I** that structures our entire reading of the later film.

Closely adapted from a Paul Bowles short story written in the late 1940s, Driver's featurette is adequately synopsized by the filmmaker herself in a publicity handout:

> . . . It is the story of a young woman, Ethel, who escapes from a mental hospital during the chaos of a nearby multiple-car accident. She is mistaken for a shock victim by a rescue volunteer who finds her trying to place a stone in a dead woman's mouth. The volunteer drives her to her sister's house. The sister is confused and angered by the sudden arrival of the psychotic Ethel. Not wishing to be alone in the house with her, the sister brings two neighbor women over. Finally the sister calls the hospital and finds out that Ethel "wasn't released at all but somehow got out." They nervously await the attendants from the hospital while Ethel, refusing to

speak, formulates a plan to stay in the house. The women are
terrified of her and are relieved when the attendants arrive.
As Ethel is being ushered out by the men, she takes one of the
stones out of her pocket and thrusts it into her sister's mouth.
The screen goes black. As it clears, the sister is being taken
away while Ethel remains in the house: "For a moment I
could not see very clearly, but even during that moment I saw
myself sitting on the sofa. As my vision cleared I saw that the
men were holding my sister's arms and she was putting up a
terrific struggle. The strange thing, now that I think about it,
was that no one realized she was not I."

Suzanne Fletcher as Ethel
in the film *You Are Not I*

    Given the overall look of the film, and the meticulously layered
construction of the sounds and images alike, it isn't surprising that Jean-
Marie Straub became an enthusiastic partisan of this film after seeing it at
the Rotterdam Film Festival in early 1982 ("I liked your film ten times better
than Roger Corman's Edgar Allan Poe movies," he told Driver). As in many
of the heroic and mock-heroic compositions of Straub and Huillet, bodies
are juxtaposed against landscapes (a row of sheet-covered corpses beside a
road actually evokes **Machorka-Muff** and **Not Reconciled** in its eerie
beauty—although the arrival of a couple of rescue vans in the same shot
suggests Benning), off-screen voices against on-screen fictions, surrealist

fantasies of the unbridled ego against documentary representations of its confinement, and momentary subjective flashes against longer and broader meditations (e.g., the powerful movement from still shots of two old women pressed against a wire fence to a *plan-séquence* that starts with Ethel (Suzanne Fletcher) walking past them—like a quick journey from Marker's **La Jetèe** to Antonioni's **La Notte**). The divided self—the art and craft of schizophrenia—thus becomes the film's method as well as its subject, and the fierce battle of wills, world-views, and intelligences between the two sisters dictates the formal separations in Driver's stark approach.

In effect, **You Are Not I** begins more or less the way **Psycho** ends— with a schizophrenic in close-up remaining absolutely still while explaining everything off-screen. That the shot of Fletcher, unlike the shot of Anthony Perkins in **Psycho**, is actually a still creates an effect of ambiguity that the

Melody Schneider as Sister in
the film *You Are Not I*

remainder of the film builds upon: because of our expectation of movement, we may initially read the still as a moment recorded on film rather than a split-second—a moment during which Fletcher is making herself as motionless as possible. In comparable fashion, the periodic uses of blackouts in the film and the synthesizer effects and music (by Phil Kline) foreground the properties of light and sound as willful constructions, highlighting the manner in which Ethel *as* a schizophrenic becomes the master of her fate by conjuring up the world around her.

Insofar as it uses narrative ambiguity and foregrounds some of its formal elements, **You Are Not I** demands a certain amount of collaborative work from the spectator. At the same time, it adopts the method of a Poe story, which requires the virtual submission of the reader/spectator to the will and power of the narrative voice. Nevertheless, the film implies that between the sisters we ultimately have to take sides—and it goes to great pains not to make that choice an easy one. The picture of domestic normality conveyed through Ethel's sister and her neighbors is almost as terrifying as the family dinner in David Lynch's **Eraserhead**, but the complacency of Edith is not very easy to accept, either. Driver told me that she saw the conflict between the sisters as basically territorial, and directed the actresses accordingly. (She asked Melody Schneider, who played Sister—and who, incidentally, was only 22 when the film was shot, although the character seems almost twice as old—to bring things of her own to the set that were precious to her, in order to make her feel more territorial towards the house. Driver also apparently rehearsed her off-screen daily routines with her so that Ethel's arrival would be felt more as a disruption.)

The film was shot by Jim Jarmusch, on whose **Permanent Vacation** and the more recent **Stranger in Paradise** Driver served as production manager. Otherwise, her background in film, apart from New York University's graduate film school (where she made **You Are Not I** on a $14,000 budget, thanks mostly to scholarship grants), is not very extensive. In college, her main interests were theater and archeology; her junior year was spent at the American School of Classical Studies in Athens, and during her senior year—at Randolph Macon Women's College, in Virginia—she wrote and directed a play about Zelda Fitzgerald called *"What the hell"–Zelda Sayre*. This may help to account for the surprising fact that the only conscious filmic influence exerted on Driver when she made **You Are Not I** was Cassavetes's **A Woman under the Influence**. ("I think it's because of the study of timing between people in that film," she told me. "It's not stylistic, it's just a gut emotional reaction—and wanting to involve an audience that much.") More recently, she cites as the two films that have most impressed her Dreyer's **La Passion de Jeanne d'Arc** and Tarkovsky's **The Stalker**, both of which might be regarded as archetypes of the European art film. Whether or not that tradition has a viable future in this country, Driver is clearly a filmmaker to watch; it'll merely be our bad fortune if we have to cross the Atlantic in order to see her future work.

...the argument thus far

Gidal and Mekas represent problematical poles in this book because my responses to their work are sharply divided. I respect and admire Gidal's work for its theoretical dimension and ethical purity more than I do for its filmic practice and the experiences that this makes possible and available, whereas I admire Mekas for his filmmaking practice and feel much more dubious about his theoretical/political positions. In each case, I strongly identify with half of what the filmmaker does and feel somewhat out of sorts with the other half. This is one reason why I have placed my conversations with these filmmakers and writers at opposite ends of this book, so that hopefully something analogous to an electrical/magnetic field might be set up between them, charging all the intervening chapters with this troubling and unresolved dialectic.

 PETER GIDAL.
Born 1946.

1967—*Room (Double Take)* (16mm, b&w, 10 min.)
1968—*Key* (16mm, b&w, 10 min.)
    Loop (16mm, b&w, 10 min.)
1969—*Hall* (16mm, b&w, 10 min.)
    Clouds (16mm, b&w, 10 min.)
    Heads (16mm, b&w, 35 min., silent)
1970—*Takes* (16mm, b&w, 5 min.)
    Secret (16mm, b&w, 25 min.)
    Portrait (Subject/Object) (16mm, b&w, 10 min.)
1971—*8mm Film Notes on 16mm* (16mm, color, 40 min., silent)
    Focus (16mm, b&w, 7 min.)
    Bedroom (16mm, color, 30 min.)
1972—*Movie No. 1* (16mm, color, 5 min.)
    Upside Down Feature (16mm, b&w & color, 76 min.)
    Movie No. 2 (16mm, color, 5 min.)

1973—*Room Film 1973* (16mm, color, 55 min. [at 18 fps],
    silent)
Photo/Graph/Film (16mm, b&w, 5 min., silent)
1974—*Film Print* (16mm, color, 40 min., silent)
C/O/N/S/T/R/U/C/T (16mm, color, 35 min., silent)
1975—*Condition of Illusion* (16mm, color, 35 min., silent)
1977—*Kopenhagen/1930* (16mm, b&w, 40 min., silent)
Silent Partner (16mm, color, 35 min.)
1978—*4th Wall* (16mm, color, 40 min., silent)
Epilogue (16mm, color, 8 min., silent)
Untitled (16mm, color, 8 min., silent)
1980—*Action at a Distance* (16mm, color, 30 min.)
1983—*Close Up* (16mm, color, 65 min.)

My first encounter with Peter Gidal's work was as a staff member of the
Editorial Department at the British Film Institute in the mid-Seventies. David
Wilson, general editor of a series of softbound BFI books, asked for my
opinion about a submission edited by Gidal and entitled *Structural Film
Anthology*. The problem was that neither Wilson nor any member of his
committee had ever seen a structural film, so they wanted to know whether
I thought it was a legitimate subject for a critical collection. I said that it was,
but certain doubts still persisted in the committee about the project—
particularly ones involving Gidal's tortured prose in his long, polemical
introductory essay, "Theory and Definition of Structural/Materialist Film." I
was offered the job of copyediting the book, with the following proviso: the
BFI would publish *Structural Film Anthology* if I could turn it (and especially
Gidal's essay) into comprehensible English. I accepted, and thus embarked
with Gidal on a series of lengthy editorial sessions that eventually led,
among other things, to the publication of the anthology in 1976.

It was somewhat later that I encountered my first Gidal film, **Room Film
1973**, at the London Filmmakers Co-op, as part of a lengthy program
involving several films as well as discussion from Gidal, Malcolm Le Grice,
and others; and the overall experience, though interesting to me, seemed
decidedly anticlimactic to my encounters with Gidal's theory. Since then,
I've seen the film again, quite recently, and am inclined to agree with Gidal
and many of his followers that it is probably his best and strongest film to
date. At the same time, candor compels me to admit that Gidal's tortuous
articulations of film syntax are even harder for me to handle as a pure
consumer than the fractured articulations of verbal syntax in his writing.
That this dual difficulty is central to his value and importance as a
filmmaker *and* theorist is clear enough to me, but I realize that it also
effectively eliminates an audience and readership bent only on "consuming" structural film—making him a rare bird indeed. Dealing with Gidal's
work on any level entails a struggle, and the benefits to be gained from this

struggle have more to do with an overall political process than a particular destination. By virtue of his radicalism—which rejects narrative in film as politically and aesthetically regressive—Gidal clarifies *and* criticizes every other filmic practice. Naturally enough, this makes a lot of people (filmmakers, theorists, spectators, readers) extremely nervous—a valuable contribution if one takes the idea of an avant-garde or front line seriously, and a total pain in the ass if one has adopted the more socially expedient policy of pursuing a comfortable, non-threatening avant-garde orthodoxy designed to protect the powerful.

To say, then, that there is no slickness (or "production values") in Gidal's films or writing would be putting it mildly. The same could be said of Brakhage, of course, but the political and ideological underpinnings of Gidal's practice make him the anti-Brakhage *par excellence*. If both film-makers can be linked to Action painting, Gidal veers noticeably from that romantic tradition by seeking to make his practice irrelevant to autobiography. As Malcolm Le Grice and others have pointed out, the romantic individualism of the New American Cinema, by turning the filmmaker into a text, merely relocated many of the central aspects of dominant narrative filmmaking and its forms of identification on a different plane. An important part of Gidal's project is to oppose that form of dominance and continuation. In some of his films, autobiographical expectations are solicited and then either confused or frustrated. For instance, a good many public discussions of **Room Film 1973** assume that the room filmed is Gidal's; this isn't the case, but Gidal himself does not usually address that issue. Also, most people believe that a prominent blurred image in his **4th Wall** (1978) is a view in a mirror of Gidal filming himself, while it is actually a color photograph of someone looking at something other than a camera!

Two critical texts are central in clarifying the principle of uncertainty underlying Gidal's methods. One, by Deke Dusinberre ("Consistent Oxymoron: Peter Gidal's Theoretical Strategy," in the Summer 1977 *Screen*), concentrates on the writing; the other, by Malcolm Le Grice (in his "Some Introductory Thoughts on Gidal's Films and Theory," written to introduce a BFI mimeographed pamphlet, *Independent Cinema Documentation, File No. 1: Peter Gidal,* issued in 1979), concentrates on the filmmaking. By juxtaposing passages from each of these essays, I hope that some of their implicit points of contact will become evident:

> *Deke Dusinberre:* . . . The overall impression is not one of linear argument, but one of fragmented comment. That comment is further fragmented by an oxymoronic vocabulary and contradictory phrase structure. [. . .]
>
> [. . .] Reiteration/repetition is a ploy which Gidal consistently uses to push the reader back off a complacent acceptance of the words themselves. Hence "Jacques Derrida has

clearly clarified what in fact is at stake in a work, in the procedure of constituting a work." Not only is there the obviously ironic stress on "clearly clarified" (Derrida! Gidal!!) but also the calculated redundancy of "procedure" and "constituting": verbs, participles, nouns of "coming into being" play an important roll in any Gidal text. One can practically feel the following sentence being dragged into being, in spurts and starts: "To begin with, radical art, an art of radical form, deals with the manipulation of materials made conscious, and with the inexpressible, the unsayable, ie, not with content, as it is understood as distinguishable and primary, positing a transparent technique." By the end of the sentence, the reader has lost a sense of the clause/phrase relationships—they all seem more or less independent. That Gidal perceives practice and theory as inextricably related is evident in that in theoretical writing—as well as film practice—he eschews a "transparent technique" to the extent of adopting an almost opaque style.

[. . .] The strategy Gidal shares with Beckett—an attack on the complacent acquisition of meaning by collapsing an apparently unified speaking subject into the fragmented voice of contradiction—has become a recognizable and assimilable fictive device over the last quarter of a century. However, to apply the same strategy to theoretical writing— where the speaking subject is still assumed to be coherent, unified, and identical with a real and specific author— currently strikes us as outrageous.[. . .]

Malcolm Le Grice: Gidal's camera movements, particularly in *Bedroom* (1971), *Room Film 1973, Condition of Illusion* (1975), and *4th Wall* (1978), however much he would want it otherwise (or however much he would like it played down critically) are at one level predicated on the sensual lure and the visual pleasure which he derives from the objects looked at (already an aware sublimation of a sexual object onto another object even before the film is shot). The camera slowly moves over the beautifully patterned bedspread (or rug, which Gidal chooses because he already finds it visually pleasurable), and even where it encounters objects with no intrinsic implications of beauty, their separation (framing) from their visual and, more important, utility, contexts transforms them into "to-be-looked-at-objects." This is one level of the inscriptions of desire in the objects, their images and in the camera's movements. But, at the same time as Gidal is lured by the objects he sees, by the images they form in the viewfinder, by the movement of the image in the frame he also resists this lure—refuses to give greater attention to an object which for some reason appeals more, perhaps refusing to indicate a response (the slight refusal may even be inscribed in a momentary hesitation on, then acceleration from, the object), or moves away purposefully, or lets the camera seemingly drift down and away. Both the lure and his resistance are inscribed minutely in the camera movement and thereby recorded as a trace in the photo-sensitivity of the film. This set of moment to moment decisions and the sensibilities on which they are based are made even more complex by a learned prediction about their likely effect (their probable transformation or re-ordering) when they are projected and confronted by a spectator. In this consideration for the image, as it is to be in its utilization by the spectator, might be found some of the reasons for the various resistances inscribed with the visual lure, into the image. "Why," Gidal might be asking of himself through the movement of the camera, "should the spectator of this film be unresisting subject to the exercise of my visual pleasures and sublimations?" He is not only resisting his own lure (resisting in a way which transforms rather than negates or ignores) but he also inscribes the possibility of resistance of the spectator. In this way, in a sense, as filmmaker, he becomes the spectator's representative—linking his attractions, attachments and resistances to theirs.

As interesting as both of the above texts are in rationalizing Gidal's methods, they need to be countered dialectically by at least a couple of skeptical observations: (1) Dusinberre's defense implicitly makes almost anything Gidal could possibly write permissible from a high art perspective (e.g., incoherence is okay, even desirable, because it "collapses the speaking subject"); (2) Le Grice's detailed rationale/explanation for Gidal's (at times) seemingly random camera movements creates an anything-goes climate of acceptance whereby scopophilia (the pleasure of gazing) or resistance to scopophilia can account for just about any random camera movement that Gidal cares (or happens) to make. At the same time, it would be wrong to place too much of an equivalence between Dusinberre's argument and Le Grice's, especially insofar as camera movements can't be taken as the only signifying practice of Gidal's films. On the contrary, the degree to which Gidal's films are determined and inscribed by many successive processes—lighting, focusing, camera movement, editing, looping, printing, etc.—implies the *absence* or *cancellation* of a unified speaking subject in the final film rather than the *collapse* that Dusinberre finds in the prose.

A further distinction should be made between the production and the reception of an effect (and/or meaning) in Gidal's film work. As mentioned above, it is very easy to misread his films, particularly in relation to an autobiographical context; and insofar as one can subsequently be made aware of one's own misreadings, the films can be very useful in revealing one's own ideological suppositions—much as Leslie Thornton's **Adynata** can perform this mirror-like function in relation to the (Western) spectator's (Western) fantasies about the Orient. In other words, because the American artworld context that helped to produce Gidal's methods is closely tied to notions of (male) autobiography via Action painting, it stands to reason that autobiographical readings of Gidal's films would be frequent, whatever Gidal's efforts to expel them.

But Gidal's project is an avowedly negative one that involves cancelling or preventing meanings as much as (or even more than) producing them. (If one walks away from any prolonged exposure to his films with *any* sort of certainty, this is the certainty that one *doesn't* know what's happening in them.) And while it isn't difficult to see this project in *some* relation to both Andy Warhol and Samuel Beckett—the two contemporary artists whose theory and practice Gidal has considered exemplary in relation to his own—it is a good deal harder to associate Gidal's work with theirs as closely as he would presumably like one to, for the enormous attractiveness of these major figures is due to that technical mastery and seduction they have *as artists* which make their forms of denial and absence both possible and interesting. Gidal, more ostensibly a theorist and less ostensibly an artist than his models, has to deal with the inevitable breach that arises between his theory and his practice. (In passing, one should note both Gidal's 1971 book on Warhol—the first written in any language—published by Dutton, and his forthcoming study of monologue and gesture in the work of Beckett, which Macmillan in England plans to publish.)

A *negative project:* "Everything is the effect of a productive labor process," Gidal told me in late 1980 when I interviewed him for *Soho News* (*see* "Cinema at a Distance," January 14, 1981), "even every cultural moment. And if the film and the process of the film are produced in a materialist as opposed to an idealist manner—both in the way it situates the viewer and in its own textual operation, in the crude material sense the way it's structured—then you can produce everything as effect, even emptying out, the fact that nothing adheres." In his theoretical rejection of every form and vestige of narrative cinema as ideologically oppressive, Gidal posits the same negativity with something like the same crudeness of effect; it is a position whereby a Carl Dreyer film becomes only a slightly better version of, say, *All in the Family.*

"I'm quite happy to admit that I am not interested in [Michael] Snow's work for 'the beauty,'" Gidal wrote in a polemical exchange with Snow about the latter's **Back and Forth**, included in *Structural Film Anthology*. "To annihilate beauty is not some kind of metaphysical statement that beauty shouldn't exist in the world," Gidal explained to me in our 1980 interview when I cited this remark. "Even to mention that would be an impossible negation, because beauty exists in the same way that representation exists. But it exists in certain codes and manifestations and positions for certain people as *their* positions. So to say I'm not concerned with beauty—that's because (A) from a puritanical point of view it's very easy to create beauty; (B) if you have a traditionally high-art education, and if you come out of a kind of history—out of painting, sculpture, theater, movies, and all that— then as far as I'm concerned it's the least interesting, least productive aspect of a practice, to create something someone else might say is beautiful.

"The worst part is, it's meaningless in the bad sense. It's the seductive element, which is separate from everything else which work is doing. It's the element which represses. In fact, the operations that exist between you and a film, or a film's operation on and through you as a viewer, or as the imaginary inhabitant of a space in a film or a narrative. Whatever it is, it's the beauty which seduces and represses at the same time. So it's the politically reactionary element in beauty I was referring to," Gidal concluded, adding, "A lot of good work *is* beautiful."

"Would it be correct, then, to call you a minimalist?" I asked him.

"I'm a purist in the sense that the work has to do with very few elements," Gidal conceded. "Very little is dealt with. I don't have a broad range at all. I went through the whole Sixties without going to double-screen, triple-screen, stereo—none of that stuff. I have enough problems dealing with single-screen. A very minimal area of concern—if that's what you mean, yeah, hopefully [the films] are rigorous and rigid almost, in a very small area." Bearing this in mind, it is worth noting the extremely high incidence of silent films in Gidal's filmography, especially after **Room Film 1973**. With the exceptions of only the 1977 **Silent Partner** (which I haven't seen) and the 1980 **Action at a Distance** (which I have), all his mature work seems as predicated on silence as Brakhage's.

Turning, finally, to the films of Gidal that I've seen, I think it's quite possible to discriminate between the best of these (**Room Film 1973, Kopenhagen/1930, 4th Wall**) and the worst (**C/O/N/S/T/R/U/C/T, Action at a Distance**). The first three strike me as superior to the latter two simply because they set up certain possibilities of fascination (hypnotic or otherwise) before disrupting or subverting these possibilities. The latter two films, by failing to engage with me on that level, place me in a position where I can't do anything useful with them at all—my only *sustained* activity is to wait for them to be over. To my mind, both **C/O/N/S/T/R/U/C/T** and **Action at a Distance** err by moving in a literary direction without sufficient filmic interest to justify this emphasis. The former presents a man putting up (i.e., "constructing") a window (as seen through another window in an opposite building) in several overlapping double-exposures. The latter presents three basically static hand-held shots—of a corner of a room, a rumpled bed, and a closed book lying on a flat surface—successively; this is accompanied by a brief poetic text that is repeated several times off-screen by a woman's voice. (A few excerpts: "Points . . . reference points . . . ports of call . . ." "I cried, I died, and that is the point. I sighed, he died, and that is the reference point. . ." "History builds character and experience builds personality. . ." In the closing credits—which are printed and scrawled, respectively—one learns that the text was written by Vivian Zarvis and read by Barbara Daly.)

"He's backed himself into a corner," Yvonne Rainer remarked to me jokingly during the interminable first shot (a corner) of **Action at a Distance**, and it's hard not to agree. Literary metaphors about "windows" and "construction" seem to constitute one such corner in **C/O/N/S/T/R/U/C/T**, while the limited materials of **Action**—including the off-screen text, which doesn't gain in interest, no matter how many times one hears it—represent a comparable impasse. Even a self-acknowledged minimalist position has its limits before what Gidal calls "[meaninglessness] in the bad sense" takes over, leaving only a void that one is interested neither in filling nor in acknowledging. Voids of this kind are not exactly scarce in Gidal's work; indeed, it would not be too great an exaggeration to say that even some of his best films are devoid of the kind of intrinsic interest that keeps even a lot of bad work intermittently interesting because of its fugitive attraction as "content." Gidal's films generally are so implacably what they are without letting themselves be anything else that they often seem to be on the verge of evaporating.

A significant exception—and one of the rare instances in Gidal's work where the interest of the "content" effectively changes some of the ground rules in his filmmaking—is **Kopenhagen/1930**. The fact that its material is a photo album of black-and-white pictures taken by Gidal's uncle—George Gidal, a professional photographer, on a vacation in Denmark in 1930— already raises issues of autobiography and history that are much more evident than usual in (Peter) Gidal's work. At the same time, the photographs themselves are sufficiently interesting from several standpoints to make the film's own methods of exploring them—via particular framings, cuts, and camera movements—stronger in their capacity to engage interest and sustained attention.

Gidal has described how what interested him about his uncle's album was the sequential order of many of the photos, which reminded him of sections of Eisenstein's **Strike** as well as certain Dziga Vertov films. The album contained between 250 and 300 pictures, out of which (Peter) Gidal selected between a fourth and a fifth and enlarged them for use in the film (which mainly restricts its focus to details within the photos, and only rarely proceeds beyond their frames and the confines of the album itself; only once, if memory serves, does one see the album as a discrete object, resting against a wall). One sees a great deal of Copenhagen and environs in these shots—all of it in exteriors usually involving crowds: one sees marching soldiers, lots of people with cameras (recalling Vertov's **The Man with a Movie Camera**), a sailboat, a drawbridge, street booths, people drinking coffee, and an oddly unexplained shot of a crowd of people in a park, most of whom are shielding their faces with their hands (perhaps from a solar eclipse). On two occasions, (Peter) Gidal* cuts abruptly to contemporary London footage of his own—a church spire in one case, a street bicyclist in another.

A non-pastoral meditative film, **Kopenhagen/1930** isn't quite as relaxing as **Room Film 1973**, with the latter's short arabesques of withdrawal, probing, drift, and retreat imposing itself as a kind of quirky massage on the eyes and brain—keeping one awake yet somehow stupefied at the same time, in a film that's every bit as chaste as Brakhage's **Wedlock House: An Intercourse**, made in the late Fifties, when Gidal himself was coming of age. "You are here, the film is there," Michael Snow said of his three-hour **La Region Centrale**, a film of continuous 360° pans around a nonhuman landscape. "It is neither fascism nor entertainment." The same is true of **Room Film 1973** and **4th Wall**, which on the contrary deal with nothing except human urban landscape, the random dishevelment of a culture-heavy room (the subject of **Wavelength** and **Back and Forth**, Snow's two previous epics of inexorable camera movement), viewed as if by a drunken, dizzy fly with the shakes who periodically passes out.

The latter comparison is a conscious act of rebellion on my part. In point of fact, anthropomorphism is just what Gidal is trying to avoid at all costs. But he probably realizes on some level that it's a losing battle, too. (Puritan that he is, Gidal watches a fair amount of American junk TV in his spare time. He grew up in Mount Vernon, New York, and Switzerland, and attended Brandeis University and the University of Munich before settling in London in the late Sixties. Although his accent sounds more redolent of Manhattan than of London to my ears, he has spent only about three of the past twenty-odd years in the U.S.). As Rivette said of narrative in early 1973, deftly anticipating his own **Céline et Julie vont au bateau**, if you throw it out by the door it comes back through the window.

There is a somewhat quixotic aspect to Gidal's position regarding some of the political ramifications of his relatively rarified and abstract work that can be regarded as either admirable and courageous because of its rigor or simply wrong-headed. The case against this position is well known; but in

---

*A (name) born out of difficulty, like that of the magnificent Laura (Riding) Jackson, a writer whose scrupulous intransigence more than matches Gidal's and whose exciting but terrifying (because exacting) passion for precision makes opponents even out of would-be allies. It should be stressed, however, that the parentheses in Gidal's case is my doing, not his.

terms of the extent to which Gidal is involved with *process* in his theory and filmmaking alike, it can be argued that there is less political mystification going on in his work than can be found in most other places. It should be pointed out, incidentally, that the still reproduced here to illustrate **4th Wall** comes not from the film but from a still camera—it illustrates in the same way a production still "represents" a Hollywood film. For Gidal, the contradiction is a useful one because it only proves that one is never in possession of any "truth" or ultimate knowledge about the image, which is just what stills pretend to convey.

4th Wall

The ultimate paradox about breaches between Gidal's theory and practice is that the single film that probably best realizes his intentions is not his own, but a film by Rose Lowder, an Avignon-based filmmaker who made her pastoral **Composed Recurrence** (see the Appendix and my closing conversation with Gidal for more details) after reading some of Gidal's theory but before seeing any of his films. Considering the ideological project that Gidal has in mind, which all of his work strives to hammer into place, into the world that we know, it is the perfect and correct and non-egotistical, puritanical resolution of an insolvable dilemma.

LOUIS JOHN HOCK.
Born in Los Angeles, California, 1948.

1969—*Los Barcos* (16mm, b&w, 10 min.)
1970—*Last Man* (16mm, color, 3 min.)
1972—*Elements* (16mm, color, 11 min.)
    Silent Reversal (16mm, color, 12 min., silent)
1973—*Zebra* (16mm, b&w, 18 min., silent)
1975—*Studies in Chronovision* (16mm, color, 22 min., silent)
    Light Traps (16mm, color, 10 min., silent)
1976—*Still Lives* (16mm, color, 20 min.)
    Perfect Roll + Walpurgis Variations (16mm, color, 8 min., silent)
    Picture Window (16mm, color, 19 min., silent)
    Mississippi Rolls (16mm, color, 25 min., silent)
1977—*Photogrammetry Series* (16mm, color, 8 min.)
1978—*Pacific Time* (16mm, color, 55 min.)
1979—*The Mirror & The Window* (16mm, color, 26 min., silent)
    Southern California (16mm, color, 70 min., silent)

Sometimes simple biographical data and filmographic detail have their own story to tell. The fact, for instance, that Louis Hock studied film with Stan Brakhage at the Art Institute in Chicago in the early Seventies is probably directly relevant to the fact that since 1972, all but three of the dozen films he's made have been silent. And the additional facts that Hock has filmed only in 16mm, and since the early Eighties has been working only in video, undoubtedly have just as much significance.

Studies in Chronovision seems to represent an important plateau in his early work, marking in a sense both the end of one kind of research and the beginning of another. Rather like the way that **Casual Relations**, the first of Mark Rappaport's features, can be regarded as a summary and synthesis of the work done in his preceding shorts, **Studies in Chronovision**, the first Hock film that is longer than 20 minutes, is a kind of anthology as well, a collection of "small" studies that he had been making over a protracted period. "The chronicle aspect of motion pictures has involved my working curiosity since my early films," he has written. "The first **Studies in Chronovision** were begun with no thought of compilation, just taking. After six years, I had accumulated several large paper bags of these studies. I was forced not only to see them as a complete film body, but to recognize the potential of temporal-based composition as a personally valid form in my film work."

A gradual shift of focus from a scientific to an aesthetic perspective clearly describes part of Hock's development, although it would be grossly oversimplifying to postulate art and science at opposite ends of his spectrum. On the contrary, his work largely inhabits the realm in which these two forms of inquiry overlap, which places him closer to the tradition of a film pioneer such as Eadweard Muybridge than to the common parlance of a narrative merchant like William S. Porter or D. W. Griffith—or, in another sense, closer to the explorations of a Dziga Vertov than those of a Sergei Eisenstein.

The time-lapse photography of **Studies in Chronovision**, made over intervals that could last for days, weeks, or months, is essentially a form of investigation into alternate time scales and what they reveal (and conceal). Changes of light in a room or landscape reveal things about the shape, color, structure, texture, and very substance of that room or landscape. This is a process that has both its structural (or structural-materialist) side and its transcendental side—the same sort of duality that can be felt in relation to Keats's Grecian urn: "Heard melodies are sweet, but those unheard/Are sweeter; therefore, ye soft pipes, play on;/Not to the sensual ear, but, more endeared,/Pipe to the spirit ditties of no tone...."

Hock's scientific, programmatic, even mechanical approach towards making unheard melodies audible—or unseen visual processes and developments visible—resembles the spiritually *laissez-faire* attitude of Michael Snow in relation to religion and politics, both of which habitually take a back seat to his personal metaphysics. But the direction in which Hock has been moving more recently seems to be diverging from this attitude, at least in relation to social engagement. (Although I haven't yet seen Hock's video work-in-progress, his *Mexican Tapes* will surely bear witness to this change, perhaps representing a plateau as significant as **Studies in Chronovision**.) Hock's **Southern California** and Snow's **So Is This** are each addressed to a wide audience, but Hock's film by necessity becomes a populist one—it is designed to be shown outdoors, in public spaces—while Snow's by necessity remains within a more circumscribed gallery nexus, and therefore a substantially different class position in relation to whom the film is ostensibly addressing.

As Mitch Tuchman put it in the *Los Angeles Times* (April 5, 1977), **Studies in Chronovision** "gauges nature's clock by one of man's. (The motion picture camera measures time, too, 24 frames per second.) He gives us common views, Arizona stucco walls, melting snow, chairs on a sunny patio. The objects (and camera) stand motionless. The 'action' is the sun's, chasing shadows. This motion, usually as imperceptible as an hour hand's, has been speeded up, so we get the whole process of a day in less than a minute." Used periodically throughout the film to separate the individual studies are shots of a changing hourglass form and coded domino pattern allowing for potential or at least conceptual re-editing of the **Studies** shots. While many spectators have complained that Hock's repeated use of this image disrupts the poetic effect, the device can be defended precisely as a means for breaking the spectator's hypnotic fascination, promoting a more analytical attitude. A kind of quick return to a neutral *terra firma*, this device can be compared to Hock's practice, as a film teacher, of flicking the lights on and off in a classroom every once in a while when he is showing a film, in order to prevent students from becoming too lost in the spectacle.

Shot between the late Sixties and 1975, **Studies in Chronovision** uses diverse locations stretching all the way from Chicago to southern Mexico (by way of Tucson, the city where Hock grew up)—with lots of other stopovers en route—in order to highlight his stop-motion procedure, whereby entire days are compressed into seconds. By contrast, all of **Picture Window** (1976), one of his more difficult and challenging films, was filmed from the fiftieth floor of Chicago's Sears Tower, where Hock programmed his camera to take one frame every half-hour over a period of a solid year. Physics and atmosphere groups have shown interest in this project: Hock recalls that when he was setting his camera up, he was a bit unnerved to find three men in grey suits standing directly behind him: "They looked real serious, as if they were going to throw me off the building. It turned out that they were trying to figure out how much the building swayed in a strong wind, and were hoping that they could use the camera in some way to find out."

The problematical aspect of **Picture Window** for the spectator is learning how to read and relate to the topographical changes in Chicago from this aerial vantage point over more than a year's time—compressed into 19 minutes, so that (roughly) each day lasts two seconds and a month goes by in about a minute. The image remains at once busy and unchanging, pulsing and random, and the distance is such that one might well be looking down at a swarming anthill...but to what avail? The lack of a clear focus or precise *raison d'être* for the experiment begins to haunt the film like an absence, forcing the eye to do more work in singling out discernible patterns (which is the film's constructive side).

A related (but more intricate and, ultimately, crippling) problem haunts **Pacific Time**, which, in contrast to **Picture Window**, manages to be topheavy with overall significance at the same time that it tends to drain and deprive many of the individual sounds and images of legible meanings. The first of Hock's two Californian epics to date, **Pacific Time** enlists artists and artworld impresarios David Antin and Allan Kaprow, both fellow professors with Hock in the Department of Visual Arts at the University of California, San Diego. Antin and Kaprow stand on a crowded street in downtown San Diego, a somewhat beat-up naval port, waiting for and then boarding a bus while reciting a couple of Platonic dialogues, including the parable of the cave. My memory of the film is less distinct than that of the other Hock films I've seen—perhaps in part because of a certain leadenness and overextension (which is relatively rare in his work) that blur the overall effect—and I've had to depend on other critics, like Sandra Mathews and Douglas Edwards, to refresh my impressions.

Pacific Time

It's the only Hock film I know that's really all over the place—with English and then Greek subtitles added to convey the dialogue between Antin and Kaprow as their talk is slowed down to an interminable crawl (and rumble/drone), a series of Felliniesque appearances by a lady in a red dress with glasses crossing many shots (filmmaker Diana Barrie), and even a grand finale in Forest Lawn. In short, while **Picture Window** might suffer from an absence or insufficiency of context, **Pacific Time** seems weighted down by a surfeit of context, footnotes clinging to many of its conceptual notions like barnacles. Only a few moments break away from this baggage and soar—e.g., the beautiful slow-motion ascent of a flock of birds in downtown San Diego, before Hock's Rosencrantz and Guildenstern board their bus.

I haven't seen **The Mirror and the Window**, the next Hock film—a triple-screen projection piece that juxtaposes the filmmaker's own face (filmed as a series of single-frame shots taken on most mornings and evenings over a ten-month period) with a long shot of a mountain range in Santa Fe, New Mexico (in which frames were taken every 20 minutes over a period of 13 months)—but Hock's own wry reflections to me about filming himself seem worth recording: "I was always curious, you know, about the vanity that prevails in the morning when you look in the mirror, and in the evening, when you say, 'My God, I'm fat,' or 'I'm skinny,' or 'I'm ugly,' or 'I look healthy,' or 'I look tired.' I always thought that you could chalk this off to vanity, that men's faces are actually pretty stable. But as it turns out, there's an immense plasticity that the face goes through. It's like some kind of modeling clay contorting around. The neck is a twisting snake, the jaws raise and lower like drawbridges, and the eyes turn around in their sockets and squint. . . ."

Southern California—the next Hock film, and the best that I've seen—is also a three-screen projection piece which is shown the same way. A single thread of film runs through three adjacent projectors aimed at the same wall. Twenty-two and a half seconds elapse between the time that the first and second panels in the triptych appear, and the same amount of time passes between the same silent image in the second and third, so that every image can be counted upon to recur twice in a 45-second cycle. (Apparently, **The Mirror and the Window** alternates the corresponding subjects of face and landscape for stretches at a time, so that three Hocks or three mountain ranges usually command the three screens at once.)

Described by Hock as a "triptych ciné-mural," **Southern California** is also identified with precise measurements, like a temporal painting: 30 feet x 7.5 feet x 70 minutes. Phenomenologically speaking, the three-screen technique produces an interesting kind of film rhythm that manages to be both suspenseful and restful, paradoxically at the same time—and oddly evocative of the movement of waves—every time the image ripples across the three projected frames. It also creates a certain analytical relationship between the spectator and the ciné-mural as three temporal stages in the same film sequence are viewed at once.

The film is called **Southern California** because it is often an anthology of the sort of things that any tourist to that part of the planet might see: the anonymous skyscrapers of downtown Los Angeles as seen in the daytime from the rotating Angel's Flight Bar atop the Hyatt-Regency Hotel; a multi-colored flower farm on a hillside close to San Clemente; a bright array of fruits and vegetables at a high-priced supermarket in La Jolla. There's even a fairly long stretch of late-night TV, including part of a Rory Calhoun western (silent, of course), **Red Sundown**, and a familiar used car ad featuring Cal Worthington and his "dog Spot." Thanks to the crisp placidity of Hock's images, his triptych format winds up giving these and other compositions an unusual kind of epic grandeur. And elliptical, contrapuntal subtitles appearing under these images quickly turn into a kind of Whitmanesque catalog of

Southern California

clichés that perfectly counterbalance the mythical images: "renowned public amusements and murals," "window to the world," "a dumping ground for weirdness?" "imported/exported/imported Mexicans," "life, liberty, pursuit of happiness," "Uncle Walt cleaned up"...

"The work is actually a documentary of the Southern California region," Hock has written. "Not the physical region, but the imaginary landscape, the mythical locale. The place that dwells in the minds of untraveled Easterners, promoted by *National Geographic*, television, and travel brochures. It is the same sort that baited Francisco Coronado's search for the Seven Cities of Cibola, El Dorado. It is the myth that populated this desert. Using doggerel language, the printed text associated with images addresses the myth from the real, concrete and stucco world on the edge of America, fronting the Pacific. The formal means of presentation acts as a documentary metaphor."

The outdoor presentation of **Southern California** is an important facet of its meaning for Hock and deserves some detailed account. As he wrote in a proposal in 1979:

> There is little reason beyond tradition to show my filmworks in theaters. They are not dramatic, they do not tell stories. Habit puts the projector behind the audience and the screen before them.... However, there are other genres of film with equally likely exhibition kinships: billboards, murals, public windows. As a detriment to profit and benefit for public access, putting film showings beyond the monetary lock of participation invites a new audience. So, from the lack of obligation to theater or commercial interests, the project with which I am currently engaged is for the streets. The screening room also quite literally captures the audience in the dark, sheltered for the spectacle, an already paid for surprise. Looking out from the stage, a theater audience is undistinguishable, excepting the popcorn, from their cousin, a moviegoing audience. The people are static. They are also waiting. My makings in the streets can be walked past or watched for their duration. The 'aesthetic receptivity' is not primed by a ticket taker or pedestal. The images and words of the work simply engage the spectators or they don't.
>
> This would seem to have a lot of political intent: truly public film rather than a commodity. Perhaps even a real lurch toward the dreams of Vertov and Moholy-Nagy. In a way, it does, and again, it doesn't. It does in that the form of the work, parallel to the reasonings and obligations behind murals, is set in a mundane context, the viewers' domain. This public context of the billboard, the bus bench, and the parked car creates the arena of presentation....
>
> On the other hand, the piece doesn't have political implications as much as simply being the logical extension of my work and the best way to show it. I want an image bigger than those existing in available theaters. I want the audience to see the film from various angles and while moving. I desire a large heterogeneous audience rather than the handful of familiar faces to see my stuff.

Over the next year or so, Hock was able to realize this dream, showing **Southern California** in several outdoor locations on both coasts. In the parking lot of the Santa Monica pier, a punk rock band called the Armaghetto Ensemble pulled up in a flatbed truck and offered to play free accompaniment. (The film was projected on a screen 8 feet high and 30 feet across, and attracted sizable crowds three nights running.) At the Los Angeles Institute for Contemporary Art, Hock projected the film into a semi-tractor-trailer. At the San Francisco Art Institute, he rear-projected it onto windows. On the University of California's San Diego campus, he used the outside of the massive Mandeville Auditorium. James Benning recalls seeing the film in Florida, with the sound of real waves as accompaniment. And subsequently, in New York—in October 1981, to be precise—Hock projected it for Staten Island commuters at the street level of the South Ferry terminal, and for kids and other Soho locals in a small park on Spring and Thompson Streets. I recall reseeing part of the film at the latter location, and it was a sight for sore eyes, not to mention a healthy antidote and alternative to the exclusivity of the New York Film Festival, which was in progress at the same time.

JON JOST.
Born in Chicago, Illinois, May 16, 1943.*

1963—*Repetition* (Salzburg; 16mm, b&w, 30 min., silent) (unavailable)
1964—*Portrait* (Casina Amata, Italy; 16mm, b&w & color, 13 min., silent) (unavailable)
Sunday (Chicago; 16mm, b&w, 20 min., silent) (unavailable)
City (Chicago; 16mm, b&w, 15 min., silent)
1965—*We Didn't Go to Unique's* (Chicago; 16mm, b&w, 30 min., silent) (unavailable)
Judith (Chicago; 16mm, b&w & color, 15 min., silent) (unavailable)
1967—*Traps* (Chicago; 16mm, b&w, 22 min.)
Leah (Chicago; 16mm, b&w, 32 min.)
1968—*13 Fragments & 3 Narratives from Life* (Chicago; 16mm, color, 20 min.)
1969—*Susannah's Film* (Soda Springs, CA; 16mm, b&w, 13 min.)
1970—*Flower* (Soda Springs, CA; 16mm, color, 7½ min., silent)
Fall Creek (Ben Lomond, CA; 16mm, color, 13 min.)

*An earlier version of this section appeared in *Film Comment,* January-February 1982.

1971—*Canyon* (Grand Canyon, AZ; 16mm, color, 5½ min., silent)

Primaries/A Turning Point in Lunatic China/1, 2, 3, Four (Ben Lomond, CA; 16mm, color, 35 min.)

1972—*A Man Is More than the Sum of His Parts/A Woman Is* (Palo Alto, CA; 16mm, color, 35 min.)

1974—*Speaking Directly: Some American Notes* (Cottage Grove, OR; Kalispell, MT; 16mm, color, 110 min.)

1977—*Angel City* (Los Angeles; 16mm, color, 75 min.)

Beauty Sells Best (Los Angeles; 16mm, color, 5½ min.)

Last Chants for a Slow Dance (Dead End) (Missoula, MT; 16mm, color, 90 min.)

1978—*Chameleon* (Los Angeles; 35mm, color, 90 min.)

1980—*X2: Two Dances by Nancy Karp* (Berlin; 16mm, color, 35 min.)

Lampenfieber (Berlin; 16mm, color, 35 min.)

Godard 1980 (London; 16mm, color, 17 min.)

1981—*Stagefright* (Berlin; 16mm, color, 74 min.)

Despite five substantial and in many ways remarkable features under his belt since 1974, and 19 shorts since 1963, Jon Jost at 40 is still a long way from becoming even an arcane household name in this country. Not that he makes it easy on anyone. His originality, technical virtuosity, and political sophistication have all tended to work against him, in fact, by showing the rest of us up—thereby banishing him from most of the restricted genre and market classifications designed to protect us from his scorn, under avant-garde and mainstream umbrellas alike. In a manner that seems exasperatingly and inescapably American, that alternately warms and chills my blood, Jon Jost embodies the dangers, limitations, and intransigent strengths of isolation more graphically than any other contemporary independent I know—with an authenticity whose challenges often leave a disturbing aftertaste.

An anarchist outsider by self-definition, whose impossibly slim budgets—$2,500 for **Speaking Directly: Some American Notes**, his first feature, in 1972-73; $3,000 for **Last Chants for a Slow Dance**, his third, in 1977—are offered like tart reproaches to other filmmakers, Jost has tended to amass a reputation more than a following in the U.S. (In England and, more recently, Germany, he appears to have somewhat more clout.)

His most recent and (by far) most experimental feature, **Stagefright**, was shot for German TV in a somewhat Dr. Mabuse/Strangelove spirit ("I wanted to lock actors in a black room for four days and see what would happen ... and orchestrate spectators' feelings with very little content"). When it turned up at New York's Collective for Living Cinema in the Fall of

1981, only a smattering of curious people showed up for the event, and a good handful of these walked out during the first 15 minutes. To the best of my knowledge, no New York publication deemed the film worthy of review—although an attack on the accompanying short, **Godard 1980**, which managed to get its title wrong, appeared in *Soho News* 12 days later, by a reviewer who smugly concluded, "I wish I could get a crack at re-editing this footage."

"Personally, I much prefer to show my films in provincial places," Jost told me in Hoboken a couple of days later, interpreting the **Stagefright** walkouts as New Yorkers being trend-conscious and fad-oriented. "I'd rather do a show in Omaha, because I feel people are more receptive there. It's the contrary of what people say."

My own first encounter with Jost's work came when I saw **Speaking Directly** at the Edinburgh Festival in 1975. Made in Oregon and Montana, it's a materialist exposition of all that the act of filmmaking entails; I can think of no other film like it. One of Jost's opening monologues, delivered at once to camera and spectator, is emblematic: "This is a movie, a way to speak. It is bound, like all systems of communication, with conventions. Some of these are arbitrarily imposed, some are imposed by economic or political pressures, some are imposed by the medium itself. Some of these conventions are necessary: they are the commonality through which we are able to speak with one another in this way. But some of these conventions are unnecessary, and not only that, they are damaging to us, they are self-destructive. Yet we are in a bad place to see this. We are in a theater."

As a radical critique of America in the early Seventies, **Speaking Directly** is as essential a document, in a way, as the collectively made **Winter Soldier** (1972)—a straight record of the confession of war crimes given by American veterans back from Vietnam—although the experiences it bears witness to are distinctly different. (Jost was imprisoned in federal custody from March 1965 through June 1967 for draft resistance.) Yet at the same time, I have certain doubts about Jost's self-willed isolation as it comes across in the film. Writing in 1975 as an American who had been living abroad for six years and who had already been deeply affected by the different attitudes toward collectivity that I'd been exposed to in Paris and London, I was at once attracted to and repelled by Jost's entrenched, lonely position, which seemed imbued with a cracker-barrel spirit that reeked of Thoreau as well as Mailer. As I put it in the Winter 1975-76 *Sight and Sound:*

> I'm wary about the lure that can be exerted by this brand of all-American confessional—the note of cranky individualism which dictates that all the most well-worn discoveries have to be reasserted anew, like home-made appliances, as if no one had ever thought of them before. It's the precise

reverse of that assumed tradition of several centuries, languages, and ideologies lurking behind every gesture which I find in Straub/Huillet. An American and contemporary of Jost, I'm constantly tempted to indulge in this rhetoric—what else am I doing now?—which may give me a high tolerance for it, extended further by a familiarity with the lifestyles and idioms.

The strange fruit borne by this maverick stance in **Stagefright** belongs to no acknowledged filmic or theatrical tradition save the magical, yet Jost clearly intends its first section to be a "kind of history of mankind and the development of consciousness." No fooling; and as Jost describes it all, it's very schematic. What follows is his edited description (with my added interjections):

Stagefright

"You see the woman's body—egg-shaped, beginnings, right? Then she sort of stumbles around and finally gets up on her feet, and by the end of the sequence she's got her body under control, and she knows it and she smiles and she walks off-screen." *(A man suddenly enters the frame from another direction as she exits, playing with our sense of spatial balance and perspective.)* "Then it's basically the same thing, but dealing with facial expression. First, he's sort of spastic, then he goes through some elementary expressions, like fear and surprise. Then he walks off, and next you see this actual mirror image where he smiles and frowns to himself. The hand comes in, the camera drops down—I wanted to suggest that expression takes some kind of self-consciousness. But the mirror itself doesn't produce a dialogue or drama.

"In the next shot you see his face on one side and his infinitely repeated image in a mirror on the other side...Then comes a mock mirror shot when he smiles and frowns at once, and you get the introduction of conflict. You no longer get a mimicking, but a disagreement." *(After the same actor applies paint to his face, there's an enormous close-up of his mouth making lip and then gutteral sounds, again moving towards greater muscular control.)* "I like the very end, when the camera pulls back and his expression really looks like a Francis Bacon character. Then he's got clothes on— another level of consciousness and repression at the same time." *(Eventually, he pulls out a book and reads a Serbo-Croatian myth.)*

"Then you go to the alphabet that you hear in different languages and then see in animated figures—again, starting from the earliest ones and going up to the story of Cain and Abel, in Hebrew." *(Blood—or, rather, Godardian red paint—splatters over the Hebrew text, and there's a dissolve to a close-up of a woman whose face bears an animated cartoon of changing make-up while one hears an audience working itself up into rhythmic applause. End of section.)*

It seems to me that **Stagefright** *is your first film that isn't about America.*

Yeah, it's the first one that isn't dealing with a specifically American background or context. It's not dealing with the German one, either—it's dealing with the universal one. It's not a pretty picture, I agree...I was just trying to deal with a more primal view of politics. Most people wouldn't refer to it as political, but to me it is. If the prime human story is that we murder one another, that's definitely a political story—but I was trying to phrase it in more primal terms, that this is something having to do with some very fundamental quality of the human species. And I was trying to deal more on those levels and deal with it so that the viewer received it the way you receive primal things—more on the subconscious level.

That somehow seems more Germanic than your other movies.

Well, in a very real way my politics have changed. Hopefully, they will continue to change as I learn more things.

In all my films, I'm always testing the limits of the audience. In **Angel City**, it was the part where [the detective] picks the jigsaw puzzle apart and gives you a very frontal lecture about what you get when you get a story. He tells you what the etymology of the word 'story' is, that it comes from 'history,' that its origins mean 'to know.' Then he gives a lecture about how story—as we think of it, fiction—means knowing the wrong things. Like, Rexon is a phony company when we should talk about Exxon, the real one, right?

Then he walks off-screen, and you just have this rather beautiful but barren shot of the blue of the swiming pool, with a woman's corpse lying on the ground. And that's the point that's hardest for audiences, for two reasons. One is that they're being shown a long, static shot where the lead actor [Bob Glaudini] walks off-screen, and meanwhile they're getting a lecture about something they don't want to hear about. They don't want to hear about the real names, or somebody telling them that they don't want to hear."

*(Angel City—a comic hardboiled detective story intermixed with an elaborately detailed social, political and economic critique of Los Angeles— cost a little under $6,000 to make. Jost's omnipresent gallows humor, extending to such sequences as an actress, who later becomes the corpse beside the swimming pool, undergoing a screen test for a Hollywood remake of **Triumph of the Will**, or a TV commercial for Rexon in which the supposedly benign president walks casually along a beach, is reflected in Jost's own frequent laughter, which some find unsettling. The hero of **Last Chants for a Slow Dance**, played by drama teacher Tom Blair, exhibits a more advanced case of the same manic, inner-directed cackle.)*

Are all your films distributed by you?

Yes, and it'll remain that way. There are distributors in America who would now like to handle my films. Unifilm wanted to take them all. But then I asked, "What are the terms?" "Oh, you provide the prints, we take 60%." I said, "How many bookings can you get me a year for all four features?" "Twenty-five." Well—I can get on the phone and do *that* in a week. There's no distributor in America who's willing to take me until maybe I'm on the cover of *Time* magazine or something. [*Laughs.*] Then, all of a sudden, I'll become of interest. Which I find embarrassing to some degree. I mean, there's no reason why **Last Chants for a Slow Dance** shouldn't book as well as a lot of Fassbinder. It's certainly no less accessible.

*(I agree. At once the easiest and most disturbing of Jost's features, and to my mind the best, **Last Chants** conceivably gets closer to the mentality of the alienated and seemingly motiveless killer than either Mailer or Capote. Broken up into extremely long takes—some of them accompanied by original country-western songs, written and sung in part by Jost himself, which are a lot more authentic than those in **Nashville**—the film chronicles the aimless wandering of Tom Bates in his truck around Montana, stopping only once to see his embittered wife Darleen, living on food stamps, who informs him during an exceptionally ugly fight in front of a bathroom mirror that their two accidental kids are soon to be joined by a third.*

Supposedly unable to find a job, although we never actually see him looking for one, Tom is cackling away to a male hitchhiker about how he "can smell pussy a mile away." When he asks, "Hey, you got pussy waiting for you?" and the younger guy responds uneasily, "I got a girl—I don't think of her like

Last Chants for a Slow Dance

Last Chants for a Slow Dance

that," Tom starts to get pissed off, gradually working himself up into a rage: "Fella, all girls are pussies...You ain't one of those funnies, are ya?" Before long, he's ranting that he's paid for his truck with his own money, doesn't have to give anybody a lift if he doesn't want to, stops, and asks the hitchhiker to get out. Throughout this one-take sequence, the camera, after focusing on the moving highway, pans over to take in first Tom and then the rider as well; the following long take pans between Darleen in front of the bathroom mirror and Tom standing beside a door behind her...After two encounters in his travels—*with a hippie and a woman he picks up in a bar— he winds up killing a man he encounters on the road with car trouble, for no apparent reason apart from the pretext of taking his wallet.)*

It seems to me that **Last Chants** *is one of the few films that combines elements of structural filmmaking with a whole other tradition that's more* *verbal and is closer to someone like Godard. And the structural and narrative aspects set up a very interesting tension in relation to things like duration. I'm curious, in any case, what structural films you've seen and how you relate to them.*

I've hardly seen any. What little I've seen strikes me as technical exercises, so I end up not being too interested—or I'm interested only if there's some technical thing I can learn from it.

Have you seen any of Michael Snow's films?

Just two days ago in Pittsburgh, I saw a reel of **The Central Region**, and then I saw **Wavelength** for the first time.

Did they seem like technical exercises to you?

Well, I didn't get bored with **Wavelength**, but I also didn't think it was all that wonderful a film. A lot of the visual intrusions struck me as arbitrary, just sort of fucking around, mainly to maintain your interest visually—all those filters and multiple printing things. It occasionally got a very striking visual effect, but it struck me as arbitrary.

What about the narrative intrusions?

Well, they were there, but they were very skimpy, and then on another level they weren't believable, because the acting was so amateurish. It was very crude that way. I mean, the idea was interesting, and somehow, cumulatively, you do end up watching it for 45 minutes. But I was surprised, after reading about it, by what I considered the sort of sloppy way it was done. All those flashes and the filters going over it were a lot cruder than I'd thought might be there. About the first reel of **The Central Region**, I dunno. It reminded me of a shot in **Speaking Directly**, the 360° landscape. And I liked it—it was very sneaky as it changed your perspective. I remember having read years ago about those jumps that occur when they changed magazines. I really wish I could have put a 7,000-foot reel on the camera. I find the cuts conceptually very disruptive. And I appreciate the technical problem, although he could have dissolved them and masked them somewhat.

*I'm curious about two sequences in **Last Chants** in which you hold a particular fixed image for a long time. One's in a roadside diner, and the other's in a room with a TV set and adjoining bedroom. I'm interested in how you arrived at these sequences and what sort of function they have for you. For me, they both stretch and manipulate the narrative-illusionist precepts of the film in a very interesting way. (I like what Noel Carroll wrote about the film, which applies especially to the latter sequence: "Jost's strength in this film is his ability to portray the experience of time of the lumpenproletariat who is outside the regimented rhythm of work and sleep, who lives without directions, schedules, and goals.")*

To me, both sequences fall into a broader overall plan for the film, which was that it should start off seeming to be in some sort of realist mode. I wanted to start off with that and then slowly push the viewer off that axis.

The first significant place where that happens is the café shot, which is a black-and-white shot with the word "café" in red, done as a multiple printing. I shot the black-and-white shot, and then I slept in the place overnight and shot the red café neon sign that was in the background, although in the picture it reads as being in the foreground. I knew it would create confusion and be an ambiguous image. Part of the reason I did it was I found it was going to be a relatively long take, and I have to throw in a little spice in the image to make you go with it. As it turned out, the improvisation that the actors did, a scene between Tom and the hippie, was quite funny, so probably it would have held without it. But for a longer strategy in the movie, it was the first step toward throwing it off this realist mode.

Then it goes into a bar sequence, then the couple go up the stairs—which is a multiple-image thing where their image and their shadow become indistinguishable. That's just a short shot, but it's usually one that's quite effective; I watch audiences, and one can just see this little ripple going through that says, "What *is* this?" Then they go in the bedroom, and here the strategy was on several levels. I knew it was going to be a very long shot—it's around 14 minutes. There's a color TV on one side (the left) in a black-and-white image, and you can hear the track of *The Johnny Carson Show,* or whatever it was—so you're listening, and it's kind of interesting, and at the same time you're subconsciously trying to look around the door on the other side of the set so you can see them fucking. *(As it is, one can see only their feet.)* Also, where the TV is situated, if you didn't have a wall there, that's where their heads would be. That was like a discreet metaphor for what their mentality was—this is the culture they live in. And within the same shot, there's also this compression of time, because it starts off at night, and within the same shot, although the TV program is continuous, it's morning.

That's one of the things that reminded me of films like **Wavelength**. *How did you do that?*

It's ABC-rolled. One roll is nighttime black-and-white stock, one roll is daytime black-and-white stock, and they're dissolved together. The third roll is the color TV. All I did was put a black piece of paper over the color TV while I shot the black-and-white. Then I blacked out the room at night, turned on the TV, and just shot it.

The intriguing thing is that you get two different time scales at once.

Yeah, there's the continuous take of the TV, which is 14 minutes, and then the rest, which is 12 hours. You see them fucking, and then there's this real slow 90-frame dissolve, and the light slowly fills the room, and the bed's now different; he's sitting on it and making a telephone call, she's in the bathroom, and you can hear water running. Then when they come out and pass in front of the TV set while it's still on, it prints through them, and they turn into ghosts. To me that had a kind of literary meaning, because in a sense they're not there, mentally.

But it was also part of the strategy to keep pushing further and further away from this realist mode. So by the time he leaves her house, this whole thing with the mug shots (*Tom looks at and reads "Wanted" notices in a post office, although we see only the notices and hear him off-screen*), and writing his postcards *(again, in close-up, to Darleen)*, and the rabbit being killed *(in excruciating close-up, this time with no discernible relation to Tom)*, all of that has no plausible relation to narrative logic. What I was trying to do was put you inside the guy's head rather than have you outside looking at him. So it was basically a step-by-step process away from a realist mode and getting you into a psychic mode of some sort.

I tried to make an honest picture of a small segment of American society. It was definitely an outgrowth of my two years in prison, where I met lots of people like that. And I'm interested in those characters. It has some connection to the Gary Gilmore case, which had happened the previous year.

*(**Chameleon**, my least favorite Jost feature, brings back **Angel City**'s Bob Glaudini, this time playing a Los Angeles drug dealer who tries to convince an artist to execute forgeries for him. Like Jost's other story films, it has a narrative only in a quasi-deceptive sense; like **Stagefright**, it seems freighted with a great deal of literary allegory.)*

*I read somewhere that the initial idea for **Chameleon** came from a shot which you weren't able to do in **Angel City**. It had something to do with color, I think. And I remember the changing color backdrops during the screen test in **Angel City**.*

Yes, and you see the same thing in the make-up shot in **Stagefright**. Actually, I think what you're talking about is something I wound up not being able to do in **Chameleon**, either. I was talking about the scene in the art gallery [with Gene Youngblood], where each shot was a different color. And originally what I wanted to do was have a continuous take, where the printer would step you through the spectrum. And the reason I didn't do it was because the continuous take wasn't strong enough on its own, and I had to cut some flat spots out of it. Also, I probably would have had to scream bloody murder at the lab I was with to go through a light change every 40 frames. Because you could gradate it so there would be no sense of steps, it would just take you right through the spectrum. The lab I'm working with now in San Francisco could do that.

When Godard and Jean-Pierre Gorin came to the U.S. with **Tout va bien** in the early Seventies, Jost arranged five West Coast screenings and drove them to each one, after picking them up in the Seattle airport. Godard saw three of Jost's shorts in Eugene—**Primaries, A Turning Point in Lunatic China**, and **1, 2, 3, Four**—and wound up forcing the San Francisco Film Festival to show them right before **Tout va bien**. Later, a local newspaper quoted him as saying of Jost, "He is not a traitor to the movies, like almost all American directors. He makes them move." To the best of my

knowledge, Godard remains the only internationally well-known film-
maker, living or dead, whom Jost respects, at least as a filmmaker. (He has
supported several lesser-known filmmakers in both America and Europe.*)
Significantly, when Jost was initially helping to set up a film project with
Nicholas Ray and Wim Wenders in 1979, which eventually became
Lightning over Water (see Jost's article in the Spring 1981 *Sight and Sound*),
Ray had already seen at least one of Jost's films, **Last Chants**, but Jost had
not recalled seeing anything by Ray.

The 17-minute **Godard 1980**, produced by *Framework* magazine in
England, shows Peter Wollen and *Framework* editor Don Ranvaud inter-
viewing Godard, who, to their consternation, backs away from endorsing
his own Dziga Vertov Group films and some of his other earlier practices:
"For a while, I made movies for other directors, or people who wanted to
be directors, who were my real audience. . . . Loneliness could be good, but
isolation is not so good."

"My experience with Godard is that he's a lot more mellow than he
used to be," Jost told me in Hoboken. "He's much better with audiences in
answering questions—he doesn't get sucked into stupid arguments that
aren't going to help anybody. I think he's learned a lot. Like I know when
Sauve qui peut (la vie) went to London, a lot of people were upset, because
they were still sitting there theorizing in a dry academic way about things
that Godard had already said goodbye to, eight or ten years ago."

*At the Collective, you were very critical of what Godard's interviewers
were saying. Are you critical of what Godard says also?*

Well, I just feel like—I'm a filmmaker, and I can sympathize and
understand a lot more what Godard's situation and thinking is. But as it was,
he wasn't getting asked good questions, because Don and Peter had
pigeonholed him. And they were too much in awe of him. He's just a
human being; if you want to ask him a question, you don't have to
apologize about it before you ask it. [*Laughs.*]

*There's one moment that's quite striking, when Godard says that even
though he hasn't been to Vietnam and hasn't been under a tank, he's been
under a truck in Paris traffic—a reference to his motorbike/truck accident in the
early Seventies. And the moment he says this, what seems to happen is that Don
and Peter become, in effect, members of a petit-bourgeois audience responding
to a Godard film: they're embarrassed, shocked, speechless.*

Well, they were taken aback. And then Peter says, "There are some
ways in which it's the same, and there are other ways in which it isn't." To
which Godard says, "For me it's just the same." And I put that in because I

---

*"... not that it's serious at all, but just in case one wonders, among modestly well known
filmmakers I like, i'd include tanner (jonas, light yrs), and now I'll forget the filmmaker's
names: tree of the wooden clogs; salvatore guiliano; gabor somebody's 'american torso' (I
guess he's not much known); zanussi's contract or maybe it was the one before that; and oh
hell here and there I like something. but usually I like unknowns more: peter hutton, robina
rose's jigsaw, rick schmidt's 1988, and . . . i liked sweet movie (censored american version).
brackets that they're operating in. All he was saying was that, with the and well you get the
drift, no?" From letter by Jost to author, January 26, 1982.

think it's provocative—especially so for people who have these political brackets that they're operating in. All he was saying was that, with the subjective experience of being under a machine, it doesn't matter where it is—if you've been under it, that's what it's like.

*I hear that this interview really affected Peter's opinion of Godard, for the worse. Considering the deadly academic effect of a Wollen piece like "Counter Cinema"—which is largely responsible for the academic fetishizing of **Vent d'Est** into some sort of primer for textbook, armchair radicalism—I personally find it refreshing that Godard, unlike Wollen, feels it's about time to turn to something else.*

Well, there's another part of that, too. Because he and Laura [Mulvey]* went out to dinner with him, and he didn't say anything.

I hear he did the same thing in New York with David Denby.† It makes sense. As far as I can tell, Godard isn't especially friendly or warm to critics who consider themselves stars.

What Peter and Laura wanted to do was sit down and have a big theoretical conversation, and I don't think Godard gave a shit.

What are we going to do about Jost, just Jost, the filmmaker as maverick? One critic of my acquaintance who hates his work has a simple solution for dealing with his combined brilliance and asocial tendencies. She assumes (or claims) that he steals his ideas from other films, then lies when he claims that he hasn't seen those films. According to this argument, there's a lipstick scene in **Angel City** that's a direct lift from **Flaming Creatures,** and the black studio space of **Stagefright** comes straight out of **Le Gai Savoir.**

I think that Jost tells the truth and hasn't seen either of the above films—which doesn't exactly prevent his work from remaining problematical, either. (In Hoboken, where these issues seem to matter less, he admitted that the opening shot of **Godard 1980**, which frames Godard from behind, comes directly from the opening of **Vivre sa vie.**) Jost openly admits that all his films are mainly part of a learning process, that he wants to get a foothold (or even a toehold) in Hollywood, that **Angel City** and **Last Chants** and **Chameleon** were all partially made to demonstrate that he could make well-acted and attractive story films for practically nothing, that his ultimate goal is to make "essay films for mass audiences."

Toward the end of **Stagefright**, after a lot more magic and allegory and reflections about acting, an actor gets a pie thrown in his face. The sequence slows down until it becomes a meditation on a nearly static image (pie-in-the-face) that seems to last forever. After one feels ready to scream and is ready to howl for blood—without ever looking away, for Jost is cunning enough to hold one's interest with the visual tease of quick

---

*A contributor to *Screen*, as is Peter Wollen.

†Film critic for *New York* magazine.

intrusions, like a stopwatch and a screwdriver that enter and exit the frame—Jost suddenly cuts to another shot, taken directly from a 35mm print of **Hearts and Minds**. It's footage of a Vietcong suspect being shot at close range through the head and is one of the most powerful and shocking eruptions of violence I've ever seen in a film. Like the killed rabbit in **Last Chants**, it both gratifies our desires for meaning and action and shows the resultant blood on one's hands in the process. As long as Jost goes on making more films just as truthful, I don't expect him to win any popularity contests.

JONAS MEKAS.
Born in Semeniskiai, Lithuania, 1922.

1950—*Grand Street* (16mm, b&w, silent) (unavailable)
1953—*Silent Journey* (16mm, b&w & color, silent) (Made
     with Adolfas Mekas; unavailable)
1961—*Guns of the Trees* (35mm, b&w, 75 min.)
1963—*Film Magazine of the Arts* (16mm, color, 20 min.)
1964—*The Brig* (35mm, b&w, 68 min.)
     Award Presentation to Andy Warhol (16mm, b&w, 12
     min.)
1966—*Report from Millbrook* (16mm, color, 12 min.)
     Cassis (16mm, color, 4½ min.)
     Notes on the Circus (16mm, color, 12 min.)
1968—*Time & Fortune Vietnam Newsreel* (16mm, color, 4
     min.)
     Diaries, Notes & Sketches (Walden) (16mm, color,
     180 min.) (filmed 1964–1968)
1971—*Reminiscences of a Journey to Lithuania* (16mm,
     color, 82 min.) (incorporates portions of *Grand
     Street*)
1976—*Lost, Lost, Lost* (16mm, color, 176 min.) (incorporates
     portions of *Grand Street* and *Silent Journey*; filmed
     1949–1963)
1978—*In Between* (16mm, color, 50 min.) (filmed
     1964–1968)
     Notes for Jerome (16mm, color, 43 min.) (filmed in
     1966, 1967, and 1974)
1980—*Paradise Not Yet Lost (Oona's Third Year)* (16mm,
     color, 100 min.) (filmed in 1977)

With each decade since the middle of this century, Jonas Mekas as a filmmaker has been reborn like a phoenix; if we split his career in two, the first half seems to have surprisingly little to do with the second half. And yet the development has been a wholly logical one, for those who care to examine it closely. Over two decades have passed since I first saw **Guns of the Trees** at the Charles Theatre in Manhattan's Lower East Side, a film that Mekas has seldom shown since. For all my negative responses at the time—prompted in no small part by the ridicule of Dwight Macdonald in *Esquire*, who had an important influence on my film tastes as a college freshman—I think it's unfortunate that Mekas has tended to keep the film under wraps in the intervening years, for I'm sure that it would constitute a fascinating period document today. It would also no doubt help to explain the path that his subsequent work has taken, by revealing another path that he chose to leave behind—a path having much to do with the European art film.

A European himself in background and temperament, forced to leave his native Lithuanian village in 1944 because of the war, Mekas became a Displaced Person who arrived in the U.S. six years later, looking for new personal and aesthetic roots. The pain of exile is in fact the central emotional element in his work, and the highly political and self-conscious **Guns of the Trees**—which registers in the memory as a somewhat strident (if heartfelt) left-wing protest "art film," highly influenced by the rhetoric of the Beat writers (particularly Allen Ginsberg, whose poetic diatribes about the state of the union are periodically heard on the soundtrack), but none the less European in many of its most prominent visual and conceptual influences—ultimately represents a route not taken in his subsequent work, just as his next feature, **The Brig**, a *cinéma verité* documentary of a Living Theatre production, constitutes another sort of rejection. Henceforth, despite certain superficial indications to the contrary, neither theatrical allegory nor naturalism nor agit-prop nor documentary is to form the essential basis of his work.

My first exposure to Mekas's mature work came about ten years ago, when Andrew Sarris asked me to review his **Reminiscences of a Journey to Lithuania**, along with his brother Adolfas Mekas's companion film, **Going Home**, for *The Village Voice* (November 2, 1972). Principally a record of Mekas's trip home to Semeniskiai after 25 years' absence (the film's central section is called "One Hundred Glimpses of Lithuania, August 1971")—preceded by footage of his first years in America (mainly the sorrowful streets of Brooklyn, shot with his first Bolex) and followed by visits to a Hamburg suburb (the site of a slave camp where he and Adolfas spent a year during the war) and to Vienna (where he luxuriates in the company of friends, including Peter Kubelka and Annette Michelson)—it remains not only his greatest work to date, but an essential key to his oeuvre as a whole, the one film that makes all the others legible. In preparation for my writing that review, Mekas at my request screened over three hours of his

Paradise Not Yet Lost. Peter Kubelka, Hermann Nitsch,
Jonas Mekas (on donkey)

preceding filmed diaries for me—basically, **Notes on the Circus** and
Diaries, Notes & Sketches (Walden). About four years later, in London, I
had occasion to review his subsequent diary film, **Lost, Lost, Lost**, for
Monthly Film Bulletin (No. 516, January 1977; *see also* Alan Williams's
excellent review in the Fall 1976 *Film Quarterly*). And in February 1983, as
preparation for this chapter, he screened all 193 minutes of his three
subsequent films for me in one marathon session—a powerful and exhausting experience.

As acknowledged elsewhere in this book, my responses to Mekas's
work are sharply divided between alienation from many of his theoretical
and political positions and an almost stupefied admiration for his talent as a
filmmaker—a conflict that his most recent work exacerbates rather than
resolves. As a "born-again" American, Mekas obviously views the American experience from the reverse side of the same telescope that I see it
through (as both a native and an erstwhile expatriate); as someone who
relinquished his bachelorhood and became a father only in his mid-fifties
(his second child, Sebastian, was born in 1982), he is similarly someone
whose relation to domesticity seems radically different from my own. And
yet if I had to cite the two artists his recent work most reminds me of, I
would pick two very dissimilar Russians, Leo Tolstoy and Alexander

Dovzhenko. Both of them, I should quickly add, are manifestly and vastly superior to Mekas as artists. For all the radical differences in class and culture between them, it is the tragic, rural, poetic lyricism of Dovzhenko and the "family happiness" in Tolstoy's prose that Mekas repeatedly evokes for me, rather than the shades of, say, Thoreau or even Brakhage (whom he acknowledges as major influences, and rightfully so).

Of course, the complex conditions of exile—articulated so strongly and unforgettably in **Reminiscences** and continually evoked in all his subsequent work—change everything. The very fact that Mekas is regarded a major poet in his native language and an eccentric foreigner in this country only begins to describe the radical discontinuity underlining so much of his life and art, the sadness that comprises an unceasing subtext. Spectators who are not fully aware of his central importance in the establishment of the American avant-garde film in the Fifties and Sixties— work informed by a saint-like devotion and fanaticism apparent only to those who have read Mekas over the years (see especially his collection *Movie Journal: The Rise of a New American Cinema, 1959-1971,* published by Macmillan in 1972), or who have read at least Calvin Tomkins's excellent profile of him, "All Pockets Open," in the January 6, 1973 issue of *The New Yorker*—are perhaps less able to appreciate the capital importance of **Lost, Lost, Lost** and **In Between** simply as chronicles and social documents (although their value as films surely exceeds those functions).

The trap represented by almost all of Mekas's mature work, which accounts for both my attraction and my ideological resistance to it, is nostalgia; whether this is nostalgia for the past (as is usually the case) or for the present (as in **Paradise Not Yet Lost**) seems a secondary issue. **Reminiscences** remains his greatest work because it is here that the lure of nostalgia as well as Mekas's willed resistance to it remain most powerful, creating what amounts to a dialectic—a tug of war that results in more than just a stalemate, but is also a taut live wire (to pursue the metaphor further) which vibrates with all the *necessary* intensity of a straight line describing the shortest distance between two points.

"The Diary Film," a lecture by Mekas about **Reminiscences** included in P. Adams Sitney's collection, *The Avant-Garde Film* (New York University Press/Anthology Film Archives Series, 1978), is full of important clues about the methodology underlying his work. In the very first paragraph, for instance, he explains how his methods grew out of the exigencies of his involvements with other films and filmmakers:

> ...I did not come to [the diary form of **Reminiscences**] by calculation but from desperation. During the last fifteen years I got so entangled with the independently made film that I didn't have any time left for myself, for my own filmmaking... I had only bits of time which allowed me to shoot only bits of

film. All my personal work became like notes, I thought I
should do whatever I can today, because if I don't, I may not
find any other free time for weeks. If I can film one minute—I
film one minute. If I can film ten seconds—I film ten seconds.
I take what I can, from desperation. But for a long time I didn't
look at the footage I was collecting that way. I thought what I
was actually doing was practicing. . . .

Perhaps the most important consequence of this strategy is that Mekas,
unlike most other diaristic filmmakers who come to mind, never seems to
turn to filmmaking as an alternative to life. The extraordinary thing about his
footage is that one feels that the events it describes would be nearly the
same if there were no camera around—which often means, in effect, that
Mekas relies largely on incorporating the strictly mechanical, "reproduc-
tive" properties of the camera into his body language; it is mainly through
his very conscious editing and use of titles, often from a vantage point
several years later, that he becomes a more deliberate and less intuitive
artist. From this standpoint, it is revealing to read what he has to say about
his conscious strategies for dealing with mechanical difficulties. The
Lithuanian footage of **Reminiscences**, for example, was shot with a brand
new Bolex, the fourth that Mekas owned, and as soon as he discovered that
it never kept a constant speed ("I set it on 24 frames, and after three or four
shots it's on 32 frames"), he sought to "incorporate the defect as one of the
stylistic devices, to use the changes of light as structural means"—an
approach that paradoxically became, for him, a step towards realism ("I
dislike any kind of mystery"):

> As soon as I noticed that the speeds were changing
> constantly (especially when I filmed in short takes, brief
> spurts) I knew that I wouldn't be able to control the
> exposures. I don't exactly mean that I wanted to have
> "normal," "balanced" lighting. No, I don't believe in that. But
> I can work within my irregularities, within my style of clashing
> light values, only when I have complete control, or at least
> "normal" control over my tools. But here that control was
> slipping. The only way to control it was to embrace it and use
> it as part of my way of filming. To use the over-exposures as
> punctuations; to use them to reveal reality in, literally, a
> different light; to use them in order to imbue reality with a
> certain distance; to compound reality. (op. cit)

It seems significant that two of the most memorable sequences of **In
Between** concern a friend of Mekas whom I know nothing about apart from
the film, Mel Lyman. The first, entitled "Mel (God) Makes Coffee," is

narrated by Mekas in his characteristic beatnik style: "It was one of those long, hot, slow summer days. Mel brought some coffee beans, but we had no coffee pots in the house." The subsequent "miracle" performed by Mel, improvising a "perfect" coffee pot out of odd parts around the house, can be taken as a metaphor for Mekas's own filmmaking, which also tries to build workable structures out of spare parts.* The exalted treatment of the minor domestic event becomes emblematic of the treatment throughout: it is the same Mel whose extended performance of a banjo solo on a Manhattan balcony effectively concludes the film, the camera moving with what amounts to a kind of steady wonder across his fingers and feet. The innocent eye is a myth that dies hard in Mekas's cinema, and he is nowhere more attentive to it than when he is dealing with the most ephemeral sort of material, as here.

Most of the other figures in **In Between** are relatively familiar, at least in relation to their milieux and periods. Allen Ginsberg singing "Hare Krishna" in Tomkins Square Park, Herman and Gretchen Weinberg, Jerome Hill, Andrew Meyer, Shirley Clarke at the World's Fair, Salvador Dali (depicted in a lengthy, self-conscious black-and-white sequence that is much more staged than most of the rest, featuring Taylor Mead as well as Dali and one off-screen rumination by Mekas which seems to be obliquely about his own exile: "Oh, Salvador Dali, what made you into a clown? Being away from my roots in Spain, that's what made me a clown"), Ken Jacobs (seen at his own wedding), Gregory Markopoulos, Gerard Malanga, Carl Th. Dreyer, even Norman Mailer and Nico. A trip to Washingon, D.C. becomes the occasion for a narration about the importance of mud puddles ("They will be here when we are gone"), and, as in much of Mekas's later work, domestic celebrations and afternoons in the park seem very preva-

---

*A colleague, Bérénice Reynaud, has offered the following commentary by Claude Lévi-Strauss on bricolage (tinkering) as a relevant gloss on Mekas's method as I've described it:
"The 'bricoleur' is...someone who works with his hands and uses devious means compared to those of a craftsman. The characteristic feature of mythical thought is that it expresses itself by means of a heterogeneous repertoire which, even if extensive, is nevertheless limited. Mythical thought is...a kind of intellectual bricolage.[...]
"Like 'bricolage' on the technical plane, mythical reflection can reach unforeseen results on the intellectual plane.[...]
" ...The 'bricoleur' is adept at performing a large number of diverse tasks; but, unlike the engineer, he does not subordinate each of them to the availability of raw materials and tools conceived and procured for the purpose of the project. His universe of instruments is closed and the rules of his game are always to make do with 'whatever is at hand,' that is to say with a set of tools and materials which is always finite and is also heterogeneous because what it contains bears no relation to the current project, or indeed to any particular project, but is the... result of all the occasions there have been to enrich or renew the stock or to maintain it with the remains of previous contructions or destructions. The set of the 'bricoleur's' means cannot therefore be defined in terms of a project[...]It is to be defined only by its potential use or, putting this another way and in the language of the 'bricoleur' himself, because the elements are collected or retained on the principle that 'they may always come in handy.'" From The Savage Mind, translated by George Weidenfeld (Chicago: University of Chicago Press, 1966), pp. 16, 17, 18. The italics are Reynaud's.

lent. The format throughout recalls a volume of short poems—each page a separate, small flight of fancy.

Thanks in large part to a somewhat more fixed time and place, **Notes for Jerome**—shot in Cassis, France at Jerome Hill's villa, mainly in 1966 and 1967—has a much more unified range of subjects and themes, and a much more melancholy undertow. Dedicated "to the wind of Lithuania," with the sounds of (and references to) the mistral* prominent throughout, the film is more clearly structured around a system of repetitions than are any of Mekas's other films, repetitions in images, sounds, and titles alike—making for an overall rhythm of vacation boredom that seems comparable, *mutatis mutandis,* to Tati's **Les Vacances de Monsieur Hulot**. (Some of the repeated titles are so familiar sounding to begin with—like "life goes on" and "siesta" and "long long ago"—that they establish a ballad-like or stanza-like effect at the outset; and the same holds for Mekas's use of patches of black leader as a rhythmic device.)

Many of the motifs—like the lighthouse seen from the villa, or the sound of Hill's piano and singing voice—structure the film as they no doubt structured the vacations themselves. According to David Ehrenstein, a critic who watched the film with me, a good deal of the film refers directly to Hill's own **Film Portrait** (which I unfortunately haven't seen)—from the lighthouse to the La Ciotat train station where Lumière's famous film of an arriving train was shot. It's hard to know how much one can attribute the film's sadness to its European setting and what this signifies for Mekas ("What Petrarch saw walking across the hills," says one title), but the repetition of certain very Mekas-like titles—"The more exquisite the beauty, the more it reminds the exiled poet of his home"—certainly plays a pronounced role. Sparing but effective uses of double-exposure and freeze-frames help to expand the film's varied rhythmic palette, which runs the gamut from Breer-like rapidity to summery stasis, from quick camera movements to the leisurely pace of fellow vacationists and other visiting friends.

Ideologically speaking, **Paradise Not Yet Lost**, also known as **Oona's Third Year**, represents a kind of acid test for enthusiasts of Mekas's filmmaking, insofar as his chosen terrain this time is more circumscribed than ever—not only because less time elapsed between its filming and editing than is customary for Mekas, but also because its focus is much more doggedly and exclusively familial than that of any preceding work. Significantly, many friends whose full names are recognizable, like Peter Kubelka, are commonly identified by their first names only, for it is their status as intimate friends at family gatherings that matters most, not their professional or vocational identities.

---

*A strong wind prominent only in the south of France.

Jerome Hill in *Notes for Jerome*

As a detailed account both of what the film is and of what it contains, Mekas's own summary—dated November 1979 and reprinted in Judith E. Briggs's 1980 monograph on Jonas Mekas in the *Filmmakers Filming* series— deserves to be quoted in full, particularly because its style closely approximates the style of the film itself:

> These three reels of my film diaries contain the film "notes" taken during the calendar year 1977, arranged chronologically. The film is divided into six parts. The first part takes place in New York. We see a lot of home life and the city. We see a lot of our daughter Oona whose third year of life this is. Some other subjects: Peter's Concert (Peter Kubelka); A Visit to Marie Deren (Maya's mother); St. Patrick's Parade; Spring in Central Park; etc. The second, very brief

Oona Mekas in *Paradise Not Yet Lost*

part, takes place in Sweden, visiting Anna Lena Wibom. The
third part takes place in Lithuania. Myself, my wife Hollis, and
our 2½ year old daughter Oona visit my mother on the
occasion of her 90th birthday. Oona meets her young cous-
ins, we drink homemade beer, we walk through the woods,
gather mushrooms and wild strawberries, we fool around.
The fourth part takes place in Warszawa, our visit to Aldona
Dvarionas, the pianist. The fifth part is Austria, visiting Peter
Kubelka and Hermann Nitsch in Prinzendorf. We taste Hermann's wine, we talk to Peter's donkeys, we visit Pater
Nicolaus in Kremsmuenster, and then we go to Italy, with
Peter, in pursuit of Michelangelo's wine, Canaiola. The sixth
part is back in New York; a visit to Willard Van Dyke, upstate;
Oona's third birthday; a fire on Broome Street; more home
scenes; the beginning of winter storms.

   The sounds: street noises, nature (thunder, rain), Oona;
Peter, Leo (Adams), Raimund (Abraham), Hermann (Nitsch),
Anna Lena (Wibom), Hollis talk about home and culture; Leo,
Peter and myself sing (Lithuanian and Austrian folk songs);
Handel, Chopin, Wagner.

   It's a diary film, but also it is a meditation on the theme of
Paradise. It is a letter to Oona, to serve her, some day, as a
distant reminder of how the world around her looked during
the third year of her life—a period of which there will be only
tiny fragments left in her memory—and to provide her with a
romantic's guide to the essential values of life—in a world of
artificiality, commercialism, and bodily and spiritual poison.

A climactic, summational pair of titles in the third reel, occurring in
September according to the film's chronological progression, sums up the
attitude expressed in the final sentence above: "that's how your father
was—a romantic in the age of science & politics"; "and so was your
mother." This is really the "point" or "message" of the whole film, insofar as
it can be said to have one; and as such, the film can be regarded as Mekas's
testament, perhaps even to the same extent as **Reminiscences** (with its own
visits to Lithuania and Austria).

   There's no question that a great deal of the film is beautiful and
affecting, particularly in its cumulative impact. What continues as a
problem for me, however, is what I see as a sort of metaphysical conceit
underlying the whole American avant-garde romantic tradition—a central
aspect of the work of Brakhage, Noren, Benning, Jost, Robert Nelson, and
countless others, which reduces the universe to a list of male possessions:
This is my wife, my child, my gun, my dog, my camera, my house, my car,
my summer vacation, my life. And while the possessiveness of Mekas (and

accompanying self-aggrandizement) has relatively little of the offensive-ness—and much less of the formal complexity—of Brakhage, it still rests on an unproblematical embrace of The Essential Verities that are somehow taken to be outside all history and ideology, an assumption of innocence that cannot help but give off a certain whiff of complacency even while it makes a certain form of simplicity and poetic insight possible.

Surely the fact that Jonas Mekas started his filmmaking career as an adult (astonishingly, he was nearly 40 when he made **Guns of the Trees**) places him apart from all or most of his colleagues. There is almost none of the insufferable macho pretension of Brakhage climbing a snowy mountain with his dog in **Prelude**, which suggests (like so much of the tradition that Brakhage helped to father in his patriarchal Zeus stance) the heroic dreams of a little boy who's never had to grow up. Behind all the childlike poetic stances of Mekas in his films is a tragic sense of life's limitations that seems closer to maturity than defeatism or middle-class inertia—a constant sense, even throughout the unceasing flow of happiness that characterizes so much of **Paradise Not Yet Lost**, that none of this can ever replace or rectify the paradise that he himself lost when he had to leave his Lithuanian village, if only because Mekas himself understands that this paradise is a child's fantasy and that the subjective world of his diary films is a constructed imaginary world that exists *in effect* only through his filmmaking.

At its best, Mekas's art has something satisfyingly practical about it. Several years ago, when I was reviewing **Lost, Lost, Lost**, a colleague found much of the film insufferable for its self-pity, sentimentality, false naïveté, and self-romanticising martyrdom. He made particular reference to a specific title in the film ("Rejected by the Flaherty Seminar, we sleep outside in the cold night of Vermont"), which is followed by Mekas's own gloss on the soundtrack:. "While the guests proper, the respectable docu-mentarists and cinéastes, slept in their warm beds, we watched the morning with the cold of night still in our bones, our flesh. It was a Flaherty morning." Yet the fact remains that Mekas's position at that point *was* that of a martyr, and the poetic positions arising from this are defensible on practical grounds: if one has to sleep outside in the coldness of Vermont, it surely makes the experience much more bearable if the morning that one wakes up to is a Flaherty morning. I'm reminded of a statement in Mekas's narration, that occurs near the end of Part II of **In Between**: "I never had enough to eat in those days....And when I *did* have enough, I played the fool."

Still playing the fool, Mekas has hours of beautiful reflections about his life to share with us in his films, and perhaps it sounds churlish to question some of the philosophical and metaphysical assumptions that make those reflections possible. If the American avant-garde is ever to emerge from its own self-absorption, Mekas's career has to be seen as exemplary, I feel, in positive as well as negative respects. His early criticism (and pamphleteering) in the pages of *The Village Voice* demonstrated an extraordinary pluralism and openness to all the varieties of cinema that seem missing from the work of most of his successors, a pluralism and openness that can still be felt in much of his filmmaking. That he has subsequently had to narrow this stance in order to clarify his own artistic identity is understandable—if regrettable in some of its long-term consequences.

 ULRIKE OTTINGER.
Born in Konstanz, Germany, 1942.

1974—*Laokoon und Soehne (Laokoon and His Sons)* (16mm, b&w, 49 min.)

1975—*Die Betoerung der Blauen Matrosen (The Infatuation of the Blue Sailors)* (16mm, color, 47 min.)

1977—*Madam X—Eine Abslute Herrscherin (Madame X—An Absolute Ruler)* (16mm, color, 141 min.)

1979—*Bildnis Einer Trinkerin (Aller Jamais Retour/Ticket of No Return)* (35mm, color, 108 min.)

1981—*Freak Orlando* (35mm, color, 126 min.)

What do I know about Ulrike Ottinger? Not much, but enough to make me want to know more. Admittedly, I've seen only her last two features. And on the basis of a single viewing about a year ago, **Freak Orlando** is a decidedly uneven film, definitely hit-or-miss in its overall thrust, and conceivably full of as many misses as hits. Like it or not, though, the film can be regarded as a climactic *summa* of the performance-oriented European avant-garde film, from Carmelo Bene to Philippe Garrel to Marc'O to the collaborations of Pedro Portabella* with Christopher Lee—to cite the names of four leading figures of excitement and interest in this category whose careers I lost track of after moving back to the U.S. from Europe in 1977. Insofar as **Freak Orlando** can be regarded as the **Monterey Pop** or **Woodstock** of the European avant-garde performance movement, it's a valuable and fascinating document to have, and one therefore has reason to look forward to its projected release in this country. . . . **Ticket Of No Return,** on the other hand, strikes me as a fully achieved work—one of the few true masterpieces of the contemporary German avant-garde cinema—making Ottinger an obligatory inclusion for this book.

---

*Portabella, actually, belongs to a somewhat more modernist and politically beleaguered species than the others, and his remarkable, black-and-white **Vampyr** and **Umbracle**, both made in Franco Spain, which I reviewed in my Cannes coverage for *The Village Voice*—June 17, 1971 and June 29, 1972, respectively—owe a considerable amount of their own brilliance to the soundtrack constructions of composer Carlos Santos.

First, though, here's a little bit about the films I *don't* know, as gleaned from Roswitha Mueller's valuable interview with Ottinger in *Discourse* (No. 4, Winter 1981/82). **Laokoon** was made with a lot of difficulty over a two-year period. (Ottinger: "I am a painter originally. The people who sold my paintings found my new medium interesting and made it possible to raise the 20,000 marks necessary to make this first film...the difficulties involved in editing seemed insurmountable at times.") And her second film, **The Infatuation of the Blue Sailors**, was made in Berlin: "It is a free association of images to the texts by Apollinaire which themselves are written in the form of a collage. I have also tried to let the texts which satirize the Comédie Française, as well as the concierge from Marseille, speak for themselves."

Madame X, her third film (and the longest to date), reportedly as variable a work as **Freak Orlando**, was financed by money from ZDF (German TV). From most accounts, including Ottinger's, it appears to be her most explicitly feminist work so far ("The *leitmotif* throughout the film is about the prohibition imposed on women to make their own experiences"), and it includes a cameo appearance by Yvonne Rainer—in Germany at the time because of the DAAD (German Foreign Exchange Service)—on roller skates, delivering a monologue written by Rainer herself.

Ticket of No Return somehow manages to be two things at once: (1) an inspired development and fusion of many of the most fruitful currents in European film over the past several years—combining elements in everything from Vera Chytilova to Federico Fellini to Lothar Lambert to Jacques Rivette to Werner Schroeter to Jacques Tati (a very democratic freak salad, indeed), and (2) an uncategorizable masterpiece so *sui generis* that influences seem hardly relevant at all to the synthesis achieved.

The nameless heroine—played by Tabea Blumenschein, a real-life clothes designer who dreamed up, designed, and made all the extravagant outfits in the film—arrives in Berlin on a one-way ticket; in the opening shot, she walks away from the camera, her bright red skirt receding like the title heroine's yellow purse in the opening shot of Hitchcock's **Marnie**, to Felliniesque music on the soundtrack, in an airport that virtually announces itself as the offspring of the Orly Airport space that opens Tati's **Playtime**. An off-screen female narrator commences the story, and only the heroine's hands are visible just before the title and subtitle (**Portrait of a Woman Drinker**) appear on the screen. Next come the credits, with color snapshots of each crew member lovingly placed next to her or his name (the sense of chuminess in both Ottinger films I've seen is an essential part of their charm, making Ottinger in one sense the Howard Hawks of the feminist avant-garde). "Berlin-Tegel-Reality," announces a female voice on the p.a. system. The heroine again walks away from the camera, this time seen from a much lower camera angle; a male dwarf passes by, just before she

Ticket of No Return

approaches a glass pane being washed by a female janitor. The airport doors slide open with a wheeze; three women dressed in prim grey outfits, known as Social Question (Magdalena Montezuma), Accurate Statistics (Orpha Termin), and Common Sense (Monika Von Cube), follow the heroine out the door, in another shot whose abrupt sounds and sharp, blocky movements seem to come out of the same comic repertoire as **Playtime**. Formally and thematically speaking, all the basic elements of the film are already present in this opening, as soon as it's made clear that the heroine has come to Berlin to drink herself to death. The remainder of the movie is merely a celebration of that decision, rendered in as many different registers and forms of celebratory pleasure as Ottinger can get onto the screen—serving up a veritable feast of depravity and irresponsibility.

In terms of plot, then, that's most of what **Ticket of No Return** has to offer: conceptually speaking, a string of episodes which repeat the same root elements, like a string of gags in a series of Road Runner cartoons (where wit always has something to do with the distinction between sameness and difference; the importance of Acme products in Chuck Jones' conceptual schemes seems fundamental). Within this relatively static framework, however, the variables—such as the heroine's wardrobe, the diverse narrative settings for her drinking, and diverse inventions in the dialogue and *mise en scène*—give the film a flamboyant, expressive range. Carrie Rickey, in an appreciative review in *The Village Voice*, offered an enthusiastic rundown of some of the heroine's ensembles: "a persimmon melton overcoat and bonnet for deplaning at Berlin-Tegel airport, an *Alphaville* of starkness and alienation; a strapless black satin gown (reminiscent of Hayworth in *Gilda*) with matching opera-length gloves and oversized bow headdress, in which she chugalugs cognac at the casino; a fucshia vicuna (I kid you not) cocktail dress with rhinestone details and matching theater jacket, which she wears to a lesbian bar where she's too drunk to boogie." (Rickey also labelled Social Question, Accurate Statistics, and Common Sense the "Greek chorus to all of Blumenschein's glamorous entrances...a trio clad in houndstooth....")

Early in her travels around Berlin, the heroine stumbles upon a woman identified as Drinker from the Zoo in the credits (played by Lutze), a bag lady who goes around with a shopping cart, whom she promptly invites to accompany her as a drinking companion. (Whether it's actually Lutze who's washing the airport panes at the beginning is not clear to me at this point, but she's clearly already there in spirit.) And the interesting thing about this character is that she comes from another genre of filmmaking—the documentary, according to Ottinger, although one could equally equate her with neorealism—in contrast to the more Hollywoodish styling of the heroine. And it is the scandal provided by the union between these two that provides the closest thing to a consecutive plot that **Ticket of No Return** can claim.

The heroine steps out in her strapless black satin gown; a yellow cab stops for her in extreme close-up (a blur of yellow crosses the screen); she takes a drink in the back seat; she sees some dwarfs. After the cab hits the bag lady in the street, forcing her to drop various things and denounce the driver, Social Question, Accurate Statistics, and Common Sense stop in an adjacent cab and prattle their disapproval. A man in an elevator shows the heroine a card trick; in the casino bar, he shows her dice tricks. After she steps away from the roulette table, she has a drink at the bar and breaks her glass; the bartender delivers a deadpan monologue to no one about her social behavior, dutifully repeated later in the film. On her way back to her hotel, the nameless dwarf in front of a fountain pays his respects to her.

Dressed in yellow, she drinks in a café the following day while the three grey sisters cite facts and figures at an adjoining table—and the value of these in explaining alcoholism to the public—while daintily devouring ice cream sundaes. The bag lady appears on the other side of the pane, is invited in by the heroine, and is served cognac. They each throw a glass of water at the glass pane, are photographed by a couple in the café, and are thrown out on the street by the management. (On the street, the couple continue to take pictures of them.) The two women repair to the heroine's hotel room, drink wine and talk and laugh, eat oranges, and lounge around on the bed; it's the most naturalistic scene in the film. "You're kind," the bag lady says in awe. "Why are you so kind?"

Waking up alone the next day, the heroine gets up in her silky bedclothes and reads in the paper about the scandal she caused in the café. After comparing her mirror reflection to her picture in the paper, she takes a drink and throws her glass at the mirror. Subsequently, she's found drinking in a nearly empty theater (occupied only by five eerie women in black, seated in another section, who turn around to look at her in one motion), served wine by a stocky usherette; in her hotel room, watching the dwarf serving food on her black-and-white TV screen (before she removes a pair of scissors from the identical fowl on her dinner tray, and stabs a picture of herself dressed as a man); at a cabaret where an operatic soprano sings about drinking; in a café where Eddie Constantine and other "artists" sit; in a room where Bavarians eat sausages and sauerkraut and listen to a yodeler; and in a lesbian bar, where one of the grey sisters notes, "The homosexual activity is an institution, a recreational activity."

Framed by two odd sequences that audibly click as they cut from the heroine in long shot on a park bench to a close-up of one of her eyes, the heroine is seen drinking in contexts that are more fantastical and extravagant: playing Hamlet drunkenly on the stage (with audience members decrying her shocking lack of discipline); sitting at an office desk getting berated by her boss for drinking (while the grey trio eavesdrop through the door); walking on a tightrope outdoors with a parasol (the grey trio marveling that she can do it drunk, without a net); on an outdoor spiral staircase at night, speaking in English and asking for a cigarette while a drummer starts a solo on a lower level which she eventually sings and chants along with, while both the dwarf and the grey trio watch on different levels; test-driving a car through a wall of fire on an empty field, with the trio again in attendance.

Later, she goes off on a ride on an aluminum-colored boat built to resemble a whale and called Moby Dick, where she's again served wine. As the bag lady, rushing to catch up with her in the early dawn, drops some of her possessions on the street, a photographer gathers them up and takes snapshots of each one. Still later, a café manager named Willy (Gunter Meisner) goes off with the bag lady, a transvestite (Volker Spengler, a refugee from Fassbinder's **In a Year of Thirteen Moons**) gets tossed from a truck and comforted with wine by women, and the heroine passes out on some steep outdoor steps just before a crowd of people descend it ("As you make your bed, so you must lie in it," says one of the honorable grey trio). In the final shot, though, the heroine's back on her feet again, in another lush location, walking in high heels across a glass mirror floor, punching holes in the mirrors on either side of her as she goes.

Like **Freak Orlando, Ticket of No Return** is a movie about body language as well as what Ottinger refers to as an inversion of narcissism; in a sense these two preoccupations are constantly being explored together. In her interview with Mueller, Ottinger noted, "Narcissism has a double face: to love *only* oneself is self-destruction. I am using narcissism as a metaphor for self-destruction. What interests me in particular is that narcissism always involves a certain amount of anxiety, anxieties which are never talked about. In this film these anxieties are drowned in alcohol. I thought about how to represent this anxiety for a long time. It seemed evident to me that she hates herself." For her literally divided stance towards notions of female identity, Ottinger thus situates herself at the same crossroads occupied in their separate ways by Chantal Akerman, Sara Driver, Yvonne Rainer, Jackie Raynal, and Leslie Thornton—a crossroads where questions of sexual roles and of reading one's self in pursuit of identity ultimately dictate the nature and focus of many of the formal decisions.

The best summary of **Freak Orlando** I can offer comes from the detailed synopsis printed in the program to the 11th International Festival of New Cinema in Montreal (Fall 1982):

> In the form of a "little theater of the world" (*Kleines Welttheater*), a history of the world from its beginnings to our day, including the errors, the incompetence, the thirst for power, the fear, the madness, the cruelty and the commonplace, in a story of five episodes.

First episode: where it is told how Orlando Zyklopa, with her seven dwarf shoemakers, special attraction of the instant shoe repair service at the Freak City department store, strikes the anvil; how she is driven away by Herbert Zeus, director of the store; then, as queen of the seven dwarf-athletes, how she climbs up on the Trojan Horse; and finally how she refuses to be the successor to a holy stylite, which leads to her death.

Second episode: where it is told how Orlando Orlanda, alias Orlanda Zyklopa, is born as a miracle on the steps of a basilicum in the Middle Ages and, with her two heads, enchants those around her with a lovely song in two-part harmony; how she can't prevent the flagellants from taking two acrobat prisoners and leading them out of the city in their procession, which leads her to pursue them with the famous Galli, a dwarf painter, up to the convent of Wilgeforte, the bearded woman saint; how she is dressed in new clothes in the department store warehouse; and how she goes through an amazing transformation while Galli paints her portrait.

Third episode: where it is told how Orlando Capricho, alias Orlando Orlanda, alias Orlanda Zyklopa, has to admit that she has been taken by a special travel offer made by the department store, announced by a seductive voice; how she learns distrust when she sees her mirror image; how she falls into the hands of the persecutors of the Spanish Inquisition at the end of the 18th century; how she has to undergo a thousand dangers and adventures, barely escaping internment in a prison; and how she is finally deported with people of every description, which Galli El Primi illustrates faithfully.

Fourth episode: where it is told how Mr. Orlando ... in front of the entrance to the psychiatric ward of a hospital, is engaged by the freak-artists of a side-show travelling around the country; how he quickly falls in love with one of a pair of Siamese-twin sisters, named Lena, which the other, named Leni, can't stand; which is why Mr. Orlando, entangled in a rather confused affair, stabs Leni with a dagger, which also inevitably kills his Lena, whom he loved so much; and how the head of the troupe is forced to deliver Mr. Orlando to death, to comply with an old tradition of the artists.

Fifth episode: where it is told how Mrs. Orlando, called Freak Orlando because of her special preferences ... is engaged as an entertainer and tours Europe with four bunnies; how she is in great demand as an attraction for shopping center openings, family celebrations, etc.; how, finally, she is engaged to do a show at the annual festival of ugliness; how she crowns the winner and bestows a trophy with the inscription, "Limping is the way of the Crippled," and, at the end of the festival, how we are told that the story is over.

At its funniest and best—a virtuoso solo performance by someone or other as Christ on the Cross that somehow manages to combine the best of both Lennie Bruce and Werner Schroeter in one very extended shot and setpiece; domestic complications in the lives of Lena and Leni, the Siamese twins (enjoyably played by Delphine Seyrig and Jackie Raynal)—it is as rewarding as much of **Ticket of No Return.** On the whole, though, as the above summary may well suggest, the film is every bit as variable as a circus, and is best approached in just that spirit—as one would approach, say, a John Waters film.

Freak Orlando
by permission of
Basis-Film

Ottinger's political focus in **Freak Orlando** is a lot closer to that of Todd Browning's 1931 **Freaks** than it is to Virginia Woolf's novel *Orlando,* from which Ottinger has taken only the notion of "an ideal protagonist...a figure who represents all the social possibilities—man and woman—which we normally do not have." But the absorption in pure spectacle that one associates with late Fellini is still closer to the mark, making the matter of the film's overall duration somewhat arbitrary, like an endlessly extendable chain of vaudeville turns. Currently in the works from Ottinger, one hears, is **Dorian Gray im Spiegel der Boulevardpresse**, which one suspects will take her whole involvement with narcissism and its inverse still further.

...the argument thus far

As noted above, Ottinger comes to filmmaking from painting, and Driver from theater and archeology. Among those who are discussed below, Rappaport can be traced back to the nineteenth century novel, Raynal was a professional film editor before she became a filmmaker, and Snow started out as a musician and plastic artist. Yvonne Rainer had a particularly distinguished career as a dancer and choreographer before embarking on film: see her beautiful and very useful *Work 1961-73*, published by the respective presses of the Nova Scotia College of Art and Design and New York University, for a detailed chronicle of that career. Yet Rainer's work in dance was already so well-versed in the techniques of mixed media that her films—like those of Benning and Snow—seem to grow out of an artworld context that acknowledges and deals with film history only in the most oblique, partial, parenthetical, and grudging of fashions. The social parameters of the avant-garde and of Hollywood may have a few amusing similarities, but (star politics to the contrary) they are scarcely identical, and it is easy to account for the natural suspicion that each group feels towards the other—and the less-than-comprehensive grasp of film history that each group tends to have as a consequence.

In the conversation that opens this book, the pluralism that was once possible in Jonas Mekas's *Village Voice* column and in *Film Culture* is recalled. Mekas's statements imply that the old comprehensiveness is no longer possible in the same way; and in the conversation that ends this book, Peter Gidal argues that this sort of comprehensiveness and pluralism (as exemplified and represented in his case by London's The Other Cinema) is no longer desirable—if indeed it ever was—for political reasons. Feeling myself that Yvonne Rainer's narrative concerns—like those of Richard Foreman in theater and Mark Rappaport in his own films—have more in common with the French New Wave than they do with (say) Abstract Expressionism, I often regret that the social divisions between these realms make such relationships harder to trace and explore than the relationship between Rainer's films and Frampton's (which is more direct and evident, perhaps, but for me less interesting). In this respect, ignorance about the artworld context is an excellent background and preparation for looking at Yvonne Rainer's movies.

YVONNE RAINER.
Born in San Francisco, 1934.

1967—*Volleyball (Foot Film)* (16mm, b&w, 10 min., silent)
1968—*Hand Movie* (8mm, b&w, 5 min., silent)
  Rhode Island Red (16mm, b&w, 10 min., silent)
  Trio Film (16mm, b&w, 13 min., silent)
1969—*Line* (16mm, b&w, 10 min., silent)
1972—*Lives of Performers* (16mm, b&w, 95 min.)
1974—*Film about a Woman Who...* (16mm, b&w & color, 105 min.)
1976—*Kristina Talking Pictures* (16mm, b&w & color, 90 min.)
1980—*Working Title: Journeys from Berlin/1971* (16mm, b&w & color, 125 min.)

The first (and, to my mind, best) two features by Yvonne Rainer, **Lives of Performers** and **Film about a Woman Who...**, are the masterful films of a dancer, performance artist, choreographer, and writer who has turned to filmmaking as a means of extending her work, continuing many of its parameters through other means. The second two features, **Kristina Talking Pictures** and **Working Title: Journeys from Berlin/1971**, as their lumpier titles suggest, are a lot less singular in their frames and impacts, and inevitably split off into dissociated sections—many of them as brilliant and resonant with meaning as anything Rainer has done. They are not projects that want to limit themselves to single genres to the degree that the preceding films do, organized as they are around the modes of soap opera, melodrama, and performance itself. These later films, which seem to want to relocate performance art in other venues—the circus, politics, psychoanalysis—are more like *Bouvard and Pecuchet* enterprises: one is served up an indigestible surfeit of texts in many forms, some of them overlapping, as in middle-period Godard or Hock's **Pacific Time** or Ottinger's **Freak Orlando** (to cite three widely divergent examples)—creating a blankness of effect at certain junctures of particular overload, oddly resembling the minimalism of Peter Gidal, who, in his spareness, starts from the opposite extreme. The main point of similarity, it seems to me, is the puritanism of both filmmakers, each obsessed with the dialectics of exposure and concealment in relation to their films and polemical positions. Gidal's dual focus on, say, the exposure of Warhol's cinema and the concealment of Beckett's prose (as connected through the political example of Brecht) can thus be seen as the near-equivalent of Rainer's equal interest in obscenity and censorship (as mediated through the apolitical influence of psycho-analysis) in all four of her features.

It's no accident that the heroine of **Kristina** comes from the circus, and that the de-centered constellation of female voices in **Journeys** all come from somewhere outside dance and theater. These latter films seem especially interested in the points at which questions of performance link up with questions of life in general outside the artworld context. That Rainer

Annette Michelson and Gabor
Vernon in *Journeys from
Berlin/1971*

nevertheless populates her films with artworld denizens and family mem-bers only extends the peekaboo dialectic of concealment and exposure, one more token of the divided self. With identity the central issue and internal debate the dominant mode, everything is up for grabs, including the spectator's focus and attention.

Rainer is only one of the many actresses in **Kristina** who play Kristina; in **Journeys**, her appearances are so fleeting that they seem at once privileged and begrudging: learning how to play the recorder in one segment, addressing to her mother an emotional videotape about a German film by Werner Hochbaum that she saw. ("By itself the monologue is somewhat sentimental," stipulates her script, which doesn't allude to the fact that Rainer herself plays these two parts.) The relocation of her performance art in **Journeys** is very much a matter of controlled generosity: allowing others the pleasure of performing, while directing them very closely. Annette Michelson and the off-screen Vito Acconci and Amy Taubin are all highly skillful performers in the film. (Contrary to what Jon Jost claims elsewhere in this book, the acting in **Wavelength**—by Taubin,

Hollis Frampton, and others—is not, in my estimation, amateurish.) And in contrast to many pure dancers and performers, Rainer is quite capable of fancy dancing on a page as well as on a stage. Consider, for instance, the following passage from a verbal trailer to **Journeys from Berlin** that I once, as an editor, had the pleasure of commissioning from Rainer. (It was originally intended for *The Thousand Eyes,* but due to complications wound up in *Millenium Film Journal* No. 6, Spring 1980.) Most of the last paragraph comes from the soundtrack of the film itself:

> Is *Journeys from Berlin/1971*. . . autobiography or fiction? Is it dadaist vaudeville or legitimate filmic research? Is its politics a set-up, a rigged game, mere window dressing thinly masking a formalist adventurism? Are its armchair terrorists and self-absorbed narcissists worthy of being made to voice serious moral-political concerns? Can I claim redeeming social value for this film? Is its emphasis on the individual act—the "attentat" or the act of suicide—in relation to totalitarian absolutism, is this emphasis an admission of the hopelessness of working for social change? Are its humanist yearnings and confessions a substitute for political practice?
>
> Without delay a short grammatical intervention: Wasn't it Gertrude Stein who said the sentence is more important than the paragraph? Flitting and dipping are more to my liking than soaring and arcing. Stumbling over the hit-and-run of the quote and the snort is more habitual to my mode of thought than the intricacies of binary logic. The latter is my nemesis, I mean amanuensis. Inadvertent puns tripped over my mother's mouth where you would have expected malapropisms. A condition in itself not totally surprising, for, as one well-known critic once said of her (mother), "She must suffer because she has no education." (Mercy, pity, compassion: gimme, gimme. [. . .]
>
> Postscript to a false ending, or another little trailer: The phone rings. The therapist answers it. A voice like Jimmy Durante raps: "My daddy called me Cookie. I'm really a good girl . . . I'm not one for fussing. Not like those movie women: Katy Hepburn facing the dawn in her posh pad with stiff upper chin. Merle Oberon facing the Nazi night with hair billowing in the electric breeze. Roz Russell sockin' the words 'n' the whiskey to the best of them. Rita Hayworth getting shot in the mirror and getting her man. Jane Wyman smiling through tears. I never faced the music, much less the dawn; I stayed in bed. I never socked anything to anybody; why rock the boat? I never set out to get my man, even in the

mirror; they all got me. I never smiled through my tears; I choked down my terror. I never had to face the Nazis, much less their night. Not for me that succumbing in the great task because it must be done; not for me the heart beating in incomprehensible joy; not for me the vicissitudes of class struggle; not for me the uncertainties of political thought. . . ."

The references to Hollywood actresses in the final paragraph only extend the ironic and ambivalent uses of material from mainstream cinema in all of Yvonne Rainer's features. **Lives of Performers** ends with an actual performance by Rainer's dance company based on imitations of stills from G. W. Pabst's **Pandora's Box** or **Lulu** that are published in the Anglo-American edition of the film's published screenplay. **Film about a Woman Who**. . . also uses film material from a book—a series of frame enlargements illustrating the shower murder of **Psycho** in François Truffaut's book-length interview with Alfred Hitchcock—accompanied by a woman's voice narrating her feelings of disgust after having seen the film. One sequence of **Kristina Talking Pictures** uses four James Cagney stills while a male voice fictionally identified as Cagney's voice in the script (and spoken by Richard Tobias) is heard, and elsewhere other movie references abound in the dialogue, such as in a discussion of Godard which contains the following Raineresque exchange:

> Kate: "I'd like to see Doris Day or Elvis Presley talk about their experiences in Dachau. Would we take Yves Montand more seriously? And what is the difference between Yves Montand facing the camera and telling us and **Night and Fog**? . . . Or a photo of emaciated corpses tacked on the wall?"
> David (with mouth full of food): "There is as thin a line between poetry and banality as there is between horror and fascination."
> Blondell's voice: "What's so poetic about Yves Montand?"

Horror and fascination, indeed, describe part of Rainer's ambivalent and puritanical response to Hollywood—a stance that seems no less evident in a paper I heard her deliver at the 1976 Edinburgh Film Festival (reproduced in *Idiolects* No. 6, June 1978), entitled "A Likely Story," which helps to clarify her relationship to narrative as well. To quote a salient excerpt:

> [. . .] Let me insert here that my own involvement with narrative forms has not always been either happy or whole hearted, rather more often a dalliance than a commitment.

The reason lies partly in the nature of the predominating form of the narrative film. The tyranny of a form that creates the expectation of a continuous answer to "what will happen next?" fanatically pursuing an inexorable resolution in which all things find their just or correct placement in space and time—such a tyranny having already attained its epiphany in the movies (I think of **Gertrud, Senso, Balthazar, Contempt, Lulu**), such a form has inevitably seemed more ripe for resistance, or at least, evasion, than for emulation.

My own forays into this territory border on a kind of banditry, the need for which has slowly evolved out of a dilemma imposed by subject matter. The dilemma has become more clarified for me on the completion of each of my three films, presenting itself in the form of basic, though variously oriented, questions, asked—and not always answered—by each of these films, and having, I would hope, wider application than my own work.

Can the presentation of sexual conflict in film, or the presentation of the experience of love and jealousy, be revitalized through a studied placement or dislocation of clichés borrowed from soap opera and melodrama? Can specific states of mind and emotion, or subtleties of social interaction, be conveyed in film without being attached, or by being only provisionally attached, to particularities of place, time, person, and relationship? And can such subject matter be presented without being "acted out"—in both the theatrical and psychoanalytic senses—via simulated dialogue and action? Are faces such as belong to Katharine Hepburn and Liv Ullman the only vehicles for grief and passion? Can a film achieve comparable impact through means other than these (faces)? And why in the world would one ever want to achieve an effect comparable to that wonder of art and nature, the smile fading from Hepburn's face? [. . .]

Considering Rainer's verbal sharpness and wit—a quality she shares with her friend and neighbor in lower Manhattan, Mark Rappaport (who has a related tendency to deal with very personal material in a rigorously objectified manner, often drawing upon the resources of self-parody with an urban self-consciousness about culture that recalls Woody Allen)—as well as her position and reputation within the artworld, it's not surprising that a veritable library of documentation about **Journeys from Berlin** has already been published, ranging from an early version of the script in *October* No. 9 (Summer 1979) to detailed interviews with Rainer and Michelson (by Noel Carroll and Sally Banes, respectively) in *Millennium*

Film Journal Nos. 7/8/9 (Fall/Winter 1980/81). But however interesting and useful much of this documentation is, it can't really compensate for the sheer intractability of the film as an audiovisual experience—an infernal machine turned against itself in which all the individual texts, no matter how interesting or relevant, exist only to be overtaken, challenged, or obliterated by other texts, through a kind of radical uncertainty principle that ultimately undermines everything in the film. After a certain point, even the words in Michelson's bawdy psychoanalytical monologues that are blipped from the soundtrack begin to seem like self-lacerations on Rainer's part—acts of seemingly random censorship which seem to reflect a mistrust by Rainer of the affective powers of her material.

Polyphony and collage are, to be sure, predominant modes in Rainer's work; there has always been a tendency for her to contradict image with sound, one actor with another (playing the same part), or simply create a vast thicket of cultural material—such as the collage of photographic material attached to a domestic wall in **Kristina**, repeatedly traversed by the camera—which defies any sort of intelligible synthesis. In fact, Rainer even

Journeys from Berlin/1971

encapsulates and parodies this aspect of her work in the multiple lateral tracks of her camera past surrealist arrays of diverse objects on a mantelpiece in **Journeys**, tracks that gracefully and enjoyably cope with this principle of overload through a linear arrangement—an approach very similar to the lateral track past an endless traffic jam in Godard's **Weekend**.

The problem is, outside such elegant structures for handling overload, Rainer never seems to know when to stop piling on the texts. Despite her reference to "dada vaudeville" in the verbal trailer to **Journeys** quoted above, it is precisely her avoidance of any of the principles of rhythmic variation underlying vaudeville which makes the polyrhythmic structure of **Journeys** ultimately sluggish in effect. This is the reverse of the impression created by **Film about a Woman Who** ..., arguably Rainer's best film, motored on a series of narrative teases and seductions of various sorts that make the spectator constantly aware of how she or he is being "taken in." **Journeys**, more doggedly bent on keeping the spectator out in the cold, despite its textual richness and density, can only shore up fragments against its ruins (to paraphrase T. S. Eliot) and defy the viewer to build something usable out of them.

Would it be fair to assert that **Journeys** is about the pleasures of performing, speaking, writing, and quoting—as opposed to **Film about a Woman Who**..., which is more about the pleasures of watching, listening, and reading? It's certainly true that the personal nexus that generates the separate texts of **Journeys** is a framework that Rainer takes some pains to keep absent from the film, forcing spectators to come up with their own connections, interconnections, and points of convergence. The problem is, it is highly unlikely that any spectator could come up with any rationale for linking all these concerns meaningfully *without* the figure and biography of Rainer herself. To demonstrate this, I have listed below most of the film's principal discourses, adding in parentheses the specific personal links to Rainer wherever I am aware of them:

1. Roller titles dealing with acts of the German government in 1977, including the imprisonments of anarchists Andreas Baader, Gudrun Ensslin, and Jan-Carl Raspe, who were later found dead in their cells. *(Rainer lived in Germany for a year during this period, on a government artist's grant, and returned on a visit only two weeks before Baader, Ensslin, and Raspe were found dead. As a child she was raised by anarchists: "When I was 15," she told me in late 1979, "Emma Goldman's autobiography was one of the great books of my life.")*

2. Extracts from a teenage girl's journal written during the early Fifties, read off-screen by a female voice. *(A journal kept by Rainer herself between the ages of 15 and 18.)*

3. To quote from the script: "an on-camera monologue by a fifty-year-old woman [Annette Michelson] designated 'patient' that from time to time becomes a dialogue with a woman, man or nine-year-old boy, all designated as 'therapist.'" *(Rainer, in her late forties when she made **Journeys**, had been in psychoanalysis for several years.)*

4. Recorder lessons. *(Rainer is the pupil, her cousin—Ruth Rainero—the teacher.)*

5. A videotape addressed by a woman to her mother. *(Rainer plays the part.)*

6. A man (Antonio Skarmeta) and woman (Cynthia Beatt) are seen walking in front of a church in various juxtapositions and configurations that

are contrasted through the editing. *(Referred to by Rainer as the "attentat" section, this block of material focuses mainly on the woman, who bears a striking resemblance to Rainer herself when seen from a distance.)*

7. Tracks along a mantelpiece full of diverse objects, including specific ones mentioned by the patient and other characters.

8. An off-screen dialogue between a man and a woman, played by Vito Acconci and Amy Taubin, about personal motives behind political actions—specifically on the part of terrorists and revolutionaries—heard over the sounds of preparing and eating dinner; quotations from the memoirs of Russian anarchists are included in the discussion.

9. Shots taken from the windows of trains and apartments in Berlin, London, and New York.

10. Aerial shots of Stonehenge and the Berlin Wall.

As can be seen, I think, from the above summary, the first six blocks of material listed above all have crucial links to Rainer of one kind or another; the following two can be seen to have links that derive from or relate to the first six, and even the last two—with the exception of Stonehenge—can be easily connected to her biographically. Yet it is the calculated suppression of these connections that gives the film its present form.

As Rainer herself has pointed out, the first 20 or so minutes of **Journeys** present all of the film's central visual material, which is subsequently only repeated—a method that can also be seen in Jean-Daniel Pollet's **Mediterranée** (discussed in the chapter on Jackie Raynal) and most of the films of Nicolas Roeg. The extremely busy surface of the film has a lot to do with the printed and recited texts that are set alongside this material; within this context, the roller titles about the German government seem to be offered up like castor oil—almost as a kind of punishment for the wit and flamboyance displayed elsewhere (such as in the patient's monologues, which correspondingly tend to depoliticize the film's internal debate). While the diversity of the visual material has something in common with the radical juxtapositions of Leslie Thornton in **Adynata**, it can be argued that the unifying role played by Babette Mangolte's splendid black-and-white photography in Rainer's first two features is sorely missing in **Journeys**—shot by no less than five cinematographers and visually less distinguished. As powerful as many of its individual parts are, Rainers's most ambitious film to date is essentially undone by its own integrity—its refusal to coast along on the personal style that Rainer alone could have brought to it.

Yet there is perhaps as much to be learned from this refusal as there is from that style. Certainly the amount of interesting feminist speculation that is already beginning to collect around the recent work of Akerman *and* Rainer suggests that the complex refusals of both filmmakers may well have implications that go beyond the range of sympathetic male critics such as myself. I'm thinking, in particular, of two recent academic papers I've read about **Journeys** which suggest fruitful lines of inquiry, both unpublished at the time of writing: Anne Friedberg, in "Split Positions," concludes with an "impossibility"—"that **Journeys** is a signifying system which means nothing"—while Kaja Silverman, in "Dis-embodying the Female Voice," singling out the distinct voices in the film of adolescent girl, patient, cooking woman, and Rainer herself, concludes that "Toward the end of the film the four voices converge more and more, until they finally seem to be participating in the same narcissistic speech." The very capacity of **Journeys** to provoke these antithetical readings, at once centrifugal and centripetal, may constitute a problem, but it remains a fascinating one.

 MARK RAPPAPORT.
Born in New York, 1942.

1966—*MUR 19* (16mm, b&w, 23 min.)
1967—*Friends* (16mm, b&w, 18 min.)
          Blue Frieze (16mm, b&w & color, 6 min.)
1968—*The Stairs* (16mm, b&w & color, 9 min.)
          Bay of the Angels (16mm, b&w & color, 5 min.)
1970—*Persepolis* (16mm, b&w & color, 11 min.)
          Chronicle (16mm, b&w, 30 min.)
1971—*Blue Streak* (16mm, b&w & color, 16 min.)
          Fluorescent (16mm, b&w & color, 21 min.)
1973—*Casual Relations* (16mm, b&w & color, 80 min.)
1975—*Mozart in Love* (16mm, color, 100 min.)
1977—*Local Color* (16mm, b&w, 116 min.)
1978—*The Scenic Route* (16mm, color, 76 min.)
1979—*Imposters* (16mm, color, 110 min.)

When the critic of a narrative film is feeling desperate, the first place that he or she is likely to turn to is a plot summary. Feeling rather desperate about my capacity to do justice to the last two features of the remarkable Mark Rappaport, I looked up the synopses and reviews of **The Scenic Route** and **Imposters** in the usually reliable *Monthly Film Bulletin,* which appeared precisely three years apart (February 1979 and February 1982), only to discover that each critic, Geoffrey Nowell-Smith and Simon Field, respectively, starts off with the admission that his own synopsis is misleading. "To summarize the 'story' of **Imposters**," writes Field, "is to misrepresent its structure, to face assumptions of causality and rounded characterization on a film that has no such preoccupations, that loves the red herring, the non sequitur, the scene for its own sake, and in which one person might not be entirely distinguishable from another."

The fact that Rappaport—a nineteenth-century figure who studied the Victorian novel at Brooklyn College and New York University before abandoning a graduate school scholarship at the latter to become a filmmaker—usually furnishes his features with more plot than one can shake a stick at doesn't invalidate Field's point in the slightest. But it does suggest one aspect of the nature of the problem involved in describing his films. And it's a direct corollary of this problem that Rappaport currently occupies that dreaded no man's land between the avant-garde and the mainstream that threatens to make non-persons out of most of Rappaport's European intellectual contemporaries as well. (I'm writing this in late February, less than a week after an entertaining black-and-white "art film" clever enough to predict its own doom in this country, Wim Wenders' well-titled **The State of Things**—winner of the Golden Lion Award at the last Venice Film Festival, contemptuously rejected by the last New York Film Festival—was brainlessly and pitilessly buried by a *New York Times* review that couldn't even tell two of the major characters apart: a movie that obviously commits the grievous error of not catering to the right crowd. In a way, for all their radical—and perhaps even irreconcilable—differences, Wenders and Rappaport share the same handicap in one respect: they make intelligent films in English that ultimately belong to a European as opposed to American frame of reference, despite the central importance of Hollywood to both directors.) And the fact that Rappaport isn't a European even though he gets treated like one only complicates the injustice.

To keep things manageable and separate, I've generally avoided listing work in video by filmmakers in this book (which makes for certain omissions—and major ones in the case of filmmakers like Louis Hock, whose recent work is all in that medium). But having seen and benefited a great deal from Rappaport's own 28-minute **Mark Rappaport: The TV Spinoff** (1980), it's hard to avoid mentioning it here, because it's the best possible introduction to Rappaport's film work that I can imagine—ideal for anyone who's encountering this filmmaker's original, unsettling work for the first time. As a very witty *précis* of what watching (and financing and making) his movies can be like, I doubt it could be much improved upon. (Come to think of it, this provides another intriguing point of comparison with Wenders, whose short film **Reverse Angle 1: New York, March 1982**, initially made for French TV, is equally helpful about **Hammett** and **The State of Things**.) At the outset, when Rappaport is trying out different kinds of music with different movie stills—just a formal variation, really, of his subsequent tryouts with different costumes, backdrops, front-projections, plots, characters, clips, and raps about his movies—he's already setting up the paradoxical parameters of his glamorously homemade cinema. ("All bourgeois dreams end the same way," snarls a character called Chuckie, played by Charles Ludlam, in **Imposters**. "Marry royalty and escape.")

It's a place where the writer-director and his resourceful actors and crew are all studiously working their asses off to furnish the audience with a kind of do-it-yourself melodrama kit, at once firmly overdetermined and subtly undermined—full of hysteria and intrigue, signifying everything. Rappaport is interested in props and scenic designs, he explains at one point, "not to recreate reality but to suggest a different one." It's no wonder that he's respected more and known better in Europe than in this country, where the zeitgeist often seems like the only game in town.

As suggested earlier, Rappaport fills most of his movies with enough old-fashioned plot to support an entire course in nineteenth-century fiction; there's also enough bitchy dialogue to stuff Joseph Mankiewicz's closet (a line from **Imposters**: "Actually, there's not much difference between being dead and being in Vermont, if you know what I mean.") He simulates opulence in his studio sets—all established within the confines of his lower Manhattan loft and generally shot by the very able Fred Murphy (who was also responsible for operating the camera in **The State of Things**)—and class in his talented cast. He then uses these elements in part like filtering screens, each of which emotionally and effectually blocks off a portion of all the others. The results of this elegant, intricately tortured process can be humorous and entertaining as well as creepy and uncomfortable. The dramas turn out to be at once so florid and so private that they can improbably suggest a full-scale opera staged at the bottom of a well, or **2001** seen on a bite-size TV screen. For the first ten minutes of **The Scenic Route** one might laugh uproariously; for the second ten minutes, one might twitch or flinch—but neither response can comfortably sustain itself indefinitely without some enormous act of repression. Stated differently, Rappaport's films are bright, impossible objects, motored by obsession and protected by wit, neither of which is effectively allowed to cancel out the other.

For a good bit of its tight, elegant construction, **The Scenic Route** depends on a European art film staple—the leading character who narrates her/his story off-screen, a direct descendant of the first-person novel, in this case a worrywart heroine named Estelle (Randy Danson). To get her plot out of the way, in standard *Monthly Film Bulletin* style, let's turn to Geoffrey Nowell-Smith's helpful synopsis (to which I've appended a couple of actors' names; others in the cast, one should note, include filmmakers Eric Mitchell and Claudia Weill):

A woman, Estelle, describes in voice-over a painting of Orpheus and Eurydice. She is then seen writing in her diary, and the voice-over continues, now describing events she remembers and is relating in the diary. Various scenes from her life are then accompanied by voice-over or occasionally by sync dialogue. She is assaulted by Jack, her estranged husband; she witnesses a stabbing in the street; she acquires a new lover, Paul [Kevin Wade], and is in his company when another stabbing occurs, this time in a swimming pool. The relationship develops: she gives Paul her ring, he gives her his address book. After the arrival of her sister, Lena [Marilyn Jones], she begins to see Paul less often, preferring to cultivate her relationship with her sister. Lena takes to picking up men in the street and bringing them home; one turns out to be Jack, causing Estelle some embarrassment; another is Paul, which is even worse, since he soon moves in as Lena's lover. Estelle consoles herself with visions of going on a journey, and with the fond belief that she is Paul's real beloved—Eurydice to his Orpheus. But more violent thoughts obtrude, including the death of the lovers at the hands of a maniac killer. No resolution to the triangle is found; Estelle returns to her diary, and comments "In my notebooks it ended like this."*

In keeping with Rappaport's nineteenth-century-novel preoccupations, one should note in passing both the theme of incest (no less important in **Imposters**) and the rather absurdly Heathcliffian romantic figure cut by Kevin Wade's Paul—quite comparable, all things considered, to Barbet Schroeder's Olivier in **Céline et Julie vont en bateau** as a figure representing the stiff, charred remnants of that novelistic (and specifically Gothic) tradition.

To Nowell-Smith's summary we should add some of Rappaport's own descriptive and analytical comments. The first paragraph is a statement written by him to introduce the film; the last four come from an interview with Tony Rayns in the February 1979 *Monthly Film Bulletin*:

Love, jealousy and revenge. All the standard components of melodrama—but a very "dry" melodrama. Expectations are thwarted and rechannelled. Instead of explanations and motivations, visual counterparts are offered. The film slides back and forth between passion and an irony which redirects it but doesn't dilute it. A film about myths and mythmaking, about the Madame Bovary in each of us, about delusions and romance in a fragile world where violence erupts randomly and unexpectedly. The film was made very cheaply in and around New York, where violence is a way of life and everyone always talks of going away.

---

*Missing from this synopsis is the fact that Lena has just been released from a mental hospital where she had been committed after stabbing Estelle's boyfriend to death a few years earlier.

The various elements only really fall into place when the narrations are there. The use of narration in low-budget films in general brings us back to finance; it's cheaper and more accessible than sync-sound dialogue. But I *like* narration: I like the fact that you can create a discrepancy between what characters say and what you see of them. It's something that we've learned from Melville, via Bresson. I think it's an incredibly rich technique; it allows you to concentrate on essentials. Plus my mind is always full of ironic double-think . . . always re-assessing, always re-evaluating.

Movies like *Out of the Past* and *Sunset Boulevard* used narration for exposition, as a device for opening the closed door, always from a single character's point-of-view. I try to use it more centrally: what happens if you use narrations from *five* points-of-view?

I once described the entire script of *The Scenic Route* to someone (not the truncated version that I put on the screen), and he thought it was very dry, very dehydrated. But there's enough material there for *five* of the melodramas that Warner Brothers used to do! Only with all the melodramatic juices pumped out. The elements of melodrama (and of theatre) that I like have more to do with painting: it's the gesture, the *mise en scène,* the lighting, the arrangement, the pregnant moment right before something happens or right after it has.

The emotional tenor is not parody. If I'm parodying anything, it's the fact that we can only respond to emotional situations in certain prescribed ways. They're the only ways we have to respond to trite elements in our lives. I guess it's more a matter of irony than of parody. I rely on associations to previous things as a kind of shorthand. It's not that audiences have to know which films I love, and I'm not interested in *hommages.* But it's all retreads—human relationships have been explored, re-explored, de-explored, and yet we still respond to the grain of truth that we recognize at the heart of these situations when they're represented on a screen. One wants the falseness to be true.

One should clarify Rappaport's statement about narration by mentioning that his notion about five points-of-view is theoretical rather than actual (although **Local Color** comes close at times to that level of intricacy, and **The Scenic Route** intermittently uses Lena as a second narrator). Nevertheless, the sort of distinction he draws between his own work and Hollywood melodrama is accurate in its broad outlines, and it's important to keep in mind that however well Rappaport knows the American cinema, his films are probably closer to the novels of Alain Robbe-Grillet than they are to the movies of Ernst Lubitsch, Joseph Mankiewicz, or George Cukor.

But as Rappaport himself indicates, it's the melodramatic and theatrical side of painting that perhaps comes closest to his concerns. And from one point of view, what could be more melodramatic and theatrical than the American flag? (Consider the cornball rhetoric of its flaunting by Robert Altman at the end of **Nashville**—the kind of pretension that invariably suckers xenophobic, all-American patriots who criticize European films for their "heaviness.") And it is the American flag whose formal coordinates are used in the obsessively reiterated picture of Orpheus and Eurydice glimpsed at the beginning—an icon and reference point that is restaged and rethought as often as the old photograph of the Chinese couple that begins and ends Leslie Thornton's **Adynata**. In certain variations of this mythical pose—a man watches an ornate woman sleeping in an ornate bed—part of the wall and bed spell out precisely those coordinates, as if to give one more expression to the European vs. American and classical vs. romantic feuds constantly being waged in this movie.

Rappaport is invariably at his best when thinking up ingenious compositions of this kind. Two other strong examples in **The Scenic Route** involve screens between people: slides of atrocities winking on and off between Estelle on screen left watching her sister Lena kissing Paul on screen right; Estelle at one end of a row of movie seats, a man at another, while enormous black-and-white close-ups of a couple kissing play on the movie screen over their heads (entailing an odd yet satisfying reversal of directions because they're both looking away from the screen). Still another striking melodramatic effect is achieved in a shot between the two previous examples, when Estelle backs away from Lena and Paul only to wind up hiding next to a gigantic black-and-white photograph of the same couple, discovered at the end of a camera movement that follows her stealthy retreat. Still later, after Paul buys a record of Gluck's *Orpheus and Eurydice,** one twice sees the ornate wallpaper in Estelle's flat rise like a curtain to reveal each sister standing outdoors in front of the same autumnal landscape; then a backdrop of snow-capped mountains also lifts behind Paul to show that he's standing in the same spot previously occupied by the other two.

The desire to be part of a work of art infects virtually every register of representation broached by the film, keeping one's distinctions between subjective fantasies and objective narrative information almost as confused as their respective emotional impacts. Paul and the two sisters dance in Estelle's living room at one point to a rock tune ("Got to Love"), and the effect is as wonderfully deadpan as the performance of the Madison by the

---

*An aria of which, "Che faro ed Erydyce," accompanies Madame de. . .'s loss of her earrings at the opera in Max Ophüls' **Madame de** ... (which, along with Visconti's **Senso** is one of Rappaport's favorite films).

Marilyn Jones and Randy Danson in *The Scenic Route*

goofy trio (two males and one female) in Godard's **Band of Outsiders**. Some of the equally deadpan lines are just as funny, particularly in their mockery of New York clichés of attitude and intonation. "I was afraid to go out—I was afraid to stay in," Estelle remarks early on in the narration, not long before she's seen walking outside when a woman with a dagger in her back falls rather promptly into her arms (echoing the United Nations corpse near the beginning of Hitchcock's **North by Northwest**). Estelle's morose follow-up comment is just as crazy in its banality: "It was the first time I ever touched someone's blood. It was also the day I got a letter from Lena...." "I think I'm ready for a meaningful affair," she says elsewhere; and Paul at one point utters a line that perfectly catches the claustrophobic, paranoid mood of pose and posture at the point of self-mockery: "I wouldn't even tell you a lie, much less the truth." "I feel uneasy with you," Estelle responds, understandably.

   Imposters isn't my favorite Rappaport film—I'd assign that place to the infinitely plotty **Local Color**, with **The Scenic Route** a close runner-up—but with a $115,000 budget and an all-star cast, it's probably the most lavish, in thought as well as deed. (Readers interested in details about the making of the film should consult my production story in the October 1979 *American*

Lina Todd, Charles Ludlam, Peter Evans, Ellen McElduff, and Michael Burg in
Imposters

Imposters. Lina Todd, Ellen McElduff, and Peter Evans (in photo)

Film.) The daisy-chain of flirtations, passions, jealousies, relationships, and correspondences between a well-to-do romantic hero (Peter Evans), a pair of murderous magicians impersonating a pair of twins (Charles Ludlam and Michael Burg—the latter a leading actor in **Local Color**), their enigmatic assistant (Ellen McElduff), and her mysterious soulmate (Lina Todd), are so complexly interwoven that after a while, *döppelgangers* proliferate like bunny rabbits.

Each couple and/or two-way pattern threatens and comments on every other, so that straight and gay sensibilities, male and female characters, and passive and aggressive roles seem perpetually at loggerheads, fighting their way through insults and betrayals into bitter, neurotic stalemates. What's even stranger is that all the males seem at times like different facets of the same personality—a characteristic that this movie shares with two of its reported thematic reference points, Proust's *La Prisonnière* and Hammett's **The Maltese Falcon** (as filmed by Huston).

A lot of the time, it's difficult to know whether to laugh or scream, and like certain other obsessive directors, Rappaport often tries to have it both ways—keeping the viewer distanced *and* testily daring the viewer to get involved and/or pissed off at the same time. Ludlam, in particular, is a superb needler who works with macabre camp as if it were a delicate instrument, stretching out his cackling effects into cadenzas.

"So many corpses, so little treasure!" wails Burg, the other weirdo magician in the movie; he could just as well be talking about the diverse deadends and rewards of narrative itself. To say that **Imposters** doesn't "work" finally isn't to say much at all. Louis Malle's **Atlantic City**, released the same year, works like a charm, but leaves one with next to nothing afterwards—like a good meal you forget about the following day, or a Jacques Demy movie that makes you feel pleasantly nostalgic about your own dreamy narcissism, without forcing any of the accompanying impostures into a state of crisis.

Imposters, a good deal stickier, leaves me with something more. After seeing it three times, it still drives me a little batty (as it no doubt should). To my taste, the women in the movie are too elliptical and remote (as are the men in **The Scenic Route**), the Peter Evans character too well armored against ridicule, and the dialogue too doggedly flashy in spots. (One character compares love and romance to an artichoke—"you peel it all away, and there's nothing left"—when what she or Rappaport apparently means is an onion.)

But there's a lot more rattling around inside the possibilities of this oddball romantic epic than one can find in most places, and viewers who like to take (and honor) bold risks should give this movie a chance. You might wind up hating it; but even if you do, you'll probably have some interesting reasons you never would have thought of otherwise. (After all, all bourgeois dreams end the same way—inside someone's head.) And either way, I can guarantee that you'll have plenty to look at, listen to, and think about, both here and in **The Scenic Route**. The fact that Rappaport has a good eye, ear, and mind already places him well ahead of most contemporary cinema. He merely has the misfortune of living in the wrong century and on the wrong continent, meanwhile making the best movies that he can.

...the argument thus far

It will be observed that the rules and criteria governing many of the decisions in this book are not so much fixed as fluid and shifting. This leads one to a consideration of the implicit contradiction between the journalistic and literary modes this book attempts to straddle—two modes that are as separate as the institutions protecting the avant-garde and the art film.

The literary mode adopted by the Serious Book obeys one time scale, according to which there is little moment-to-moment fluctuation. One respects the long view, the fixed set of exemplary figures and absolutes which one expects to outlast the season. The journalistic mode, on the contrary, is entirely of the moment, and sacrifices the integrity of the long view in the interests of immediacy. For the weekly columnist, it is essential that the goods on display each week be made to seem equally important, insofar as they and the columnist equally "fill a need," "perform a service." Hence the journalist has to lie by claiming to assign final evaluations to goods when in fact he or she is merely assisting in the process that turns them all into instant commodities, whether good or bad, while the critic, more literary in stance, has to lie by claiming the sort of comprehensive knowledge and wisdom that is usually available only to the journalist.

Writing as someone who is literally caught between these conflicting modes and professions, I can enjoy the security of neither, but can at least attempt to claim some of the authority of both. But it should be acknowledged that being a journalist today on the subject of the avant-garde is light-years away from what it was 20 years ago. One need only compare Jonas Mekas's writing in *The Village Voice* in the Sixties to J. Hoberman's consumer guides today in order to realize how unthinkable a figure like Mekas would be in today's service-oriented *Voice*, where the dictates of the marketplace speak a lot louder than the musings of anarchists or poets.

This brings me to the special case of Jackie Raynal. By most of the rules set down in this book, her recent output as a filmmaker is less substantial than that of many others. Yet her importance as a figure in the international avant-garde is such that it would be a crime to leave her out, for more reasons than one. As a programmer for Carnegie Hall Cinema and the Bleecker Street Cinema in New York, with important links to Europe, she has been more responsible than any other individual for the exposure in this country of major films by Chantal Akerman, Scott B and Beth B, Marco Bellochio, Marguerite Duras, Jean-Luc Godard, Ulrike Ottinger, Yvonne Rainer, Jacques Rivette, and Wim Wenders, among many others. As a filmmaker, she straddles the categories of avant-garde and mainstream through her professional background as a film editor—much as Yvonne Rainer, through her former career as a dancer, straddles the separate worlds of avant-garde film and performance art. Raynal's filmmaking career has been sporadic in large part because of her pioneer efforts in programming, and to deal with her here I have to expand my parameters somewhat in opposite directions—back a dozen years to the making of her first feature, **Deux Fois**, and forward to the projected completion of her second feature, **New York Stories**. It is an exception worth making.

JACKIE RAYNAL.
Born in Poilhes, France, 1940.

1965—*Merce Cunningham* (16mm, b&w, 30 min.)
      (co-directed by Étienne Becker & Patrice Wyeis)
1971—*Deux Fois* (35mm, b&w, 75 min.)
1980—*New York Story* (16mm, b&w & color, 30 min.)

    Deux Fois was shot in 35mm and in black and white by a professional film editor on a visit to Barcelona and environs in 1969; it features Raynal in practically every sequence and has no plot of any sort. Instead of a story it comprises a flow of sequential events that formally rhyme with each other in a variety of ways, so that the title is a succinct representation of the method involved (although there are certain things that the film gives us three, four, or five times, too, always with distinct variations). Consequently, on one level the film is a kind of elementary editing puzzle that asks, "How did I get from this long-take sequence to this one that follows it?" and/or "What are the sexy forms of duplicity between these two sequences—their secret points of agreement and accord, as well as their strongest points of tension?" It's a film, in other words, about a couple, and about coupling— there is a man who appears with Raynal in many of the sequences—as well as about repetition. It's also, as Raynal has noted herself, "about the representation of the image of woman as a sign."

    Perhaps because Raynal made **Deux Fois** after a long stint of editing commercial French narrative films, there is a liberating feel to it—a sense of ease regained, of identity tasted and slowly chewed. Raynal's self-absorption—which occasionally suggests a flipped-out, female version of Jacques Tati's Hulot character—luxuriates in the space that it affords itself like a puppy in clover. "All the images of our imaginations are real," Raynal declares in an early autonomous sequence. At their best, the sequences of **Deux Fois** are like neatly sculpted, delicately lit arenas where different versions of this postulate can be staged, by Raynal and spectators alike. Solipsistic, masturbatory games, to be sure. But isn't the camera a solipsistic

Jackie Raynal
in *New York Story*

instrument and moviegoing largely a masturbatory activity—regardless of their manifold alibis and social excuses (which is what most film criticism is all about)? **Deux Fois** is perhaps an avant-garde film first of all because it allows itself no shame whatsoever for reveling in the pleasures to be found in those simple facts.

The following is a revised and somewhat updated version of an interview that Sandy Flitterman and I conducted with Raynal for *Millennium Film Journal* (Nos. 7/8/9, Fall/Winter 1980-81) and its introduction.

"Should you come to our capital, do stay at the Algae Hotel," intones a woman's voice over crisp 16mm color images of the Plaza Hotel, shot by Babette Mangolte and elliptically edited by Suzanne Fenn with a rhythmic grace that reminds us of Resnais. "The service there is impeccable, the cuisine excellent. Enjoy these advantages and do not worry about anything else." Eventually, this surrealist text by Tibor Tardos—translated by Carlos

Clarens—begins to show its true colors as the voice relates the unhappy experiences of a few guests at the Algae. One, for instance, finds, on the thirtieth floor, aquariums over 100 yards long, "stocked with thousands of large fish, all harnessed to the same steel cable," which is linked, in turn, to the express elevator. And we learn that a "foreign lady accidentally lifted the edge of the carpet covering the hotel's luxurious corridors and discovered that it was made of whale's skin, sheltering in its three-inch-thick blubber an incredible mass of wriggling maggots" while, in a fluid movement, we see the corner of a carpet being pulled back, and some-thing—we're not sure what—visible on its underside. A similar uncertainty occurs when the narrator describes another guest ripping apart the seams in a blanket and finding inside "a network of blood vessels through which coursed a rather warm, reddish liquid, propelled through the tiny vessels by imperceptible spasms."

This is the prologue to **New York Story**, a film started after Raynal received a CAPS grant in 1978. Originally planned as a series of sketches called **New York Nights**, the film has taken a different direction ever since Raynal decided to expand her first episode—entitled "Cable Car Couple"—to feature length by chronicling all the events that led up to it. Playwright and film critic Gary Indiana has assisted with the dialogue, and as this book goes to press, **New York Stories** (as the feature-in-progress is now to be called) seems relatively close to completion. All the shooting has been done at this point, and only the final editing of the new material remains.

The black-and-white "Cable Car Couple," also shot by Mangolte, has a rather cock-eyed New Wave flavor. Some of its phantasmagoric and self-referential aspects also remind us of some of the more "deconstructive" cartoons of Tex Avery in the Forties, and not merely because of the alliterative title. It features Raynal herself, as a French filmmaker named Lulu Blanchot living in New York, and her husband Sid Geffen—who runs the Carnegie Hall Cinema and the Bleecker Street Cinema, where Raynal often works as a programmer—as Lulu's husband, also known as Sid.

In a long take we see them enter Manhattan together via a Roosevelt Island cable car after getting married. After an intertitle, "Six months later," we find them having breakfast in Geffen and Raynal's Central Park South apartment. The subsequent action is more or less framed by references to a dream that Lulu has about a meatball, which for her symbolizes sexual frustration. Sid obligingly offers to find her a young lover, and most of the remainder of the episode depicts his quest. He goes to see a fortune-teller whose face is shrouded in darkness (played by Raynal), and then to a movie theater (the Carnegie Hall Cinema), where he falls asleep during Keaton's **Sherlock Jr.** and has a curious dream (a remarkable silent film pastiche featuring both himself and Lulu, who is dressed as a man and sports a moustache; subsequently, a seedy bartender in the lobby (Gary Indiana) recommends the silent film organist (Jim Dredfield) as a lover for Lulu.

Meanwhile, back in the apartment, Lulu spends her time reading a newspaper (a *New York Post* consisting exclusively of headlined front pages), watching TV (where Sid appears, without explanation, along with diverse commercials), and painting pictures. When Sid returns with the organist, she shows that she's momentarily forgotten her request, but Sid convinces her to enjoy her dream now that she can fulfill it, and says that he'll see her in the morning. In the hallway outside their apartment, after exchanging pleasantries with a neighbor, Sid steps into what he believes to be an elevator but proves to be an empty shaft, where he falls many flights to his death. The film returns to color for the final shot—a close-up of a meatball—over which Lulu remarks, "And it all happened because of a meatball." The closing credits appear over popular French accordian music.

In 1972, following the second public screening of **Deux Fois** at the Toulon Festival, where it won the Grand Prix, Noël Burch described the film in *Cinema Rising* (No. 2) as "a deliberately elementary meditation on certain basic film functions which may be said to underlie editing as such—expectation, frame-scanning, perceptual memory, relationships between on- and off-screen space, all explored in a series of autonomous shot-sequences of exemplary simplicity." Analyzed in considerable detail in the first issue of *Camera Obscura* (Fall 1976, pp. 11-51) and more recently cited by two *Cahiers du Cinéma* editors, Jean-Claude Biette and Louis Skorecki, as one of the key films of the Seventies, **Deux Fois** remains, with Jean-Daniel Pollet's **Mediterranée**, one of the most neglected French avant-garde films west of the Atlantic.

SANDY FLITTERMAN: I see on your resumé that you had some experience as a still photographer between 1961 and 1963.

JACKIE RAYNAL: Yes—I did about 2,000 pictures on two separate continents. The first time was in Mexico. I was really learning what still photography was then, because I was shooting everything with a Rolleiflex, which has the format of a painting—square rather than rectangular. I also did many, many photographs in Tunisia, where I co-produced **Heraclite l'Obscur** a few years later. But I quit the job because I didn't enjoy it: it was too mechanical most of the time.... Long before that, I used to make films with my father. I used to hold the camera and set up the little scenes we did. My father ran a summer camp for underprivileged kids, sponsored by the government. He ran it for the C.G.T., the blue collar workers' union, for free every year. We used to produce a play each month for the parents to see, and then we'd film it. But don't think there was any conscious relation between this and my later work! I wasn't so much interested in film at that time; I just recall shooting those 16mm films.... The first film I ever saw in the city was an operetta, **Violettes Impériales**, with Luis Mariano. I was ten years old, and it was the first time I ever came to the city. Before that was **La**

Belle et la Bête. I remember very well, my father went in an old truck to a little station where the bus used to drop off packages on the road, and the landscape was pretty much like Scotland, or the moors in **The Bronte Sisters**.* And he brought along **La Belle et la Bête**; we had a ciné-club at the camp every Friday and Saturday night, and he showed this incredible film. I guess the ciné-club started when I was 8 and went up to when I was about 15. And the location of the camp happened to be a castle—a huge old medieval castle! So it's very funny...I think **Deux Fois** was influenced very much by Buñuel and probably also by Cocteau: the mirrors, for instance. Of course, it's been advertised as a feminist film because of my being there on the screen 98% of the time; but the film could be read quite differently and associated with Buñuel. A lot of Americans don't understand—they think that the whole film was shot in Paris, which is not true. It was in Spain, in Barcelona, at specific places, like the church—it's a film about the church, too.

SF: You end with a portion of *La Vida es Sueño*, the Calderon play...

JRa: Yes, right. But that was more an influence from Rivette. I wanted to introduce a play into my film, and to actually film a decor on the stage. So when you see the shot, the framing's a little crooked and tilted. I did it on purpose, to have a different angle—

SF: To emphasize that it's on a stage?

JRa: First of all, to emphasize that it's on a stage. Second of all, it was supposed to have come after the scene where I walk in a straight line from the country church where there is a light coming from a mirror. That's an effect from Cocteau, where you have this silver and this strange light coming from it—you know, when it's dawn and you have all this dew. I told the cameraperson I wanted to have this reflected light from the mirror in the background of the shot. And this straight perspective line could be another broken line, like the one I shot in the theater.

SF: There's another sequence in the film that's very stagey—in the arch.

JRa: Yes. That's part of the *décor* of the theater, what you see in the reverse-angle, in fact—an open doorway where there is nothing in front of us and the light is very dark.

JONATHAN ROSENBAUM: To go back about seven years before **Deux Fois**, to your early work as an assistant editor: did you see very much of Renoir while working on **The Elusive Corporal** in 1964?

JRa: No, only twice. He was sick at the time and living in Hollywood. He came twice and was always wonderful, but he didn't work at the editing

---

*A film by Andre Téchiné.

at all. Renoir is like Chabrol—working as an editor with him doesn't give you many choices. At least **La Corporal Epinglé** was like that. Rohmer was different. In the early days it was difficult, because he was such a master of economy. He claimed that the actor was often best in the first take. I'm not sure if that's true with the way he made **Perceval**, but at the beginning, the films were all very economical.

JRo: Is editing a good preparation for a filmmaker?

JRa: Oh yes. Now I think I miss it a lot. For me, editing is like a film's second breath. Look at **Mediterranée**.*

JRo: What was the experience of working on that film like?

JRa: It was a great experience for me, because I was really an assistant editor at the time on commercial films. **Mediterranée** was made by someone, Jean-Daniel Pollet, who already had experience with a big-budget film that was also very personal, a film that he doesn't want to show now—**La Ligne de Mire**, a very romantic title and a very romantic story. And the way that he shot it—without using a union crew and spending a lot of his own money—caused a big scandal in Paris. Artists were talking about what rich kids could get away with; unionists were saying you must not make a film without union people. And finally the film was so different that when it was released, critics said, "My God, it's a fantastic film!" So Pollet left Paris, and when he returned with all this new footage, he didn't really know what to do with it. I worked for seven months on the film, and he'd already been working for a year before I started! It was an ideal film for an editor, because it's a film about editing—voice, music, sound. And it wasn't always clear what was narrative and what was non-narrative. Jean-Daniel had the narrative idea of the young girl being wheeled into an operating room for heart surgery—the voyage of that table she's on—and that's all he had. He wanted to have a voice-over commentary about Mediterranean culture, all these dead places. And he had so much wonderful footage! Volker Schlöndorff was the cameraman; he and Pollet met completely by chance in a village, somewhere like the south of Italy. And the producer of the film was Barbet Schroeder, who asked me to do some further editing: first for Rohmer on several films [**La Boulangere de Monceau, La Carrière**

---

*"A medium-length film by Jean-Daniel Pollet with a text by Philippe Sollers. A series of images, filmed in various countries around the Mediterranean (a Sicilian garden, a Greek temple, a fisherman, a young girl on an operating table), reappear throughout the film, in a different order each time, held for different lengths of time, constituting a sort of mythical narrative in which each image serves as something like an ideogram. The order of these shots was not predetermined before shooting but established, by trial and error, in the montage." Footnote to interview with Jacques Rivette by Bernard Eisenschitz, Jean-André Fieschi, and Eduardo de Gregorio, in *Rivette: Texts and Interviews*, (London: BFI, 1977), p. 40. *See also* pp. 75-78, and discussions of the film in *Godard on Godard*, Noël Burch's *Theory of Film Practice*, and *Cahiers du Cinéma* No. 187.

de Suzanne, Nadja à Paris, and, later La Collectionneuse] and then for Paris vu par...[a sketch film with episodes by Chabrol, Douchet, Godard, Pollet, Rohmer, and Rouch]. Then there was Barbet's own first feature, More, which I refused to edit because I couldn't stand it. He was disappointed—and, you know, it was a big risk, because how could I do that to Barbet, who gave me my start? But it was very fortunate that I turned down that film—although now I have second thoughts about it—because it was just at that moment that I hit upon the idea that led to my own first film, Deux Fois.

JRo: What about Heraclite l'Obscur (1968) and Acéphale (1969)?

JRa: They weren't really my films in the same way. I co-produced them, but they were more or less part of my association with Patrick Deval, whom I was living with at the time. He was making films and I was helping him. I was involved in those films very much. But Deux Fois was, by contrast, a real breakthrough. The very fact that I did that type of film when I was involved with all those commercial people—I mean, even Rohmer didn't go to see my film! (Laughs.) I was an outcast.

SF: I read somewhere that the film was edited in the camera.

JRa: Yes—I only did two days of editing. Of course when I came to America and described how I did the film, some people said, "Oh, that's been done several times."

SF: Regarding the sequence in the pharmacy, when you enter three separate times to buy soap: were you experimenting with different ways of telling an anecdote by changing the lighting?

JRa: Yes, I wanted to do that experiment. At that time, I was learning from Philippe Garrel how much you could change a scene through the lighting. For editing, lighting is always a problem.

SF: What was working with Garrel—as editor and assistant director—like?

JRa: He was like a terrorist. He was very nice when you were working alone with him, but at that time he was working with lots of other people. He used to go into the laboratory and force technicians to do things they'd never done before. At that time, Godard was totally the father of Garrel, while Garrel was totally the enfant terrible. During May '68, Godard had an Alfa Romeo with a 35mm camera, and he and Alain Jouffroy and Garrel went around shooting footage—I forgot what film it was for, but because of the Alfa Romeo, the police left them alone. You had so many unexpected alliances then; it was like a revival of the surrealist period in the links that were being made....Garrel was a very good cameraman, and he did all the lighting himself on his films. He likes to control everything like an artisan. If you watch him edit, you'll see that he does things very simply—most of his editing is done in the camera. And he influenced me a great deal formally. I worked on both **Le Revelateur** and **La Concentration**.

JRo: How did your short **Merce Cunningham** (1965) come about—the film you made with the cameramen Étienne Becker and Patrice Wyeis?

JRa: I was very interested in Robert Rauschenberg at the time—I didn't know much about dance—and a friend working at the Alexander Iolas Gallery told me that Rauschenberg, Merce Cunningham, and John Cage were coming to Paris. I was living with one of the cameramen. So we decided to shoot everything, all the rehearsals, every day at the T.E.P. [*Théâtre de l'Est Parisienne*]. Then I spent three months editing it with someone else. We did the film with no money at all; then, when we had a $2,000 bill at the lab, a producer came along and took over the control of the film entirely—I'll never make that mistake again, I was very inexperienced. The film's been seen very widely, both on TV and non-theatrically.

JRo: Your filmography lists one other film by you, in 16mm, that's both unfinished and lost—**Shiva Puri** (1975). Was that shot in India?

JRa: Only part of it. I had footage shot in the desert in Algeria—it was like an independent version of **Lawrence of Arabia**, and I was Lawrence! I wanted to film a sort of ceremony in each country, and to participate in the ceremony in each case. It was a mixture of autobiography and fantasy, like **New York Story**. I met a guy like a caliph who caught scorpions and snakes and extracted their poison; he sent it to Germany where it was used as medicine. I had a scene, a fantasy, where he was taking me away on a horse in the desert—after which I took a swim at the Hilton while he sent off the poison. Then I went back to Paris, which is where the footage was eventually lost. Then I went to India and Nepal, where I wanted to cross over into China. In Tibet, I filmed in a monastery. It was all really a mixture of fiction and documentary.

SF: What made you come to the States?

JRa: I always wanted to come here. I had a very good first impression when I was here in 1961. Then I traveled all over New Mexico—I lived in a commune there and in San Francisco. And finally, I had a boyfriend who was here and invited me over—I'd invited him over to Paris many times, and he said, "It's your turn now." And when I came here he became very violent, and we stayed together two months and that was it. My plane ticket was stolen, and then I met a wonderful friend who was an editor too, Suzanne Fenn. She convinced me to stay, and we decided to live together. That was in 1975. We wound up editing together an atrocious commercial feature, **Saturday Night at the Baths**.

JRo: How did you arrive at the combinations of autobiography and fiction that you have in your new film?

JRa: As soon as I started filming, I discovered that I wanted to hide myself again. I see a lot of problems—I really have no confidence in myself, I become abstract. That's why I think that I succeed in the prologue—because it's abstraction, but at the same time, it's me; it's totally what I like. And it's not autobiography—or, rather, it *is* only in the sense that it's really what I think about New York in certain ways. Because my first film was autobiographical, I started to do something completely different, a totally fictional narrative. But then I discovered that I cannot speak—I cannot do good dialogue because my English isn't good enough, and I can only recount what my view of New York is. So what better experience to depict than that of a filmmaker living in New York, getting a job on a commercial homoerotic picture? Someone who lives with a character like Sid. There's some slight change, but Sid's presence is there; it's much more interesting. Sometimes I discover that I hate the film: when I was doing the scene at the bar in the café at the Carnegie Hall Cinema with Sid and Gary, I said, "My God, I'm stuck here with the camera on the tripod, I can't move, I have to do a *champ contrechamp* [angle and reverse-angle]—it's a narrative film." It's a constant fight between me and the exterior world that influences me.

JRo: I'm thinking about the autobiographical book I just finished writing [*Moving Places*]. It's like a kind of socialized psychoanalysis—one that involves more than just one's self and a therapist, but a whole crowd of people....

JRa: To me, the film is in a shape that astonishes me. It seems to go off in so many different directions. Gary's writing all the dialogue now for the earlier part of the film. I really want to include a few of my responses to New York. I want to describe a few things, like the gay world—by which I mean I want to describe a couple of gay men. It's so funny how much of the straight world they reproduce. Besides which, I find I don't like New York. If I didn't have dear friends here, I'd leave. It's such a masculine city, and there's so much temper—destroy, build; destroy, build; it's really like a phallus, this town.

SF: For one thing, the skyscrapers are really an image of that.... Your prologue sets this kind of tone in a way because of its eerie nightmare quality.

JRo: One aspect of the prologue I like is how you manage to turn New York into another city—something like what Godard does with Paris in **Alphaville**. It's a lot like surrealism for me.

JRa: Yes, for me also—but at the same time, realism too, because the

Plaza Hotel is the heart of New York. After the prologue, the film will be about my staying in New York, living in a Soho loft, then living in a boat near the Statue of Liberty with Sid—which is autobiographical, because the first time we met was on a boat. It's going to be like **L'Atalante!**—(laughs)—I hope. I'll shoot this part in another style.

SF: I really like the way the surrealist texts work with those lush and beautiful images of the Plaza in the prologue. In a way, the voice is like a travelogue, so that when the absurd images (like the maggots under the carpet) appear, they catch you by surprise. It's the kind of shock you get when naturalism is combined with the absurd.

Sid Geffen and Jackie Raynal in *New York Story*

JRa: In the prologue, when you hear the voice, you don't really listen because you're struck by the image. But at the same time, all of a sudden, you wonder what you're listening to. Because it's off the image, the narration isn't exactly changing the image. You show a little bit of the carpet, a little bit of the mask, a little bit of the nerves—you know, the "circulation" of this carpet—but not up to the point where you see the whale being skinned alive! (Laughs.) Especially with that voice, which sounds very much like she's doing an advertisement for the Hilton. It belongs to Leslie Cockburn. It's a beautiful voice.... And I'm very pleased with what Babette [Mangolte] did at the Plaza. We fought many times, because I wasn't clear. At the scene in the café, everybody was first of all passed out—it was six o'clock in the morning. Actually, if you look at Sid without the sound, you will see that sometimes he's asleep. They were so tired. I couldn't believe it, I pinched myself and said, "My God, I'm doing a narrative film." You know what I mean?

A brief postscript about **New York Stories**, which is presently being completed. **New York Story** was shown at the New York Film Festival in 1980, and subsequently won a prize as Best Short Film at the Melbourne Film Festival in 1981, which helped to finance further shooting. A lecture by Raynal, "The Difficult Task of Being a Filmmaker," which includes more details about the shooting of this short, was published in *Idiolects* (Nos. 9/10, Winter 1980/81), and the script of the projected feature was published by *Framework* (No. 18, 1982). In December 1981, I was asked to play a small part in the film as a film critic, and invited to rewrite my own dialogue— which I did with Veronica Geng, another critic who plays a critic in the same scene. March 1983, about a week before completing this book, I was able to see rushes of part of Raynal's newly shot material. It would be premature to comment on any of it in its unfinished state, except to note that a very long, improvised take between Raynal and Geffen on a houseboat, which re-enacts their first meeting, probably contains the best acting in the film. For the rest, we will have to wait and see.

JACQUES PIERRE LOUIS RIVETTE.
Born in Rouen, France, 1928.

1949—*Aux Quatre Coins* (16mm, b&w, approx. 20 min., silent) (unavailable)
circa 1950—*La Quadrille* (16mm, b&w, approx. 40 min., silent) (unavailable)
1952—*Le Divertissement* (16mm, b&w, approx. 40 min., silent) (unavailable)
1956—*Le coup de Berger* (35mm, b&w, 28 min.)
1966—*Paris nous appartient* (35mm, b&w, 140 min.)
        La Réligieuse (35mm, color, 140 min.)
        Jean Renoir, le Patron (16mm TV film, b&w, 260¼ min.)
1968—*L'Amour fou* (35mm, b&w, 252 min.)
1971—*Out 1: Noli me Tangere* (16mm, color, 760 min.) (unavailable)
1972—*Out 1: Spectre* (16mm, color & b&w, 255 min.)
1974—*Céline et Julie vont en bateau* (16mm blown up to 35mm, color, 192 min.)
1976—*Duelle* (35mm, color, 118 min.)
        Noroît (35mm, color, approx. 145 min.)
1980—*Merry-Go-Round* (35mm, color, 155 min.
1982—*Le Pont du nord* (16mm blown up to 35mm, color, 135 min.)

Perhaps no single figure in this survey dramatizes the contradictions of the avant-garde film as an institution and social force better than Jacques Rivette—a major filmmaker who has consistently been denied credentials, recognition, or any sort of protection by the "official" avant-garde establishment, even though his work has generally been shunned just as consistently by the mainstream power structures. Who, then, gives a damn about Jacques Rivette? More people than either establishment cares to acknowledge or deal with. As someone who has written a good deal about Rivette, programmed his films in three countries, and edited the only book devoted to him in English (or French), I can report that everywhere I go, I meet passionate Rivette fanatics.

In London, I once met an American who dutifully translated most of Rivette's old *Cahiers du Cinéma* reviews in his spare time, simply for his own amusement. I also once shared a Hampstead maisonette with a brilliant Israeli-born lecturer in philosophy of art whom I took to a screening of the

Jacques Rivette and Kika Markham during the shooting of *Noroît*

four-hour **Out 1: Spectre**; he spent most of the rest of the night telling me why it was the greatest film ever made—only a sleepless day or so before he temporarily flipped his lid and tried to chop down part of our kitchen wall with a hatchet. A friend who lives in Texas, collects and sells movie posters, and issues intense and thoughtful "auteurist" catalogs of his collection from time to time, has been intermittently working on a video remake of **Out 1: Spectre** for several years. A Belgian Rivette freak of my acquaintance was recently sent from New York to Paris by *Vanity Fair* to interview the director; I hear that he returned empty-handed, but will be writing the piece anyway. I know many women who consider **Céline et Julie vont en bateau** their favorite movie about female friendship, and Bernadette Lafont once told John Hughes, another one-time Rivette buff (see his delirious reflections on the now out-of-print *Rivette: Texts and Interviews*, published by the British Film Institute in 1977, in the May-June 1978 *Film Comment*), that Rivette "is a kind of Mao and his films are a Cultural Revolution. . . ." A Cuban friend currently living in Miami has a gigantic **Duelle** poster taped to his ceiling. In Brittany, during the shooting of **Noroît** in 1975, I chatted with a Scandanavian journalist and Rivette aficionado based in Rome who told me disquieting anecdotes about the shooting of **L'Amour fou** in 1967, some of which she also apparently watched.

These are only a few of the Rivette crazies I've run into, and like any true Rivette obsessive I could undoubtedly extend my list for days if such possibilities were available to me. The fact that none of them is supposed to exist or matter or have as much taste or *savoir faire* as any of the official traffic cops who rule avant-garde (as well as "art film") discourse only makes them that much more passionate and fanatical about their cult enthusiasm: the unexpected mob scenes that occurred at the last New York screenings of **Out 1: Spectre** and **Merry-Go-Round**—probably Rivette's best and worst films, respectively—with dozens of people having to be turned away on each occasion, only testify to the resilience of this growing "secret" society over the past several years. It may help to account for the curious, anomalous position of Rivette as a filmmaker who still manages to get new films financed, even though he frequently can't get them shown: like all the great film and filmmaking obsessives, his work thrives on legends, and the 13-hour version of **Out 1** is almost as scarce a Holy Grail as the longer versions of **Greed**.*

Considering the fact that only Rivette's first feature has ever been released in this country with any seriousness—and nothing has been released at all since the belated and very half-hearted launching of **Céline et Julie** by New Yorker Films several years ago—it's hard to know what constitutes "new" or "old" work in this context. I've restricted my range here to his last three features. (Readers interested in investigating the previous one, **Duelle**, should consult my article with Gilbert Adair and Michael Graham in the Autumn 1975 *Sight and Sound* about the shooting of **Duelle** and **Noroît**, and my reviews of **Duelle** in my Edinburgh Festival

---

* The effort of a few American critics to link up Jean-Jacques Beineix's **Diva** with Rivette, while no doubt well-intentioned, seems to me to be based on a fundamental misunderstanding of Rivette's aesthetics. My own two primary choices of recent films that could be called properly (and interestingly) Rivettean in a "commercial" context would be Alan Rudolph's **Remember My Name** (which Rivette himself has identified as an imitation) and the controversial middle section of Wim Wenders' **The State of Things** (including a semi-deserted "house of fiction" as resonant with narrative meaning as the country houses in **Out 1: Spectre** and **Céline et Julie vont en bateau**—not to mention the curious "first-person narrator" house in Eduardo de Gregorio's **Serail**, which turns the convention of the fiction-laden house into an actual female character that devours its hero).

coverage in the Winter 1976/77 issue of the same magazine and the September-October 1976 *Film Comment*.)

If every new Rivette film generally marks a decisive break as much as a discernible development, Part III in the projected but subsequently aban-doned **Scènes de la vie parallèle**—the second and last film made in the tetralogy, after **Duelle**—reinforced that principle with a vengeance when it received its world premiere at the London Film Festival in 1976. Rather like the pitiless Chuck-a-Luck in Fritz Lang's **Rancho Notorious**, enlisting new players and expelling old ones with every spin of the wheel, Rivette's precarious games have always been predicated on enormous risks; but unlike that vertical roulette board, they are not necessarily played to be won. Demonstrating this fact with shocking clarity, **Noroît** enters a treach-erous, kaleidoscopic no man's land where the very notion of judgment in any ordinary sense—the director's or ours—largely seems beside the point. The old-fashioned term for this realm is "experiment."

What are some of its ingredients? (1) A pirate tale fashioned out of diverse parts of **Moonfleet, House of Bamboo**, various samurai sagas, and Tourneur's **The Revenger's Tragedy**, set on "a small island in the Atlantic, off the coast of a larger one" in no locatable period, and structured, like **Duelle**, on the successive elimination of every character, developing towards a confrontation between a "moon ghost" and a "sun fairy" (although without very much of the mythical baggage underlying **Duelle**, save a few references to it in the closing sections). (2) A few English lines of Tourneur, violently wrenched out of context and recited by the avenging ghost Morag (Geraldine Chaplin) and/or her accomplice Erika (Kika Markham), as incantation, as simple quotation, or in a hammy style suggesting **Land of the Pharoahs**—playing, like Eduardo de Gregorio's dialogue, on a variety of uncanny emotional registers that, along with facial and body movements, range from the nightmarish to the parodic. (3) Music improvised by a visible trio who contrive to blend "modern" and "primi-tive" elements on an assortment of instruments, with a use of direct sound throughout offering another broad palette of possibilities, from the wind and sea to the squeaks and squishes of the lavender leather pants suit worn by Giulia (Bernadette Lafont), sun fairy and head of the pirate clan. (4) A systematic development towards ritual, dance, fantasy, gibberish, and total abstraction of the narrative through camera distance and darkness—coupled with facial masks, red filters, and silent 16mm black-and-white footage in the aggressive last sequence—all of which periodically makes it difficult or impossible to identify certain characters and transforms the coordinates into those of pure spectacle. Even the film's supposed English subtitle, **Nor'wester**, sounds more like a perverse joke than a significant clue to anything—rather like the fake Middle English subtitles used to translate parts of the gibberish French in the closing sequence.

Noroît contains the most beautiful images and sounds of any Rivette film, and the fewest indications of what a spectator is meant to do with them, apart from look and listen. When I watched a week or so of the film's shooting, I was amazed by the unnatural amount of sinister suspense that could be generated during successive takes, especially whenever the three musicians were playing, because their improvisation guaranteed that one could never be quite sure how any take would register—despite the lack of any improvisation in the plot or dialogue and the careful working out in advance of the camera movements.

The existential tension generated by this uncertainty—a hallmark of Rivette's style from film to film, whatever the differing strategies for bringing it about—has led many critics to draw a blank on the film, or even to retreat in terror (like the critics of Cahiers du Cinéma, who have avoided writing about the film). The disquieting implications of the film and its "images of castration" (as a film about female pirates) have perhaps led many commentators to conclude that any sort of analysis might be messy and embarrassing—as if it weren't a film at all, but a form of unsuccessful psychoanalysis.

While the plot is generally easier to follow than the one in **Duelle**, the shifting levels of mood and tone produce a sustained uncertainty of response—reaching an apotheosis in the mutual stabbing and subsequent laughter of Giulia and Morag in the final shot, which perfectly encapsulate the film's clashes and contradictions. On the level of identification, a subjective pan from beach to fortress in the first sequence initially designates Morag as the viewer's reference point. But in a film that seems executed according to principles of discontinuity, plot itself—by sheer virtue of its continuity—ultimately becomes the least relevant aspect of its experience. And by the time Morag is back on the beach near the film's end, by the time a comparable pan across the Atlantic is abruptly introduced in the middle of another camera movement following Erika around a room in the fortress, the subjective reference has significantly been raised (or reduced) to the level of abstraction, like a phrase in a foreign tongue.

Many of the preoccupations can be traced back to Rivette's seminal review of Lang's **Beyond a Reasonable Doubt** in Cahiers du Cinéma (No. 76, November 1957). There one finds the notion of a "totally closed universe" (all the more paradoxical in **Noroît**, which abounds in spectacular vistas and spacious interiors), where a director who "always looks for the truth beyond the probable ... looks for it here by entering the improbable." Equally present is an aesthetic of self-destruction, whereby each scene is restricted into a succession of "pure moments" and whereby anything that might fix them to reality is "reduced to a condition of pure spatio-temporal reference, without embodiment." In these moments "the characters have lost all individual value, are no more than human *concepts*," defined only

Noroît

by what they say or do. We are left with the strictly material space and existential duration in which an actor moves. (In fact, in reference to the subsequent **Merry-Go-Round**, Rivette told David Sterritt of the *Christian Science Monitor*—a perceptive and faithful Rivette supporter—"I care more about the grace of the actors' gestures and the quality of their voices than what they actually do or say." To my mind, the most radical innovation of **Out 1: Spectre**, because of this interest, is the effective obliteration of any distinction between "good" and "bad" acting: everything becomes potentially interesting as "behavior.")

These are, of course, the conditions of the theater rehearsal, examined at length in **Paris nous appartient**, **L'Amour fou**, and **Spectre**, where the actual end-point of "performance" is never reached. The radical departure of **Noroît** is to resume that inquiry (with improvised music assuming the role of the relatively "fixed" percussion in **L'Amour fou** and **Spectre**, which increases the almost primitive sense of perpetual tryout) *without* the narrative-illusionist pretext of the rehearsal to "place" it, apart from a few perverse instances that work more as *displacements*: Morag's murder of Regina, which serves as "rehearsal" for its re-enactment by Erika and Morag before Giulia and her court; the rehearsed swordfight between Ludovico (Larrio Ekson) and Jacob (Humbert Balsan), merging imperceptibly along with the music into a performance staged to confound Erika. (Considering the ambiguity of behavior in relation to "real" rehearsals, I should cite my own mislabeling of the production still from **Noroît** on the cover of my Rivette book—unfortunately unavailable for reproduction here—as "Rivette directing Babette Lamy and Danièle Rosencranz," when further reflection revealed that he is actually directing an unseen Geraldine Chaplin—showing her how to whisper into Lamy's ear.)

The most characteristic rhythmical pattern set by the delivery of lines and music, the movements of actors and camera, is one of stopping and starting, with odd-shaped pauses falling in between, while the tempos often tend to be either slower or faster than those favored in most Western dramaturgy, and somewhat closer to those associated with dramatic and ceremonial forms found in Japan. Both of these strategies converge in the climactic "masked ball," lit by bonfires and punctuated by pageant-like repetitions—a choreography of confrontations and crossing vectors isolated in time and space, whose counterpart in **Duelle** is the central dance hall sequence, where the mirror breaks and the goddesses meet.

The madness and hysteria of the Tower of Babel is basic to every Rivette film, from **Paris nous appartient** to **Le Pont du nord**; the maniacal giggling of **Céline et Julie** which irritates some spectators is merely one of the less sinister manifestations of it. Prior to **Noroît**, each film distanced this aspect by providing an audience with a phenomenological world to cling to; even **Duelle**, thanks to its cozy *film noir* references, nostalgic piano music, and Cocteau quotations, intermittently allows one to "enter" its reinvented Paris as a potential inhabitant. But the increased remove from any semblance of "lived experience" in **Noroît**—which makes it a much more exciting and daring work than any Rivette film since **Spectre**—also leads to a certain shrinkage of possible affect whereby the film becomes a "documentary" of a *tournage* and *montage* on the one hand, a capitulation to Babel itself on the other. Acknowledging the brilliance of William Lubtchansky's photography, the precision of the frontal camera movements and long takes (both evocative of Mizoguchi), the caustic bite of de Gregorio's dialogue, the dancer's grace of Ekson, the chilling laughter of Lafont, the howls and mimes of Chaplin, the beauty of Markham, the savage power of the music—and, above all, the continual shifting of gears, placing one at a tangent to all these elements as they struggle independently or collectively towards representation—one is nevertheless obliged to ask just where Rivette's experimentation is headed.

So far, **Merry-Go-Round** and **Le Pont du nord (North Bridge)** have provided only partial answers. Each can be regarded in a different way as a step back from some of the radical implications of **Noroît** and an attempt to find new ground as well. Neither film to my mind is an "essential" Rivette work, although both certainly have their interesting facets.

Merry-Go-Round came about through a rather unexpected occurrence: Maria Schneider announced that she wanted to make a film with both Rivette and American actor Joe Dallesandro. At this point, Rivette, recovering from a nervous collapse that halted the shooting of the third feature in **Scènes de la vie parallèle** only a few days after it started (a love story starring Albert Finney and Leslie Caron), decided to make a thriller as a sort of interlude from the tetralogy. Once again, he had as his producer Stéphane Tchalgadjieff, the remarkable Russian-born producer of **Out 1** (both versions), **Duelle**, and **Noroît**—as well as many other exceptional and unusual films over the past several years, ranging from Bresson's **Le Diable, Probablement** to Duras's **India Song** to Straub-Huillet's **Fortini-Cani**. In addition, Rivette re-enlisted many of his former collaborators, including scriptwriters Eduardo de Gregorio (who had worked on **Céline et Julie, Duelle**, and **Noroît**) and Suzanne Shiffmann (who had worked on **Spectre**), director of photography William Lubtchansky, and editor Nicole Lubtchansky (the former's wife, who had already worked with Rivette as editor on every one of his films since **L'Amour fou**, excepting only the shorter version of **Out 1**).

Some of the secondary actors chosen were also veterans of previous Rivette films, including Danièle Gegauff (née Rosencranz) **(Noroît)**, Françoise Prévost **(Paris nous appartient)**, Michel Berto **(Spectre)**, and Hermine Karagheuz **(Spectre, Duelle)**; others included Sylvia Meyer, Maurice Garrel, Dominique Erlander, Frédéric Mitterand, Jean-François Stévenin, and Pascale Dauman. And Rivette once again hired musicians to work on the film—in this case, bassist Barre Phillips and bass clarinetist John

Surman—but this time chose to integrate them with the fiction in a completely different manner, cutting back and forth periodically between the story and the two musicians improvising their free jazz in a dimly lit studio—with only very brief overlaps, if memory serves, of their music heard off-screen with the film's action.

Tom Milne synopsized the film as follows in the Winter 1978/79 *Sight and Sound:*

> In New York and Rome, a man and a woman who do not know each other (Joe Dallesandro and Maria Schneider) each receive a summons to the same mysterious assignation in Paris. No one turns up at the rendezvous, and their contact—his girlfriend, her elder sister—proves to have disappeared in sinister circumstances, possibly kidnapped. They duly set out on the trail of a dark conspiracy, filmed largely with a subjective camera: not quite so systematically as in *The Lady in the Lake* (there are objective shots and sequences), but along the same lines and designed to shade the atmosphere of mutual suspicion into a kind of fantasticated terror.
>
> Originally, the idea was for the couple gradually to rediscover their childhood in the sort of regression planned, but never finally realized, for *L'Amour fou.* Instead, their fear now creates a sort of parallel universe, and the suburban surroundings of the thriller, "the dangerous, sad city of the imagination," gives way to a natural world (sand dunes, a forest) into which they each project the other and where they are assailed by hounds à la Zaroff, snakes, a medieval knight, and suchlike terrors of the mind. [...]

The above account, based on an interview with de Gregorio while the film was being edited, may differ in one or two particulars from the finished film, but is substantially what I recall seeing at Manhattan's Museum of Modern Art in February 1980. Rivette himself, who was present at the screening, told me he regarded it as his worst film, and I would be inclined to agree, although I regret not having had a second look at it. From all the accounts that I've heard, the project was largely sabotaged by a lack of compatibility between Schneider and many of the others working on the film, including Rivette and de Gregorio; an original plan which involved a certain amount of improvisation from the actors had to be discarded more or less in midstream, and, as it stands, the strongest and most arresting portions of the film, at least in memory, tend to be those not involving dialogue (and, in many cases, those not involving Schneider)—particularly the use of music and the sequences in the sand dunes and forest alluded to by Milne. In the latter, significantly, Hermine Karagheuz *replaces* Schneider—a tactic recalling Buñuel's in **That Obscure Object of Desire**— and the mainly silent confrontations between her and Dallesandro have an abstract and quasi-comic aspect that to my mind recalled Road Runner cartoons. Otherwise, the complex and paranoid plot is not easy to follow, especially in its latter stages; and rather than attempt the impossible task of paraphrasing it here, three years after seeing the film, let me conclude this account with Rivette's own statement about the film that was included in the program notes:

> I like a film to be an adventure: for those who make it, and for those who see it. The adventure of this filming, I must admit, was a bit fitful: the course which was established at the outset was corrected many times, in response to contrary winds, lulls, or gentle breezes. I only hope that the finished film, with all its detours, keeps something of the dangers of the crossing, of its uncertainties, of its unclouded moments—even if, at the end, one notices that perhaps the voyage has been circular: like a "merry-go-round."

Rivette has described **Spectre** as an updated critique of **Paris nous appartient**—his first feature, about political conspiracy—ten years later, and **Le Pont du nord (North Bridge)** as still another updated version of the same theme. It also seems to announce an end, temporary or otherwise, to Rivette's preoccupation with modernism in the other arts (particularly music and theater), which reaches a certain culmination in **Noroît**, pointing in the direction of a more popular narrative (and hence less radically avant-garde) tradition. In this respect, one could say that **North Bridge** reaches back towards **Céline et Julie** in the same general way that **Noroît** reaches back towards **Spectre**—and hence could serve, like **Céline et Julie**, as an excellent introduction to Rivette's work as a whole. One therefore had hopes that **North Bridge**, by getting a U.S. release, could serve as an Open Sesame in this country for Rivette's more difficult work. But these are conservative times, and even though Rivette's audiences in this country have repeatedly shown themselves to be well in advance of most American critics and distributors, their enthusiasm is not enough to grant **North Bridge** an opening. (A comparable deadlock seems to keep even a cult favorite like **Céline et Julie**, which *does* have a distributor, firmly under wraps as far as theatrical showings are concerned: in New York, at least, the film is never revived by New Yorker Films in *any* of its revival programs—to the extreme frustration of many buffs who discovered Rivette via **North Bridge** at the 1981 New York Film Festival, but can't see any more of his work.)

For a detailed plot summary of **North Bridge**, let me once again turn to one of my colleagues—David Ehrenstein, writing in the July 20, 1982 *Los Angeles Reader*:

> Just out of prison on a robbery charge for which she claims to have been set up, Marie (Bulle Ogier) is ready to start her life anew. When she meets up with Baptiste (Pascale Ogier), Marie gets her chance to do so, though not in the form she probably had in mind. A thoroughly wacked-out punkette given to ominous, haughty stares and Bruce Lee karate stances, Baptiste is convinced that she has been chosen to be Marie's "protector" after their paths cross three times in the street. "Once is an accident, twice is chance, three times is fate!" A Rivette paranoid in the grand tradition, Baptiste, when queried about her past, claims to come from "elsewhere." Seeing secret policemen whom she calls "les super-Max" on every corner, she babbles on endlessly about the plots that supposedly spin about everyone on earth. "We're all under very careful surveillance, you know."
>
> Friendless, at emotional loose ends following her incarceration, and nearly crippled by a claustrophobia so severe that she is unable to stand being indoors for even the shortest period of time, Marie really does need someone's help and protection. Moreover, the curious behavior of her gambler boyfriend (Pierre Clementi) begins to make Marie suspect that Baptiste's nutty ideas may have some truth in them. The viewer at this point is inclined to agree. What's the mysterious black valise that Marie's lover Julien keeps so closely guarded? Why is he perpetually making brief assignations with her, then suddenly rushing off on some appointment or other? Who is the strange man (Jean-François Stévenin) who keeps popping up on streetcorners near Baptiste and Marie?
>
> Stealing the black valise, the two women discover a file of numbered newspaper clippings about recent political scandals and the unsolved murder of a leftist leader, plus a map of Paris inscribed with a strange circular design. In an ingenious attempt to break the code, Marie and Baptiste convert the map into a game board and use it to traipse around the city investigating the out-of-way spots to which it leads them—building sites, vacant lots, an abandoned Hebrew cemetery. At each location they encounter the

unidentified stranger, now accompanied by another nameless gentleman clad in an official-looking, dark business suit.
Baptiste's conspiracy theories have slowly but surely been
transformed into reality.[. . .]

The file of clippings concerns specific scandals of the Giscard
d'-Estaing regime, and the locations refer to various municipal corruptions
associated with that period (e.g., the ruins of slaughterhouses in La Villette
which were built and then demolished before they could be used, due to
safety hazards). Rivette has indicated that the film was made prior to the
French elections and with the pessimistic expectations that the same regime
would remain in power; so the unexpected election of François Mitterand
obscured and blunted part of the film's intended impact. Rivette conceived
of Marie as a continuation of the anarchist character played by Bulle Ogier
in Fassbinder's **The Third Generation** (1979), after she gets out of prison.
Her claustrophobia was occasioned by the film's cut-rate budget, which led
to the decision to shoot the film exclusively in exteriors.

Working once again with Suzanne Schiffmann (scriptwriter) and
Nicole and William Lubtchansky (editor and cinematographer, respectively), as well as with two leading actresses whose off-screen relationship
is more than professional (Pascale Ogier is Bulle's daughter, just as Juliet
Berto and Dominique Labourier were friends prior to making **Céline et
Julie**), Rivette turns his complex plot into an absorbing and offbeat
travelogue of Paris, beginning with a stone lion (le Lion de Delfort) and
virtually ending with a children's slide perceived as a dragon. In mystical
terms, one might even add that Marie's little red *Plan-Guide de Paris* neatly
assumes the same function as Julie's book of magic spells in **Céline et Julie**
in summoning up her shadow-double (in Marie's case, Baptiste). And in
keeping with the tradition of **Paris Belongs to Us** and **Out 1: Spectre**,
North Bridge opens with a title announcing a precise date, coupled here
with a witty paraphrase-parody of the title at the beginning of **Star Wars**:
"Long ago and far away/October or November 1980."

An explicitly quixotic fairy tale, **North Bridge** leads from such
enchanted moments as Baptiste putting her capsized motorbike out of its
misery—cutting a wire to stop its motor the way that a cowboy shoots his
wounded horse—to Marie's encounters with Julien/Clementi (amorous) and
Max/Stévenin (political), ending up in such fantasy realms as Baptiste's
weird, "naturalistic" confrontations with a spider's web spun out of a
fiberglass sprayer and the children's slide perceived as a dragon (which,
incidentally, exhales fire). For former bank robber and prison convict Marie,
waiting around for her dreamboat Julien to bump her off, Paris is a
conspiratorial spider's web, a marked city map, and intermittently a kid's
game of "Chutes and Ladders" (known as "Snakes and Ladders" in
England). For Baptiste—an abstract cipher without a past, for whom "life is a

reign of terror," projecting her staccato teenage body through angular karate stances, headphone music, and ugly industrial faces—Paris is the tail of the dragon, a city of eyes to be defaced (she habitually slices the eyes out of people in posters) and spies named Max to be faced. ("A maximum of what?" someone asks her, and she replies, "A maximum of Maxes.")

Together, Marie and Baptiste constitute one more Rivettean female couple whose mysteriously fateful and existential encounter transforms Paris into the city of their mutual desires. But the Paris of **North Bridge**, interestingly enough, isn't the same city as the Paris of either **Duelle** or **Céline et Julie**, just as the equally different Paris of **Spectre** isn't the Paris of **Paris nous appartient**. As Dave Kehr—who had the good taste to put **North Bridge** as well as Straub-Huillet's **Too Early**, **Too Late** in his ten best list for 1982—pointed out in the Chicago Reader, "Of all the survivors of the French New Wave, Jacques Rivette remains the most thoroughly unpredictable (Godard is predictably unpredictable). His critics charge him with changing his theories too quickly from film to film, but it seems to me that an inconsistency of approach is more of a virtue than an evil in the search for new ways of making movies."

...the argument thus far

Past a certain point, the old-fashioned adages about what is supposed to be good and bad in movies—things like believability, "good" acting, principles of conventional editing, literate dialogue—can begin to seem forced and arbitrary, as potentially harmful to adventure and exploration, as the rules for playing bridge. Certainly everybody's entitled to play bridge every night of their lives if they want to; but it's not the only game in town. Of course the rules for "good moviemaking" mean something; they are valid for plenty of reasons, and to say that one sometimes gets weary of them after years of submitting to their dictates as a dutiful viewer is not to argue that they should be discarded *a priori*. What needs to be discovered in greater depth is the kind of complex pleasures that can be had on occasion by moving beyond the boundaries of these standards:

—submitting to the breakdown in distinctions between "good" and "bad" acting in all of Rivette's films since **Spectre**, and encountering the fascinating spectrum of *behavior* that this erasure makes possible, like stumbling upon a new musical scale for the first time and learning the beautiful melodic possibilities arising out of this seeming atonality;

—accepting the disappearance of single focal points ("keeping an audience's attention") in the restaurant sequence of Tati's **Playtime**, which enables one to find and even help to create in the dance of one's wandering gaze the secret balances and imbalances of one narrative line dovetailing into another across the crowded floor, empty pockets of space and inaction that suddenly blossom into events like the sped-up growth of flowers, effecting unexpected symmetries or interruptions or both;

—coming upon the naked artifice of props, actor-props, and schematic plots in the late films of Fritz Lang,* and recognizing in this discovery the fact of one's own fascinated gaze, which can persist even after all concern for the characters (both Lang's and the spectator's) have vanished, leaving

---

*Der Tiger von Eschnapur, Das Indische Grabmal (1958), and Die 1000 Augen des Dr. Mabuse (1960).

175

the skeletal mainsprings of narrative continuity and attention in a primal active space (a precarious and momentary balance, to be sure, but how else to define the cosmic algebra and geometry of Lang's very Germanic notion of sublimity, a phenomenon of abstract essentials?);

—experiencing the perpetual rediscoveries of space, movement, objects and the relation of all three to one's shifting perceptions in the three great camera-movement works of Snow, where the apparent "absence" of what one usually goes to movies for gets replaced by its dynamic equivalent, but this time taking root equally in the seeing mind and in the seeing camera, the "content" of the film itself springing out of the quasi-sexual partnership of these two parents, camera and body/mind defining one another endlessly in ecstatic, reciprocal acts of recognition.

MICHAEL SNOW.
Born in Toronto, 1929.*

1956—*A to Z* (16mm, blue & white, 4 min., silent)
1964—*New York Eye and Ear Control* (16mm, b&w, 34 min.)
1965—*Short Shave* (16mm, b&w, 4 min.)
1967—*Wavelength* (16mm, color, 45 min.)
         Standard Time (16mm, color, 8 min.)
1969— ◄――――――► *(Back and Forth)* (16mm, color, 52 min.)
         Dripping Water (16mm, b&w, 10½ min.) (made in collaboration with Joyce Wieland)
         One Second in Montreal (16mm, b&w, 26 min., silent) (may be projected at sound speed, 17 min.)
1970—*Side Seat Paintings Slides Sound Film* (16mm, color, 20 min.)
1971—*La Region Centrale* (16mm, color, 190 min.)
1974—*Two Sides to Every Story* (16mm, two-screen, color, 8 min.)
         "Rameau's Nephew" by Diderot (Thanx to Dennis Young) by Wilma Schoen (16mm, color, 260 min.)
1976—*Breakfast (Table Top Dolly)* (16mm, color, 15 min.)
1981—*Presents* (16mm, color, 90 min.)
1982—*So Is This* (16mm, color, approx. 60 min.)

A few particulars about what follows: On September 15, 1982, I taped an interview with Michael Snow at his home in Toronto. Eight days later, in New York, at a screening of **So Is This** at the Collective for Living Cinema (my first look at the film), I presented Snow with a transcript of our dialogue.

---

*An earlier version of this section appeared in *Afterimage*, No. 11.

The following evening, when I returned for the second screening of **So Is This**, Snow handed me back the transcript with a few corrections, additions, and other changes. Roughly half of that material is printed below, in alternating sections with my notes and responses to this text—a dialogue with a dialogue, as it were.

Late afternoon, I find myself in Snow's living room—only a couple of subway stops from the middle of downtown Toronto, yet it seems downright rural; across the streets are railroad tracks, and when a train rushes by at one point, it feels exactly like the country. There's a similar kind of city slicker/just plain folks dichotomy in the cozy room, which is full of characteristic Snow objects. Next to a trumpet on top of its case is the elegant little grand piano at which Snow's mother recites biographical information about Rameau in Spanish in the third sequence of **"Rameau's Nephew"**—the same piano at which Snow will today play some limber bebop à la Bud Powell to relax a couple of hours later, explaining that he often selects bebop because he can't play Bach. There's a front door that isn't being used, or, rather, a front door that has been turned into the concept of a front door (a different kind of use): over its inside surface is attached a color photograph of a painting of the same door, seemingly the same size as the real one except for a curious anomaly—that also in the photograph, in front of the painting, is a hand holding a lit match that's gigantic, many times larger than life. For a related effect, look at Snow's three giant fingers curled around the "door" (actually a photograph of a door) on the back cover of his 1975 book *Cover to Cover*.

It's a room that, like Snow, is warmly, enjoyably, even deliciously absorbed in and turned in on itself—like a stanza of Walt Whitman, perhaps; very North American, in any case. It's likely a place where Snow does a lot of his reading—his main form of cultural consumption these days, he says, apart from listening to tapes of his weekly sessions with his local improvisational musical group, CCMC: there's a wall full of books, and in our conversation Snow speaks of recently reading a lot of ancient literature (Euripides, Aeschylus), philosophy both ancient and modern (Aristotle's *Politics* and books about it, including *Mind and Madness in Ancient Greece*, Derrida's *Disseminations,* Baudry's *Le Dispositif,* Lyotard). Not so long ago, Snow attended a Lyotard conference in France, organized around the question, "How does one judge?"—a conference, he says, at which Derrida physically recoiled from a screening of **Presents**.

The last time I interviewed Snow (*see Film Comment,* May-June 1981) was also in Toronto, right after he showed me **Presents**. Since then, **Presents** has made the rounds of other big cities, and the responses have been decidedly mixed, to say the least—particularly in relation to the film's third and longest section. In *The Village Voice,* J. Hoberman took me to task for referring to it—prematurely, he thought—as a masterpiece in *Soho News*

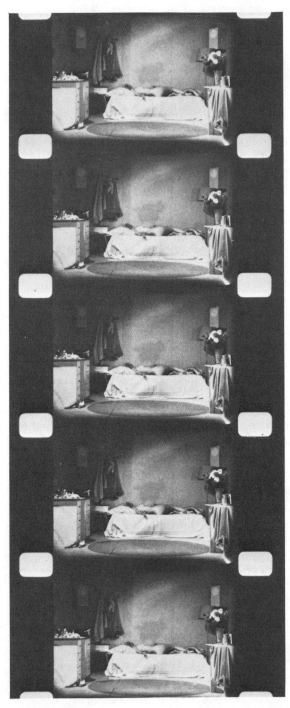

Presents

Presents

a few weeks earlier. Questioned critically about "the male gaze" at the Collective after a screening, Snow grew defensive, and it's clear that some of the negative responses to **Presents** continue to gall him. They gall some others, too: in the Collective's *10 Years of Living Cinema* catalog, published in fall 1982 to accompany a two-month retrospective from which Snow's work was conspicuously absent, Tom Gunning concludes his essay "Looking Backward: Ken Jacobs Presents the Past" with the following:

> Jacobs deals with films as a trace of what was present and now is absent. The image is not fulfilled with an aura of full presence, but rather through the act of being presented, here and now, to an audience. As I end this essay I must meditate on the absence from this retrospective of Michael Snow's *Presents,* a film which deals with many of these issues from another perspective, and certainly one of the most important films shown at the Collective for Living Cinema, a film misunderstood and abused. I feel I can write for this program in good conscience only if I lodge this protest.

It's been said that Snow is sensitive to criticism. Another way of putting it would be to say that, unlike many filmmakers, he both thinks about and responds to criticism—two concrete ways of demonstrating his sensitivity. (When I met him for the second successive year at the Edinburgh Film Festival, in 1976, I was rather surprised to discover him responding in detail to my critique of **"Rameau's Nephew,"** which was published in Sight and Sound the previous winter. During our recent conversation in Toronto, he was looking forward to an engagement of issues related to Teresa de Lauretis's article on **Presents**—"Snow on the Oedipal Stage," in Screen, vol. 22, no. 3—at an upcoming conference in Milwaukee.) And he thinks enough about my skeptical comment to add two further paragraphs to his Toronto response in New York.

JONATHAN ROSENBAUM: I find that the most difficult aspect of the last and longest sequence in **Presents** [the hour-long assemblage of handheld moving-camera shots], the thing that made it hardest for me to get into the film, are the drumbeats heard at the beginning of each shot.

MICHAEL SNOW: Um-hm. Well, I can understand that in a way, because what it does is it sort of flattens it. On the one hand, the drum beat is always the same tonality, so it establishes a kind of picture plane, I think. And things kind of advance or recede from that, but it tends to equalize in a way, even though the lengths of the shots are all different. So it isn't rhythm, it's never rhythm. Yet there's a sense of being equalized because of that tonality. But that's proper, you see, because they are equal, on one level. They're all film, the subjects have all become film, they're all this particular thing, which has a certain power. It should be—I hope—knowledge of the reduction that's involved might be a little sad. It is sad. They're ghosts, those things. There's not really that much there, in a way. There's a kind of deflation of the medium. Everything's disappearing constantly. Films give the impression of keeping something, but what they keep is so minimal. It's just like everything else, it's just going. You catch everything out of the corner of your eye, really, and this film makes that more extreme. In life this can seem a sad thing, and you don't want to be told that, but the medium of cinema, it seems to me, is quite properly concerned with fate. I mean, what is a more appropriate content for a medium that is a temporal structure that's determined? That's another thing I've been finding out about Euripides, especially The Bacchae and The Trojan Woman—they are just so staggeringly fantastic. The whole element of fate that's in Agamemnon, too, it's in all these things; it's in cinema. I hope it's in all my films. The mystery of going and not knowing where you're going, but the way is predetermined. I mean, some people think they know, but I don't think they do. (Laughs.)

The nature of the drumbeat is very much involved with the dialectic *in the film.* The tonality does establish a sense of two-dimensionality, thus equalizing all the shots. At the same time, happening at every *cut,* they individuate and isolate each shot, but the violence of the sound emphasizes the material nature of the cut. As in the memory selection of important images, it becomes a question of the spectator's emphasis on one of the levels of materiality and illusion that are all in constantly shifting emphases.

The compound functions of the handheld pan and the drumbeats are analogous to the function of individual brush strokes in Cézanne's paintings; they are hand-made smears of colored material on a surface but also are illusionistic representations. To me this reconciliation is a most important (*necessary*) and difficult problem of film and of all art-making.

Reviewing Jerry Lewis's **Hardly Working** *in Soho News, I argued that Lewis, Snow, and Godard shared an interest in fields rather than plots. Due to a typo, the "p" was dropped, making the point a matter of property rather than aesthetics. "Lest there be any further confusion," I wrote in a letter to correct this error, "the sort of field I have in mind is the conceptual kind—visual, aural, mental—that an artist thinks in (e.g., the exhaustion of space as action, in separate sequences of, say,* **Presents, Le Gai Savoir** *and* **Hardly Working***)." This was mainly an allusion to the second and most popular of the three sequences in* **Presents,** *filmed on a movable stage in a studio, in which an entire set is demolished by (1) an off-screen machine jerking the set, actors and all, back and forth, and (2) the camera proceeding into the set's interior and literally attacking much of the remaining wreckage.*

Exhaustion, I might have added, is a theme that haunts all of Snow's work. What are **Wavelength, Back and Forth,** *and* **La Region centrale** *but the simultaneous exhaustion of a loft, a classroom, and a non-human landscape, respectively, as well as of the spectator? Ditto* **"Rameau's Nephew"** *and sound/speech,* **Breakfast** *and groceries (in which the camera assaults a painterly—as opposed to theatrical—still-life),* **So Is This** *and silence/words— all films that devour their own subjects, genres, and procedures. The slide and tape* **A Casing Shelved** *exhausts a bookcase, the recto-verso projection piece* **Two Sides to Every Story** *exhausts the space of two rooms (the one it was made in, the one it's projected in).*

Snow himself looks rather exhausted, too, at the same time that he seems very much alive—a bit like the city/country paradox. (The trouble is, in order to be a North American conceptual artist you have to be all things to all people— all people and all things being alternate versions of one's lonely self.) His eyes have a sunken look, but in mid-September he's a couple of months away from becoming a father, and proud as a peacock about it; Peggy Gale, the expectant mother—curator, critic, and editor of the much respected Performance by Artists—*is cheerful too. Snow likes to laugh a lot these days, and in a way one can see humor becoming a much more dominant force in his work with*

"Rameau's Nephew" and **Breakfast**—although after a first screening of **Breakfast** and **So Is This** at the Collective, during which the audience was in an almost constant state of manic hilarity, Snow remarked during the question-and-answer period that he doesn't think these films are all that funny.

Actually, humor can be seen performing a specific role of renewal in Snow's work after the camera movement trilogy of **Wavelength, Back and Forth**, and **La Region centrale**, a hedge against exhaustion. How could he (or we) ever get through the 260 minutes of *"Rameau's Nephew"* by Diderot **(Thanx to Dennis Young) by Wilma Schoen** without the puns? (How we get through it with all the puns is another matter.) Or consider his recent publication High School (1979), done in the form of a spiral notebook—a sketchy conceptual joke book full of Snow's mainly adolescent kind of humor, flashes of which are also evident in **Presents** and **So Is This**. (Literally flashes in both cases—in **Presents**, the fleeting bits of Little Annie Fannie nudity on the part of the actress/model in the first two sections; in **So Is This**, when "tits" and "ass" are flashed almost subliminally in single frames in the midst of a sentence about the Ontario Censor Board, who gave Snow a lot of trouble with *"Rameau's Nephew"* as well as **Presents**.)

Insofar as conceptual art and puns are ultimately about "everything" (cf. Finnegans Wake or the behavioral puns in Rivette's **Out 1: Spectre**), Snow has found himself engaged in social questions in spite of his dogged apoliticism. If an ostrich is a formalist, he/she must find that even the inside of the ground tells one something about the outside, and in comparable fashion, it would seem that Snow's consideration of the "climate" that his films and other works enter involves him willy-nilly in ideological questions. "There's a lot of violence involved" in making a film, he concludes below: not quite the same thing as Jon Jost's evocation of "the iron ore pits of Minnesota," "the steel mills of Gary, Indiana," "the gold mines of South Africa," and "a camera factory in France" involved in the making of his own **Speaking Directly: Some American Notes** (1973), but perhaps a step along the same general path. Or, if not, an acknowledgment of the very different kind of violence that can be involved in the reception of a film.

JR: Do you find that most people prefer the second section of **Presents**, where the set gets destroyed?

MS: Yeah. But not consistently—I know quite a lot of people who like the last section, too. I think, for me, I thought of it as a loaded or trap kind of film. And I think it's working. *(Laughs.)*

JR: Could you elaborate on that?

MS: Well, I think the climate of the last few years... A lot of people have been on a kind of Möbius strip that's made up of ideology and entertainment. And I think that—I don't know, this is really presumptuous—

but I feel there's been less free seeing or less open seeing amongst cognoscenti of film in the last few years, and more tendency to want to see what you already know in the sense of affirmation of the correctness of your views. And that's a cultured thing—there's a stage of sophistication in a certain sense. But it's a little damaging sometimes...I very rarely consider the climate that my films go into, but this is the first one where I really thought about the environment it's going out into.

JR: And you wanted to confound some of these expectations.

MS: Yeah.

JR: How was the movement of the set in the second section effected?

MS: The set was built, and it's on rollers. It was pulled from side to side by two forklifts; then there's a part where the set gets lifted up and moved towards the camera. The mechanical aspect of it is not shown, but I think you have to be aware that there's the power of the machinery involved.

There's a whole thing about tools and about motion in **Presents**. There's every kind of hand tool, and then there's structures, all kinds of structures—buildings which relate to the kind of construction that's involved in making the film. Fundamentally it's about creation and destruction. There has to be something that has to be chopped off, something that has to be smashed or flattened. How do you make these films? Where does that come from? It has to be gouged out of the ground. There's a lot of violence involved.

Some of these things are not explicity stated, but they're kind of bubbling in **Presents**. Like destroying a set is a creative act in a sense, because flattening is a two-dimensionalizing, and so on. But it's the reverse of making the set, which involved even more violence, because most of that stuff is wood, it had to come from somewhere, and it was all hacked and hammered and sawed. I mean, which end is which? It has a lot to do with power. And that gets involved with the fact that there's a machinery for looking—the film itself...The part where the set moves is literally a role (and "roll") reversal on the relationship of the camera to the subject.

*If I have a problem with Snow's formalism, this mainly has to do with the political uses that right-wing critics and filmmakers, from P. Adams Sitney to Paul Schrader, are potentially able to make of it. Clearly there are materialist as well as transcendental ways of dealing with modernist film work, from Dreyer to Bresson to Godard to Straub-Huillet, and it disturbs me to contemplate the possibility of some compatibility—some very North American marriage of convenience—between Snow's structural concerns and the unspeakably racist, sexist, and quasi-fascist positions of Schrader in **Taxi Driver**. (That racism, gun worship, and structural concerns co-exist in the film has first been pointed out by Patricia Patterson and Manny Farber, in their exemplary article about the film* *in the May-June 1976* Film Comment. *The question of whether these things are mutually supportive—in the same way that, as I argue elsewhere in this book, in my conversation with Mekas, the structural concerns and progressive political critique support one another in Tarkovsky's* **The Stalker**—*seems more debatable; and considering the traces of structural concerns in the editing of the home movies in* **Raging Bull***, Martin Scorsese is just as implicated in these contradictions as Schrader is. In any case, such considerations are not irrelevant to the issues raised by Snow's remarks below.)*

On the other hand, I think that Snow deserves to be applauded for his political candor—a virtue he does not share with many of his contemporaries in the avant-garde. How many conservative armchair Marxists and leftist Royal Families in our midst, especially in Europe, would admit for a second to being aristocratic in their theory, practice, and ideology? Admittedly, by exempting himself from a political arena Snow can afford to be honest, as many of his colleagues presumably can't be. Nevertheless, it is not unreasonable to hope that a serious, leftist avant-garde position can grow out of a form of honesty that goes beyond public relations, rhetoric, and careerism; and if this hope is warranted, Snow's lucidity may indeed show the way more clearly than the work of many of his more politically vocal contemporaries.

Consider the concrete social pressures involved: Europeans are encouraged more to be political than North Americans in this area of debate, creating a certain warping of impulses on both sides. But consider, too, the ways that Snow is seemingly beginning to respond to pressure from across the Atlantic in **So Is This**—by acknowledging and responding to a specific social context both inside and outside the screening situation. His own discourse about this apparent change is ambiguous: after showing the film for the second time at the Collective, he says, among other things, that there is political commitment in the film, but not about El Salvador; that "the essential thing [one is] doing in a film is shaping light and time"; and that "it turns out to be your own voice silently reciting the text of the film, one word at a time, although it's under someone else's direction." Is there a political commitment in making **So Is This** a partially collective and shared as well as individual experience, in a way that his earlier films are not? Considering the wider audience and closer understanding made possible by this approach, I think one can argue that there is—within certain limits.

Much the same can be said for Flight Stop (1979), a photographic sculpture of 60 fiberglass geese landing, each one suspended from three wires, in a formation whose progressive "cinematic" patterns resemble those of a zoetrope—Snow's most well-known and popular work in any medium, located in downtown Toronto's Eaton Centre, an enclosed shopping mall. A social work insofar as it functions with maximal effectiveness inside a public arena—which, in the case of a shopping mall, also happens to be private property—Flight Stop resembles **So Is This** in both its serial and cluster patterns (the former using geese, the latter using individual words on a screen), which bear some eerie *relation to the crowds/audiences attending to them. Peter Gibian's two-part article, "The Art of Being Off Center: Shopping Center Spaces and Spectacles," which mainly centers on* Flight Stop—*an essay printed in* Tabloid #4 *and* #5, *which Snow both likes and recommends—describes this work in nearly utopian terms ("visionary freedom in enclosure"), and clearly some of the same happiness of group activity is implied in the cheerful progressions of* **So Is This**.

A recent court action involving Flight Stop, *by the way, indicates that Snow is quite capable of being socially aggressive and engaged when the integrity of his work is involved. During the last Christmas season, after the Eaton Centre tied scarlet ribbons around the necks of all 60 of the geese as part of its Christmas decoration, Snow went to the Ontario Supreme Court in protest and, after a hearing, Judge Joseph O'Brien ordered the ribbons removed by the following Monday morning—a decision widely criticized in the Toronto press.*

JR: How do you feel if anyone sees your work in a religious way? Does that bother you?

MS: No, it doesn't. I think if you don't recognize that certain kinds of examinations of reality bring you to a stage that asks for a metaphysics, you're being stupid. Because even semiotics heads towards being a religion. What does it go towards except the Word, the Word of God? I don't have any specific religious beliefs, yet I've found often that there's a limit to the capacity to judge both in and out because of what we are. What is it that's doing the judging? We don't know these things, we really don't. And I think you have to be sort of humble about it.

JR: Ideology doesn't seem to be acknowledged too much in your work, at least as a frame. How do you feel about it?

MS: Well, everybody's always in the time you're in—there's no stepping out of it. But fortunately that isn't as constricting as it might sound. There really is a lot of variety in life! But I think artists have always gotten away with something in relation to their patrons and audience in general— that it's essentially, in the old-fashioned craft sense, an individual or individualistic thing, even when you're the leader or the general of an army (which *is* the way a film or opera can be made; there are executive kinds of creation, too). But I think it comes down to a very personal kind of leadership. So my ideology tends to end up being—like the content of my films in a political sort of a sense is really a kind of—I guess it's aristocratic, in a way. But I'm thinking of the aristocracy of artists.

JR: How do you feel about asserting yourself within a particular political struggle *as* an artist?

MS: I have a lot of trouble with that because I know that I don't know anything. I can be indignant, too, but I really know that it's very difficult to find out what happened. And I *have* become involved in certain things where I felt that I knew enough to take some kind of action. Like, I don't know whether you heard anything about the Montreal Corridart business. There was a kind of street exhibition which had very good installation kinds of work. It wasn't like a Washington Square show but had really quite marvelous things; it was during the Olympics. And the mayor decided he didn't like it, and one night he had it all destroyed, without talking to anyone. It was quite a lot of work by some of the best artists in Montreal, and they all went to court. They lost the case—the judge's verdict was quite amazing; it made it all a question of taste. But anyway, they had to raise money and stuff like that, and I tried to help with that, because I was close enough to know something about it. But I don't hardly ever read the newspapers, and I don't watch television, although I always know what the catchword is. I mean, there's a little something about that in **So Is This**—it says there's going to be no political commitment or talk whatsoever, there will be no mention of El Salvador; because when I made the film, that was what was the main thing in what's called "the news"; if I'd done it two weeks later, I would have said the Falkland Islands. Now it would be Beirut, I guess . . . But I don't know. They're far away. I'm not saying that a lot of people aren't getting hurt. But I don't know what the fuck's going on.

JR: What I'm thinking about, though, is that in addition to being part of the history of representation, your films are also quite simply part of history. So when someone looks back at **So Is This** and sees a reference to El Salvador, that will be a way of placing it in history.

MS: I'd like to add that my use of the words "El Salvador" in **So Is This** is not callousness; it's an attempt to make the spectator be "in the now" with the film. THIS is a most *present* word, but around that there are several mentions of distant times and places (ending with the 4th century B.C.). What is important in the work (of art) is stronger than such references. The film says it was made in April 1982, talks about certain "local" problems (censorship), but all with a view to *using* these subjects to make what's more important, THIS work.

Everything dates, but you can try to step out of time a little bit. Photographs and tapes as soon as they're made are just immediately full of nostalgia.

JR: There seems to be a real difference between Europe and North America in relation to ideology. Within Europe, it's seen as inescapable.

MS: Yeah, I think that's true. And maybe it *is* Canadian of me, in that we have no power and are partly kind of colonized by foreign businesses, mostly American—and that's been our policy, that we've had the same government for thousands of years (joke). So maybe my attitude is related to the fact that I'm not in the mainstream of political history, that I don't exist in it—although there are plenty of people here who say they do, who follow everything and are active.

In the past, I've had problems locating Snow within the history of cinema, which has led me to conclude that he belongs more in the history of representation—a lofty badge of identity that solves certain problems and creates certain others. I regret the facility of my remark above about Snow's film being "part of history" (*what* history?), but at the same time I would defend his right to define that history as the history of art (which he does), and not according to some alternate theory of representation (such as "the news"). It seems significant that Snow doesn't own a television set; that undoubtedly makes certain things possible, too. (**So Is This** can be regarded as a pre-McLuhan work in more ways than one.) Close attention to "'local' problems" is not one of them. But at the moment when perception itself becomes a political question, Snow's work functions politically.

 JEAN-MARIE STRAUB.
Born in Metz, Lorraine, 1933.
DANIÈLE HUILLET.
Born in Paris, 1936.

1962—*Machorka-Muff* (35mm, b&w, 17½ min.)
1965—*Nicht Versoehnt* (35mm, b&w, 53 min.)
1967—*Chronik der Anna Magladela Bach* (35mm, b&w, 93 min.)
1968—*Der Brautigam, die Komodiantin und der Zuhalter* (35mm, b&w, 23 min.)
1969—*Othon* (16mm, color, 83 min.)
1972—*Geschichtsunterricht* (16mm, color, 85 min.)
Einleitung zu Arnold Schoenbergs "Begleitmusik zu Einer Lichtspielscene" (16mm, color & b&w, 15 min.)
1975—*Moses und Aron* (35mm, color, 105 min.)
1976—*Fortini-Cani* (16mm, color, 88 min.)
1977—*"Toute rèvolution est un coup de dès"* (35mm, color, 11 min.)
1978—*Dalla Nube alla Resistenza* (35mm, color, 105 min.)
1981—*Too Early, Too Late* (16mm, color, 105 min.)
1982—*En Rachâchant* (35mm, b&w, 8 min.)

I.

During the five-month period when most of this book was written, I also curated a two-week season of films revolving around the work of Jean-Marie Straub and Danièle Huillet between November 2 and 14, 1982 (the filmmakers themselves were around for the second week)—an event discussed in detail in my dialogue with Jonas Mekas. Part of this work involved editing and partially writing and translating a publication intended to serve as a kind of catalog to this event. Thanks to the institutional support of Films at the Public and Goethe House (New York), The American Film Institute, Media Study/Buffalo, and New Yorker Films, it was possible to produce the publication and distribute free copies to people attending the event.

It seems worth pointing out that, despite a couple of mishaps involving prints, the event was a considerable success in terms of overall attendance by the second week, the number of walkouts relatively few. The programming structure of the Public necessitated consecutive double and triple bills nightly, which were shown without interruption—making each evening an endurance test *a priori,* quite apart from the separate challenges posed by the films—and yet a surprising number of people came for the duration.

It seems neither possible nor desirable to reproduce the season's catalog here—although I *have* elected to reprint my own text about **From the Cloud to the Resistance**, originally written for (but not published by) *Soho News* in July 1981, as the first part of this chapter. To contextualize it briefly, the article makes specific references to (1) a column by Andrew Sarris that appeared in *The Village Voice* the previous week, (2) a college course I was teaching at the time, and (3) a 1962 essay by Manny Farber, "White Elephant Art vs. Termite Art" (available in his collection *Movies*). It is entitled "Transcendental Cuisine."

In a characteristically gross and funny episode about a *haute cuisine* establishment in William S. Burroughs's *Naked Lunch,* we're told at one point that "Robert's brother Paul emerges from retirement in a local nut house and takes over the restaurant to dispense something he calls the 'Transcendental Cuisine'.... Imperceptibly the quality of the food declines until he is serving literal garbage, the clients being too intimidated by the reputation of *Chez Robert* to protest."

It's a passage that often comes grimly to mind when I contemplate The Art of Movies as it's officially defined in our Transcendental Culture. But insofar as the analogy with film actually holds, I'm afraid that things are even worse off in my profession than in Burroughs's Swiftian nightmare. At least the clientele of *Chez Robert* smells or suspects the presence of something rotten, while by and large, the possibility that we're all consuming literal garbage seems less likely to cross the standard film buff's mind. Worse still, the possibility that better fare actually exists somewhere, even though it rarely finds its way to our plates, seems scarcely to have occurred to most moviegoers. They certainly haven't been helped or guided much in this process by critics, whose professional loyalty seems to belong more to the garbage merchants (who treat them to free meals) than to their fellow hapless consumers.

I'm one of those garbage freeloaders and consumer guides, too, even though every once in a blue moon a real movie comes along, something capable of changing my life, and it makes me gag a little on the others. I even have trouble holding the real movie down as a total entity, especially at first, because it's generally too much for me. I have to break it down into manageable units first, and I get only bits and pieces; friends, critics, and cohorts help me find others; still other parts slide perpetually out of grasp, remain elusive. I'm the reverse of that critic on a rival weekly—the one who just referred to me, flatteringly, as "Some of the people who have written recently on **Juke Girl**"—who categorically states, "I cannot even begin to evaluate a movie unless I have seen it from beginning to end."

It's a reasonable-sounding statement, but one predicated on closure—the kind of movie which doesn't change your life much except by extending it a little, which is the kind we both usually get paid to promote. He clearly *isn't* talking about Snow's **Région centrale** or Tati's **Playtime** or Godard and Mieville's **Numéro Deux** or Jean-Marie Straub and Danièle Huillet's **From the Cloud to the Resistance**, which are too radical as movies to begin or end in the ordinary sense. The latter film began for me many weeks ago, when I booked it for my Seminar in Current Cinema at NYU, continued when I checked out translations of the two Pavese books it uses from a library, was overturned when I saw it with students and friends last week, and is still in dazzling progress. **Playtime** hasn't ended yet, either; to "evaluate" it, one has to look at a lot more than other movies.

From the Cloud to the Resistance, an interesting, descriptive title that lucidly traces a passage between the two mythological and political possibilities of film itself—from the idealism of the medium, where stars are like gods in the sky and transcendental fiction is bigger than life (Part I—Pavese's 27 poetic, difficult 1947 dialogues between gods and mortals, six of which are used in the film) to the material resistance of the earth and human and animal life to aggression and oppression imposed from above (Part II—Pavese's last book before his suicide in 1950, a novel about the Italian resistance against Mussolini). Common to both parts is the same lush, brightly lit countryside and Pavesean imagery: blood, stone, trees, moon, bonfires, fields.

It should be stressed that this beautiful, intractable, 1979 Cézanne-like landscape film is being distributed non-theatrically in the U.S. by New Yorker Films, and is not going to open here, perhaps not ever. Straub and

Huillet are major European filmmakers, but ever since their **Moses and Aaron** showed at the New York Film Festival in 1975, and was reviewed in *The New York Times* as *Aaron and Moses* (a title Vincent Canby persists in getting wrong even today), their subsequent films—two shorts and three features—have been almost totally ignored in this country, and will continue to be. **From the Cloud to the Resistance**, one of their very best, hasn't a ghost of a chance of opening here.

The incapacity of New York to deal with it on any level is not surprising or unprecedented, given the personal stake we all have in keeping up the garbage flow (our Transcendental Cuisine) and shunning the very possibility of a movie that requires a certain kind of work and engagement. For one thing, it forestalls the convenient digestibility of a beginning and end that clearly separates it from life....

According to an Italian anthropologist who visited my class, **From the Cloud to the Resistance** is post-Pasolini in its relation to linguistics. (The relevance of Straub-Huillet to Pasolini and vice versa is problematical but unavoidable, because the issues of *translation* on multiple levels and a Marxist, dialectical relation between antiquity and the present seem central

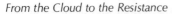

From the Cloud to the Resistance

to both.) Part I features formalized deliveries of a wide variety of regional dialects, while in Part II the non-professionals speak in the local dialect of Piedmont, the northern region where the action is set.

One of the most remarkable sequences in Part I is a dialogue between Oedipus and Teresias shortly before the former's misfortunes begin. The camera is stationed directly behind them on a wagon drawn by oxen that's being pulled along a lovely country road by a male peasant. The peasant is never once mentioned or acknowledged by either speaker, yet he's the constant, bobbing center of all the long takes recording the dialogue and its silent aftermath—the precise equivalent of the off-screen cameraperson behind the speakers (another ignored worker setting the whole show in motion), who are conversing mainly about sex and blindness, and there's a stunning moment at the end of the conversation when Oedipus prays to god that he won't become blind, just as a beautiful clump of red flowers— rhyming with a red toga over Teresias's left shoulder—appears on the right side of the road. Earlier, their discussion of sex occurs under dark tree branches punctuated by flickers of light, before returning to a bright patch of road that, as critic Gilberto Perez points out to me, traces a full circle.

Perez—whose essay "Modernist Cinema: The History Lessons of Straub and Huillet" in the October 1978 *Artforum* is an invaluable guide to their work—informs me that the long car ride through Rome in **History Lessons** (1972), a clear forerunner of this gorgeous sequence, is also circular, and notes that the rear-view mirror at screen center framing the driver's eyes offers a parallel to the peasant/camera dichotomy. Offsetting one thing with another—including the visible with the non-visible—is basic to Straub-Huillet's strategies. And I like what another critic, Serge Daney, says about material resistance itself being a constant theme of their work— the resistance of texts to bodies, of locations to texts, of bodies to locations. (This is already implicit in the very title of their first feature, in 1965, **Not Reconciled**.)

Straub-Huillet seem to identify with only two characters in their new movie—a baby wolf* in Part I who appears to be dying (occasioning a dialogue between the two hunters about Lycaon, the man the wolf once was before Zeus punished him) and a little boy who survives the death of his family in Part II. The monumentality of their best compositions is like the obstinate will that has enabled them to raise money and produce all 11 of their beautiful, impossible films—as hard and angry as granite, as implaca- ble as Fritz Lang or Carl Dreyer or Kenji Mizoguchi, often brutally thwarting our desires (such as holding the most handsomely framed and colored

---

*"The only small mistake of your article: it is not a 'baby' wolf, but an adult normal one— coming from the Abruzzi—; it was the rock, the stone, which was very big...." From a letter by Danièle Huillet to author, 18 May 1982.

interior shot in the movie—a summary of eight rugged anti-partisans standing at a bar, singled out in preceding shots—for scarcely an instant, so that it hits you like a brick). Yet the tenderness of their work ("This is a gentle Marxism in the metaphysical realm," writes Pamela Moorehead, one of my students) perhaps places it within the termite range, as coined by Manny Farber, and outside the whole bluff of White Elephant art.

The weather was beautiful in Washington Square Park before and after I saw **From the Cloud to the Resistance**; the movie didn't make it that way, but it made me see, hear, and feel more of it. According to the present state of received ideas, the right-wing formalism of Carpenter, De Palma, and Lucas/Spielberg is "good clean fun," not politics or ideology, while the left-wing formalism of Godard or Straub-Huillet is supposed to be pleasureless politics, no fun at all—torture to critics who hate to think too much, hence impossible for most of us to see.

But the talent of the good-clean-fun guys mainly has to do with their capacity to make me either forget or enjoy the fact that they're shoveling garbage. They haven't got anything to say to me about the weather outside. And the absence of Straub-Huillet and other exemplary termites here has also meant the absence of what might have produced some thrilling criticism. The silence of Manny Farber and Patricia Patterson for the past four years as film critics (their last published article, significantly, was on another undistributed masterwork of the Seventies, Akerman's **Jeanne Dielman**) can probably be explained in part by the quarantine placed on the kind of movies they appreciate and support the most—a quarantine collectively maintained by a community of "scholars" who despise the possibility of having to think too hard.

"For all their usefulness, termites can never be entombed in the Pantheon," a local and celebrated garbage collector recently had the considered loftiness to announce. No, thank God, but at least they can eat away at the crumbling pillars supporting that Pantheon—which may prove to be more useful in the long run. Who wants to be entombed, anyway, except for people who are already dead? Next to that transcendental version of Forest Lawn, I'll take Straub-Huillet's material resistance in a flash. The fact that most of us are unable to see it is our problem, not theirs—White Elephant criticism (which is all we have, alas), not Termite Art.

II.

Of all the films discussed at length in this book, **Too Early, Too Late** is conceivably the one that has had the strongest impact on me, although I have seen it only twice. After having seen it the first time, in Spring 1982, I was sufficiently impressed to put the film at the end of my "all-time" top ten list for *Sight and Sound's* international critics poll later the same year. Consequently, it seems paradoxical yet unavoidable that of all the films dealt with here, **Too Early, Too Late** automatically qualifies as the most difficult *and* elusive to write about. My two previous efforts have yielded only a few inadequate and hastily conceived sentences in the introduction to my Straub-Huillet catalog, and a somewhat more reasoned paragraph in the conversation with Jonas Mekas which opens this book. The notes below cannot pretend to be more than an interim report; further and more extensive analysis will have to await a future date:

(a) First, a few concrete facts about the film. For the first time in a Straub-Huillet film, the texts used are all read off-screen, making separate versions in different languages possible without any recourse to dubbing. Hence the film exists in four separate versions, with the same two people— Danièle Huillet and Bhagat El Nadi—reading the three texts in each one: English, French, German, and Italian. Consequently, it is the first Straub-Huillet film that can be seen in an English-speaking country without the distraction of subtitles. Otherwise, the sound in the film, as is usual for Straub-Huillet, is all direct.

(b) A few more facts: The first text, read by Huillet, is an excerpt from a letter written by Friedrich Engels to Karl Kautsky describing the impoverished state of the French peasantry on the eve of the French Revolution—accompanied by a shot moving through a busy Paris intersection. Then come longer excerpts from the *Cahiers de Doléances,** while we see the various places in France that are described as they appear today— ranging from spots just outside Lyon and Rennes to more rural places including Tréogan, Mottreff, Marbeuf, and Harville. These sequences, filmed by a mainly panning camera in June 1980, are practically all devoid of people, giving them, in Straub's words, a "science fiction, deserted-planet aspect." The second part of the film, roughly twice as long, uses a more recent Marxist text about the Egyptian peasants' resistance to the English occupation prior to the "petit-bourgeois" revolution of Neguib in 1952—a more journalistic text by Mahmoud Hussein, author of *Class Struggles in Egypt.* In both sections, it is suggested that the peasants revolt too soon and succeed too late. Once again, the locations cited in the text are filmed by Straub-Huillet (the shooting of this portion was done in May 1981), basically the sites of revolutionary struggle, again mainly rural. Here the camera occasionally remains motionless—most noticeably in the longest single take in the film, which shows workers leaving a factory in

---

*These "notebooks of grievances" were written by the mayors of those villages prior to the *"Reunion des États Generaux"* in 1789, held because of the fiscal crisis occasioned by Louis XVI's desire for further taxation. The meeting turned into a trial of the monarchy as certain representatives of the clergy and the nobility (such as Mirabeau) joined forces with the others—the bourgeois representatives of the *"Tiers-États"* (the Third Estate)—to launch the French Revolution. For the average French pupil, these facts are as well known as the Boston Tea Party and the War of Independence are to an American. (For all of the above information, I am indebted to Bérénice Reynaud.)

Too Early, Too Late (Part II)

Cairo. But there are also a certain number of slow lateral and circular pans, as well as more rapid views from a car moving through various villages. (The only shot taken from a moving vehicle in the first part, if memory serves, is of the busy Paris intersection.) After this section is a sort of Egyptian coda containing unsubtitled newsreel footage from TV of a speech relating to the 1952 revolution, followed by a downward pan that passes from a skyscraper in contemporary Cairo to waves from the Nile beating relentlessly against the shore.

(c) Central to the unique impact of **Too Early, Too Late**—which Dave Kehr, the very perceptive critic of the *Chicago Reader,* called "the most sensually captivating film" he saw in 1982—is the resonance it gives to specific places, particularly in the second part; no other film has come even remotely close to making me feel I've been to Egypt, which this film does. A lot of this has to do with tempo, rhythm, pacing: the sight and sound of a donkey pulling a cart down a road towards the camera is recorded in long shot and at leisure, with no sense of either ellipsis or dramatic underlining according to any principle other than the placement of camera and microphone in relation to the event. The extraordinary result of this technique is that one almost feels able to *taste* these places, to contemplate

Too Early, Too Late (Part II)

them—observe and think about them. Some spectators find this activity tedious; many of the first spectators of Jacques Tati's **Playtime** complained about it in a comparable manner, claiming that "nothing happens." Yet the significant relationship between Straub-Huillet's long shots and Tati's is that something is *always* taking place in them, if only the spectator can learn to watch and listen without expecting to be led by the nose through the sequence.

Discovering this capacity in one's self is part of the experience the film potentially offers. Is there any other film about the countryside and landscape—barring only such special cases as James Benning's work and Snow's **La Region centrale** —in which something is *always* happening in the shot? It's the absence of plot and characters that causes one's initial feelings of loss, absence, and/or boredom; yet once the feel and complexity of these places begin to seep into one's consciousness, without the confusions and distractions of a story or a too-rigid thesis that might regiment or codify them, something at once mysterious and materialistic starts to take place. (Many American critics, myself included, have committed the error of identifying the mysterious aspect of the film as "religious"— an assumption I believe a European critic with more familiarity with a

Marxist tradition would be less likely to make. It is ideologically interesting that Americans find it difficult to recognize any intense practice that is not capitalistic under any category except religion or mysticism. The intensity of Straub-Huillet's materialism may indeed seem "religious" and/or "mystical," but such labels in this case may well run the risk of confusing more than they clarify.) **Too Early, Too Late** may have no characters, but it is the most densely populated and *inhabited* of all Straub-Huillet's films—a paradox that the entire film is structured around.

(d) Questions of camera distance in **Too Early, Too Late,** like those in **Playtime**, are ultimately moral questions, as well as practical ones: how does one see what one needs to see without exploiting either the spectator or the person being filmed? (Many related questions of tact are broached by the landscape paintings of Patricia Patterson.) Serge Daney has some relevant things to say about this in his lovely newspaper review of the film for *Liberation* (20-21, February, 1982), entitled "Cinemeteorology," which I translated for the Straub-Huillet catalog:

> ... [In overpopulated Egypt], the fields are no longer empty, fellahs work there, one can no longer go anywhere and film anyone any which way. The terrain of performance again becomes the territory of others. The Straubs (whoever knows their films realizes that they're intransigent on this matter) accord much importance to the fact that a filmmaker should not *disturb those whom he films.* One therefore has to see the second part of *Too Early, Too Late* as an odd performance, made up of approaches and retreats, where the filmmakers, less meteorologists than acupuncturists, search for the spot—the only spot, the right spot—where their camera can catch people without bothering them. Two dangers immediately present themselves: exotic tourism and the invisible camera. Too close, too far. In a lengthy "scene," the camera is planted in front of a factory gate and allows one to see Egyptian workers who pass, enter and leave. Too close for them not to see the camera, too far away for them to be tempted to go towards it. To find this point, this *moral* point, is at this moment the entire art of the Straubs. With perhaps the hope that the "extras" thus filmed, the camera and the fragile crew "hidden" right in the middle of a field or a vacant lot would only be an accident of the landscape, a gentle scarecrow, another mirage carried by the wind.
>
> These scruples are astonishing. They are not fashionable. To shoot a film, especially in the country, means generally to devastate everything, disrupt the lives of people while manufacturing country snapshots, local color, rancid back-to-

nature museum pieces. Because the cinema belongs to the city and no one knows exactly what a "peasant cinema" would be, anchored in the lived experience, the space-time of peasants. It is necessary therefore to see the Straubs, city inhabitants, mainland navigators, as *lost*. It is necessary to see them in the middle of the field, moistened fingers raised to catch the wind and ears pricked up to hear what it's saying. So the most naked sensations serve as a compass. Everything else, ethics and aesthetics, content and form, derives from this.

To Daney's second paragraph, two personal footnotes should be added. Danièle Huillet, who sent me a copy of Daney's review, added one small caveat: "Jean-Marie is a 'Stadtkind' [city-child] but I grew up in the country, though born in Paris...." And Sara Driver has suggested to me that **Too Early, Too Late** may indeed be more Huillet's film than Straub's, reflecting her country background—just as **En Rachâchant**, again according to Driver, may be more Straub's.

(e) As I suggested earlier in this book, **Too Early, Too Late** inverts the usual relationship in a Straub-Huillet film between landscape and text—the landscape becoming the film's central text, the verbal text becoming the film's "setting." Practically speaking, this reduces the relative importance of the verbal texts in the films—although when I mentioned this notion to Straub, he countered that nevertheless the film could never have been made without those texts. And the documentary side of this—which is of course the major element apart from comedy separating Straub-Huillet's use of long shots from Tati's in **Playtime**—has specifically musical implications. The uncontrolled movements of people, animals, and weather function on this terrain like improvisations that play against the "composed" framings and camera movements, somewhat in the manner of jazz. When I proposed this parallel to Straub, he replied that a principal reference point for him and Huillet while shooting the second part of **Too Early, Too Late** was the late quartets of Beethoven—particularly the use of suspensions and slow tempos. The very slow pans, according to Dave Kehr, always move in the same direction as the wind, and it is largely the sense one has of the film's profound attentiveness to the material world that makes the film so singular a documentary—calling to mind the three quotations cited by Straub before the screening of the film at the Collective for Living Cinema on April 30, 1983:

D. W. Griffith at the end of his life: "What modern movies lack is the wind in the trees."

Rosa Luxembourg: "The fate of insects is not less important than the revolution."

Cézanne, who painted Mont Saint-Victoire again and
again: "Look at this mountain, once it was fire."

III.

The two most recent shorts by Straub-Huillet, "**Toute revolution est un
coup de dés**" ("**Every Revolution Is a Throw of the Dice**") and the
untranslatable **En Rachâchant**, made respectively in 1977 and 1982, also
deserve some mention here. Both films project a kind of laconic wit that is
common to virtually all their shorts (excepting, perhaps, only **Introduction
to Arnold Schoenberg's Accompaniment to a Cinematographic Scene**,
whose tone is too doggedly somber)—a kind of violent abruptness that
seems entirely appropriate to their rebellious stances and subjects.

The title of the first comes not from the film's central text—Mallarmé's
poem "*Un coup de dés jamais n'abolira le hasard*" ("*A throw of the dice will
never abolish chance*")—but from Michelet's statement about the Paris
Commune of 1871, and the film is set near the graves of several Commune
heroes in Pere Lachaise, commemorated on a wall plaque traversed by the
opening camera movement. Nine readers, glimpsed collectively on a
hillside only once in a flash (like the partisans at the bar in **From the Cloud
to the Resistance**), proceed through the poem in almost militant cadences,
with a cut to a new reader for every change of typeface in the poem.
Women read the portions in lower-case letters while facing screen left,
men read portions in capital letters while facing screen right; a long look at
working-class rooftops teeming with TV antennas, as seen from the
cemetery, follows the 43 shots devoted to the poem. The shotgun marriage
effected by this rigor is at once freakishly comic in its inexorable deadpan
and mysteriously haunting in its lingering suspensions.

En Rachâchant, taken from a children's book by Marguerite Duras
(which Straub originally discovered in Amsterdam, in English translation),
returns to the hard-as-granite black and white of **Machorka-Muff** and **Not
Reconciled**—shot in 35mm by septuagenarian Henri Alekan, the memorable cinematographer of Cocteau's **Beauty and the Beast** and Wenders's
recent **The State of Things**, as a sort of "study" for Straub-Huillet's next
feature (also in 35mm black and white), based on Kafka's *Amerika*. Here, in
the most directly comic of Straub-Huillet's 13 films to date, the same length
as a cartoon, a solemn nine-year-old Ernesto in glasses (played by Olivier
Straub, the co-director's nephew) defies his parents and teacher alike, by
refusing to go back to school in an exacting sing-song voice. After a brief
burst of Schönberg's music over the credits—as emblematic of the Straub-
Huillet oeuvre here as the burst of Bach is at the end of **The Bridegroom,
the Comedienne and the Pimp** (the best of all the shorts)—a pan across a
stringent kitchen where the mother is peeling potatoes introduces us to this
adorable brat, who a few shots later, in an equally stringent classroom,

identifies a picture of Mitterand over his male teacher's desk as "*un bonhomme*" (some guy). Asked by his teacher to identify a framed butterfly, he replies, "A crime." Asked whether a globe of the world is "a football or a potato," he semiotically replies it's a football, a potato, *and* the world. "An idiot, that's what he'll be," his mother remarks in the same empty classroom, not long before Ernesto takes his leave. Neatly encapsulating what might be regarded as the Dennis the Menace side of Straub's personality (which makes him as cantankerous in his way as Akerman) just as surely as **Too Early, Too Late** bears witness to the rural watchfulness of Huillet, **En Rachâchant** promises that their encounter with Kafka, to be filmed in Germany and the U.S. in 1983, will surely be something worth waiting for.

...the argument thus far

Two months prior to the completion of this book, I had my first exposure to the work of Leslie Thornton, at a screening of what she regards as her four most important films: **X-Tracts**; **All Right You Guys**; **Jennifer, Where Are You?**; and **Adynata**. On the basis of the first and last of these (and, to a lesser extent, the third), I felt I had to include her in this book. Yet considering the limited amount of time I had left, with over a third of the book still to write, I decided with some arbitrariness that she would have to be the last new inclusion. (Sara Driver was another relatively late addition.) By this time, I should add, I had been invited to teach two courses at the University of California, Berkeley during the following Spring quarter—a job that necessitated completing this book at least two weeks ahead of its April 1 deadline—and one of the projected courses, it was quickly decided, should be a spin-off of this book. This meant in effect that only shortly after deciding to write about **Adynata** for this book, I had it programmed at the Pacific Film Archives in Berkeley as part of a course I would be teaching a few weeks later. Such, at any rate, are the kind of things that institutions generate—institutions in this case referring not only to Millennium, the University of California, Pacific Film Archives, and Arden Press, but also this book and my rather crazed freelance career in relation to all four. (Readers who object to this kind of autobiographical background should be reminded that it is the very suppression of this sort of information that falsifies most kinds of film criticism, even while it makes it more "usable," by naturalizing its *constructed* coordinates—a principle I have tried to demonstrate at much greater length in my book *Moving Places*.)

LESLIE ANN THORNTON.
Born in Knoxville, Tennessee, 1951.

1974—*Face* (Super-8mm, color, 10 min, silent)
1975—*X-Tracts* (16mm, b&w, 9 min.)
1976—*All Right You Guys* (16mm, b&w, 16 min.)

1977—*Howard* (16mm, b&w, 30 min.)
Fiddlers in May (16mm, color, 28 min.)
1979—*Minutiae* (16mm, color, 55 min.)
1981—*Jennifer, Where Are You?* (16mm, color, 10 min.)
1983—*Adynata: Murder Is Not a Story* (16mm, color,
30 min.)

X-Tracts and **Adynata** have one very interesting and crucial aspect in common: they are montage films structured around the possibility of an auto-critique, the activity of reading one's self. The fact that Thornton performs this work in **X-Tracts** is what gives the film interest; the fact that we are able to perform this work in relation to **Adynata** is what gives it an even greater interest and importance.

The first film—split into three sections and six sub-sections (each section containing shots whose lengths are exactly the same)—starts with the text of Thornton's own journals, which is broken up into three separate sets of equal units, or linguistic equivalents. ("I was thinking of morphemes and phonemes," Thornton told me.) The very different (though no less fragmented) **Adynata** begins with a "text" that is no less internalized—the fantasy construction of an Other, built around an East of the mind, an imaginary Orient. In both cases, the approach seems comparable in some ways to the processes undergone in, by, and through the films of both Peter Gidal and Yvonne Rainer, which exercise a rigorous form of abstraction and analysis on private, personal, and subjective material so that the autobiographical content is absorbed only by being made unrecognizable, censored, unattainable—usable, finally (if at all), only as something else.*

Less than a third as long as **Adynata**, **X-Tracts** gives the impression of having been drawn from just as wide a pool of material. The whittled-down effect is, if anything, even more ruthless, especially in the sound editing, which makes each aural unit as distinguishable and separate—a thing that starts and stops, isolated in its completeness—as every shot. It is sound, in fact, which begins the film: a male voice counting slowly to six over black leader, the sound recording audibly recommencing for each successive digit. As the voice counts to six a second time, fragmented close-ups of separate body parts appear in sync with the digits, and fragments of Thornton's own speech—broken down into indecipherable units—overtake and replace the male voice towards the end of the series, while other images come along to replace the body parts.

---

* Not long after writing the above, I received a note from Thornton which alluded to the relation between her work and Gidal's—occasioned by Gidal's recent visit to San Francisco, where Thornton currently lives and teaches: "[We] seem to have a hard time with each other's work. I was struck by something though—that what he discards, clears away and represses I embrace, exaggerate and indulge, yet in many ways some basic concerns are similar—the inquiry into conditions of representation, the refusal to be located, the obsessive transgressions. His work in its silence & persistence demands vocalization and mine in its cacophony engenders a muteness." (February 1983)

Adynata

Over the nine minutes comprising and composing **X-Tracts**, speech gradually becomes less fragmentary and more comprehensible (and the sound units are correspondingly of increasing duration), while the images become more fragmentary and more difficult to identify (and the visual units are of decreasing duration). The black-and-white footage—shot very quickly in and around Thornton's house in Connecticut—focuses, like the extracted journals, on Thornton herself, her immediate environment and ordinary activities—sitting in a rocking chair, putting on lipstick in front of a mirror, closing shower curtains several times (as seen successively from different angles), walking down a country path, smoking, bathing— although a man and/or a dog also figure in many of the shots. Camera angles, speeds, and kinds of movement vary considerably, with the notion of traversal frequently recurring: Thornton and dog crossing through woods, shadows crossing both a wall and the ground, the camera repeat- edly panning up past Thornton to man and dog in a living room, or across a body in a bathtub. At one privileged moment, sound and image seem to cross paths in literally reverse directions: the camera pans from right to left just before a speech fragment says "left to right."

Over the same nine minutes, the succession of speech fragments from the equivalents of grunts and interjections to more comprehensible units of meaning tend to become increasingly referential to the film itself and the analytical possibilities of verbal segmentation (both familiar preoccupations of Godard). "The movement," "I still," "concentrated," "in contrast," "doesn't change," "both," and "constructed" are all early comprehensible units; later, when the fragments seem to overlap each other slightly, the units become less comprehensible again. Finally, when they stretch out into longer durations of ascertainable meaning, there are times when two or three successive units contain the syllables of a single word: "signifi—"/"—cant," "Leslie," "by an external form," "a language speaks only to...," "out of necessity, I have become an instrument," "through comparative sound units," "a syl—"/"—lable," "de—"/"scrip—"/"tion."

All Right You Guys—co-authored by and co-produced with Desmond Horsefield, as was **X-Tracts**—enlists the services of Thornton's kid sister (Eleanor) and her best friend at the time (Liz). Over six separate sections, this time numbered as such in introductory titles, one woman speaks, her voice appearing in and out of sync, while another off-screen asks her questions like "Why don't you go out with men?"; a woman is shown tapdancing with and without accompaniment (and the sounds of her dancing subsequently accompany a shot of her standing still); a couple dances in short fragments in and out of sync with harpsichord music; a woman's lips whisper "All right, you guys, this is it" in extreme close-up; a baby is fed in a highchair; and quick snatches of previous shots are reprised (along with black leader, and individual sounds that are instantly repeated in an echo effect).

The film's net impact is rather jumbled and confused; Thornton told me that she "wanted something sinister about the ordinary" to emerge in the film, but the effect is somewhat more diffuse. It was in reference to **All Right You Guys**, apparently, that one of Thornton's teachers, filmmaker Ed Pincus, referred to her as a "primitive." (Earlier in the Seventies, one should note, at the State University of New York at Buffalo, she studied with Paul Sharits, Stan Brakhage, and Hollis Frampton.)

Jennifer, Where Are You?, made five years later, seems more successful, although it is no less difficult to follow. At the beginning of an article that admirably charts the reasons for (and conditions of) that difficulty (The Downtown Review, Fall/Winter/Spring 1981/1982), Su Friedrich succinctly describes the film as follows: "The dominant image is a tight close up shot of a small girl engaged in various activities: playing with lipstick, a mirror, matches. These shots are separated by black leader from other, upside down, images. The soundtrack consists of music, natural sounds (footsteps, water, etc.) and a man's voice repeatedly asking the title question." Clearly, the question of identity signaled by the lipstick and mirror is as central here as it is in **X-Tracts**, even if Thornton uses a little girl rather than herself to broach the question. But despite the persistence of certain images from this movie in my memory—the little girl's blue handmirror, her clown-like red lips, the rhythmically edited succession of lit matches—I can't find much to say about it, and can only refer the reader to Friedrich's excellent review, which rightly locates the film's project as ideological, particularly in the relationship between the off-screen male voice asking the same question repeatedly and the little girl's autonomous activities. To cite here only two of her summary points:

> ...A film such as *Jennifer*...works because it makes us *afraid*, not in the interests of confirming our fears but in the hopes of making us so vulnerable that we finally become *angry* about the questions, the noise, the camera, and the presence that belies an essential absence.
> [...] Throughout *Jennifer, Where Are You?*, Leslie Thornton makes it clear that terror and evasion are an inadequate but nostalgic sublimation of the need for genuine communication. And she makes it clear that we must break the cycle, or be broken.

The title **Adynata** is a word that Thornton came across in Lanhan's *A Handlist of Rhetorical Terms;* it means "A stringing together of impossibilities; sometimes a confession that words fail us." The other point of departure is one of the film's first shots—a photograph of a Chinese Mandarin and his wife, taken as a formal portrait by M. Miller in 1861 and tinted yellow. (According to Thornton, the initial impulse that led to the film, apart from coming across this term and photograph, was reading Edward Said's *Orientalism*.) After some black leader, one begins to hear the sounds of a plane and an indistinct rustling that continues over a strange succession of subsequent images: a map that appears to be a diagram of the inside of a transistor radio, but could just as easily represent a city (actually, an aerial photograph of Berlin taken from a Soviet bomber); a spinning globe of the world in black and white which the camera approaches (evidently "found" footage); then a fade-in to a still color shot of a greenhouse in the Bronx or the Brooklyn Botannical Gardens, succeeded by a drastic tilt and swerve of the camera as it lurches forward and footsteps are heard; a cut to a closer subjective shot of the camera moving forward, feet visible at the lower edge of the frame; the sound of the footsteps continuing over a static close-up of a red flower....

The above summary of the beginning attempts to collate notes taken during three viewings of the film and subsequent information given to me by Thornton. Such a summary falsifies the experience of viewing the film, which is a lot less anchored and more treacherous in potential meanings than the above description suggests. The fact that the opening photograph is of a Chinese Mandarin and his wife and was taken in 1861 is fundamentally as external to that experience as the information that the "map" is an aerial photograph, or that the greenhouse filmed is in the Bronx or the Brooklyn Botannical Gardens. One should emphasize, on the contrary, that the lack of precise references for such images forces the viewer's imagination and unconscious to make their own connections and assumptions, which reveal all sorts of ideological positions and forms of ignorance about the Orient. Rather in the spirit of the French writer Raymond Roussel, who never left his stateroom when he "visited" Africa, and whose novel, *Impressions of Africa,* is about the country constructed in his imagination, Thornton's project is partially to construct an Orient of the imagination—an activity the spectator must also perform to some degree, merely in order to make the film legible.

This means, in effect, that one's misconceptions and uncertainties about what one sees and hears are not a distraction from the film's focus but part of its subject, as is the case with all the earlier Thornton films I've seen. On a phenomenological level, this connects Thornton's work rather unexpectedly to that of Robert Breer and to the Godard of **Numéro Deux**, in which the very process by which meaning is produced becomes the narrative motor: the metamorphosing figures of Breer and the verbal puns and double images of Godard operate in these terms much like the various editing and mixing strategies of Thornton, to yield a semiotic activity that is continually in progress—hence a subject that can be examined. From the vantage point of a critic trying to annotate (and thereby represent) **Fuji**, **Adynata**, and **Numéro Deux**, all three films are equally elusive to verbal paraphrases of their impacts, for each refuses to settle down into the fixed coordinates of a summary or synopsis. In its own way, each insists upon keeping us on the move.

Before trying to illustrate how Thornton achieves this a bit more concretely, it might be helpful to turn to portions of her own description of the film, written as part of a grant proposal when she was contemplating a couple of possible sequels to **Adynata**—some of which serves as a useful *non*-phenomenological summary of the film's contents (such as the last paragraph), and some of which attempts the reverse (such as the first):

> Observing a photograph of a Chinese Mandarin and his wife, a formal portrait taken in 1861, one notices that, while the man appears wholesome and animated, the woman seems quite lifeless by comparison, her features made up in the stylized manner of a "china doll." Yet her presence is compelling.
>
> In *Adynata*, the configuration suggested by the photograph becomes the initial point of departure for a sustained play of fantasy, speculation, fiction. The Orient within which events take place is an impossible one, a world of

exquisite beauty and mystery, artifice, deformity and obsessiveness, an Orient signified by exoticism and difference.... A subtle eroticism and violence pervades, like an uncanny cross between the narratives of Maurice Blanchot and Sax Rohmer. [...]

Adynata is primarily concerned with surfaces, beginning with the representation of the Chinese couple in the photograph, speculations, fantasies on their lives, their world. The image consists of individuals mimicking the positions in the photograph, establishing characters' identities through a series of repetitions and ciphers (a figure in an ornate robe is glimpsed walking through sculptured oriental gardens, voices, parts of bodies intercede, a murder scene). A series of complementary opposites—male, female, past, present, sound, image—construct a minimal and fragmentary narrative, an open text. [...]

The sound track is an intricate, evocative mix of environmental sounds and some dialogue which informs and oftens dominates the image. Included are rare ethnographic recordings of Chinese opera from the 1920's, old 78RPM love songs & blues, a Cuban rhumba, some Bach, the "Hartz Mountain Canary Orchestra" and TV-style background music; an assortment of crickets, birds, thunderstorms; & a passage in which English and Chinese are mixed over each other, both obscured, and synced with the gestures of the characters, their lips not moving.

Shot, Thornton wrote me, mostly in New York and environs, plus "a little in San Francisco," and produced at the facilities of Millennium Film Workshop in Manhattan for less than $2,000, **Adynata** is a film that secretes its own rules and laws as it goes (e.g, the man in the initial photo appears on the right, the woman on the left, and this sexual/spatial rule is developed in various ways throughout—with even Thornton herself briefly playing both parts in costume, in separate shots, with and without the white makeup). The film proceeds over its mosaic of elliptical details like a Ouija board, with a kind of logic that seems internal and external at the same time.

Found and stock footage of diverse kinds is worked into the overall pattern—faded, pinkish stock from the 1950s (budding underwater plants, an American with earphones in a sound studio, figurines on a medieval clock); an Oriental dance shot off a TV screen, accompanied by rock-and-roll—as well as old and probably heat-damaged stock along with a salad of other types and tones to film the same botannical gardens. In one of Thornton's climactic inscrutable blends towards the end, an optically distorted refilming of the end of Truffaut's **Shoot the Piano Player** is accompanied by a weird mix of soundtracks from **The Bride of Franken-stein,** a TV cop show, and a Betty Boop cartoon—yielding a complex form of signification run riot. Yet in the kinds of new and unparaphrasable language thus created, many different expressive registers are possible. The many fade-ins and fade-outs tend to make the fragments more serial and discrete, like beads on a string. On the other hand, when Thornton lingers over a heavily made-up and whitened face—like that of German filmmaker Karen Luner (in authentic nineteenth-century Chinese dress) or her own—with Hollywoodish pseudo-Oriental music in the background, there's as much dreamy contemplativeness as in an early Werner Schroeter film.

The only audible instances of English in the film are fleeting passages in "Moaning Low," a 1920s pop tune, and an excerpt of rock-and-roll, neither of which registers as more than incidental. Otherwise one hears a Korean soap opera, sees a pair of hands placed inside Oriental slippers, traipses through assorted bits of *Chinoiserie* and Japanese garden, and flips (in sped-up motion) through an illustrated book about foot-binding. The theoretical fascination with the East informing such French studies as Julia Kristeva's *About Chinese Women* and Roland Barthes's *Empire of Signs* seems to lurk in the background of this experiment in ideological self-scrutiny, a form of textual production that ultimately transforms all the materials in its path into a new source of knowledge.

APPENDIX:
22 MORE FILMMAKERS

All sorts of determinations have led to the choices of the individual subjects of the 18 previous sections—some of which are rational and thus can be rationalized, and some of which are irrational and thus can't be. To say that I could have just as easily picked 18 other filmmakers would be accurate only if I had equal access to the films of every candidate. Yet some of the arbitrariness of the final selection—particularly in relation to the vicissitudes of American distribution and other kinds of information flow—has to be recognized. So, I have listed below 22 more figures I would like to have picked—if this were a perfect universe where all cultural artifacts were uniformly visible and available, as *The New Yorker* and *The Village Voice* (among others) pretend. Once again, the order is, approximately, alphabetical.

TOM BRENER. As I suggested in the section on Jonas Mekas, a surprising number of North American avant-garde films seem to center on the same general obsessions as **The Deer Hunter** or **Manhattan**—namely, a boastful inventory of male possessions: This is my hometown, my house, my rifle, my dog, my flag, my Bolex, my woman, my art, my Louis Armstrong, my Shelley. The great thing about Tom Brener's lovely 12-minute 16mm study of a rural autumn landscape, **Pilotone Study I** (1976), which I saw in 1981—no heavy ideas but some great russet tones—is its graceful avoidance of that syndrome.

Spaced out in quasi-structural terms between stationary and moving medium and long shots within each segment, a beep sounding over each splice, the film proceeds from leaves (raking, burning) to highway (with passing cars) to the dance of a friendly dog behind a fence in relation to the unseen photographer—eventually winding up with more raking and burning of leaves, at night, the sky modulating between lavender and orange behind silhouetted trees. So far as I can see, no possessions anywhere.

RANDY CASHMIRE. A bit of autobiography seems unavoidable here. A graduate student of Brener's at Bard College, Cashmire showed me his remarkable 16mm short, **Cashmire Confidential**, in Brener's garage late one night during the Autumn after I saw **Pilotone I**. If memory serves, the film was made around the late 1970s, and I saw it in 1981. I had come up to Bard, my alma mater, to deliver a lecture about my first book, called "Placing Moving Places," and it was largely this context of autobiography in relation to cinema that led to my meeting Cashmire and seeing his film. A work at once hermetic and powerful, peculiar and personal, Cashmire's confessions involve not only himself as an actor (shades of Brakhage), but boldly recycled fragments of such films as **Psycho** and **2001** that constitute part of his consciousness, not to mention a portion of his filmic flesh. (Part of the film's originality relates to the sheer materiality of its eccentric impact.)

I would love to see Cashmire's film again. If I ever get an occasion to program it somewhere in an autobiographical context, I would be tempted to pair it with an equally invisible first film in 16mm by **PETER BULL—The Two-Backed Beast, or the Critic Makes a Film** (1979)—which uses me playing myself (in San Diego, 1978, while writing Moving Places), being interviewed by Bull and two other graduate students (Jim Randall, Dan Boord) about an imaginary film called **The Two-Backed Beast** which I had to invent out of whole cloth, and which they then tried to shoot and integrate with the interview in various ways. Obviously I can't be objective, but the few friends who've seen it tell me it's a good student film and an entertaining 45 minutes.

EDGARDO COZARINSKY and **EDUARDO DE GREGORIO** are both extremely intelligent and original Argentine-born filmmakers based in Paris whose 35mm films reach American shores less often than they should. I still haven't been able to see Cozarinsky's second feature, **Les Apprentis Sorciers** (1977) or de Gregorio's more recent **The Aspern Papers** (1982), both of which I'm sure have a certain interest. Fortunately, thanks to the New York Film Festival, I have seen de Gregorio's 1980 **La Memoire courte (Short Memory)** and Cozarinsky's 1982 **La Guerre d'un seul homme (One Man's War)**—two of the most formally sophisticated political films made during the past decade, in their very different ways. If I had easier access to the work of either of these filmmakers, I would have devoted an entire chapter to him. Linking them together is a bit unfair to both—despite the fact that they are friends, and worked together on the script of **Short Memory**—although there's no question that a leftist reorientation of Borgesian metaphysics is involved with their otherwise separate enterprises, placing them also within a certain proximity to Rivette.

Only considerations of space and inaccessibility of prints have obliged me to omit from this book a detailed discussion of **MANOEL DE OLIVEIRA**, the Portuguese director whose 265-minute, 16mm **Amor de Perdicao**

(**Doomed Love**, 1978) has to be counted among the great experimental narrative films of the Seventies. "In his films, which show affinities with Pasolini, Buñuel and Dreyer, he always demonstrates a lively avant-garde impulse," wrote the programmers of the Forum of Young Films at the Berlin Festival in 1981, which elected to present a complete retrospective of the director's work, spanning half a century, when he was 72 years old, arguing that it was in fact the avant-garde impulse in de Oliveira's films that made them "young." Happily, another complete retrospective of de Oliveira's work is planned by New York's Museum of Modern Art in 1984. For a more detailed account of de Oliveira in the meantime, see Carlos Clarens's perceptive interview with him in the May-June 1981 *Film Comment* and my own article about **Doomed Love**, "The Masterpiece You Missed," in the June 3, 1981 issue of *Soho News*.

MARGUERITE DURAS is another obvious exclusion in this book, necessitated by the complete unavailability of all her recent work in this country. It's symptomatic of her neglect that it wasn't easy to come by the following list of her films since **Le Camion (The Truck)** in 1977: **Aurelia Steiner** (1979), **Le Navire Night** (1979), **Agatha ou les lectures illimitées** (1981), **L'Homme Atlantique** (1981), **Le Dialogue de Rome** (1982). In the past, I've seen three Duras films that I believe could plausibly be called masterpieces: **Nathalie Granger** (1972), **India Song** (1974), and **Le Camion**; all were shown at the New York Film Festival, but have yet to receive American distribution. (When last heard of, the only English subtitled print of **The Truck**, Duras reports, was lost in the mail.) Meanwhile, most of our "intellectual" film critics are much too busy worrying about the deep-dish implications of a Brian De Palma or whether we'll all go to see **Tootsie** to be ready for someone as tough as Duras and her exquisite wit and humor. (Pauline Kael's unexpected defense of **The Truck**—occasioned, apparently, by a freakish occurrence of her having seen such a film, on a rare visit to Cannes—has had no visible sequels or consequences, not even from any of Kael's several faithful disciples. But leftist and intellectual interests of any sort do not seem like high priorities in Kael's stable of preferred critics.)

In recent years, the late **JEAN EUSTACHE** has become just as over-looked in the U.S. as Marguerite Duras, and one still awaits (without much hope) the local appearances of his **Une Sale histoire** (1977), **La Rosière de Pessac 79** (1979), **Odette Robert** (1980), **Avec passion Bosch ou le jardin des délices de Jérôme Bosch** (1980), and **Les Photos d'Alix** (1981). To the best of my knowledge, all these films are shorter than feature length. The only one I've seen is the first—on my last visit to Paris, five years ago—a 60-minute oddity that deserves at least some acknowledgment here. It is the only film in the history of cinema, to my knowledge, which has to be shown in two separate film gauges—the first half in 35mm, the second half in

16mm. In the first part, closely scripted, Michael Lonsdale tells a group of friends a "dirty story" about peeking through a crack under the door of a ladies' room in a café in order to see women urinating; in the second part, completely unscripted, Jean-Noël Picq tells the same story to a group of friends. The paradox is that the 16mm documentary version, which supplies all the scripted material for the 35mm fictionalized version, is shown second, complicating our own responses to the material. ... It's highly unlikely that anything else in Eustache's filmography can compare with the towering (if disturbingly reactionary) achievement of **La Maman et la putain** (**The Mother and the Whore**, 1973)—a 219-minute epic of post-New-Wave disillusionment which I reviewed in the Winter 1974/75 *Sight and Sound*— but an eventual retrospective of his uneven yet singular work over here would certainly be welcome.

HOLLIS FRAMPTON. An important filmmaker whose collected essays are due to appear the same year as this book, whose 16mm work is not exactly neglected by the Michelson-Sitney power axis. In relation to my bias against male possessiveness as a preoccupation of the North American avant-garde, his extraordinary **Nostalgia** (1971) is a key statement and act of *dis*possession. (Leslie Thornton's **X-Tracts** can be regarded in certain respects as an honorable descendant of **Nostalgia**.) I'm also somewhat interested in his **Zorns Lemma** and **Critical Mass**, but still have a lot of catching up to do regarding the rest. And I'm even worse off when it comes to Ernie Gehr, another important structural filmmaker whose oeuvre I scarcely know.

PAULA GLADSTONE. In Gladstone's mainly black-and-white, hour-long, Super-8 **The Dancing Soul of the Walking People** (1978), possession *and* dispossession both happily become very much beside the point. Shot over a two-year period, 1974-1976, each time the filmmaker went home to Coney Island ("I'd take my camera out and walk from one end of the land to the other," she reports in *Camera Obscura* [No. 6]; "I'd talk to people on the streets and film them"), **The Dancing Soul of the Walking People** is basically concerned with the space underneath a boardwalk, a little bit like the luminous insides of a translucent zebra on a sunny day—an interesting kind of space, at once public and private, that is traversed by receding strips of light, camera pans, and people, in fairly continuous processions and/or rhythmic patterns.

   Playing against these traversals is the repeated sound of galloping hoofs, some lyrical jazz arrangements (Duke Ellington with a scat singer, George Russell, Anthony Braxton, Stravinsky's *Firebird* rearranged by Alice Coltrane), "Under the Boardwalk" by The Drifters, conversation about Coney Island, and some funky black- and male-oriented poetry, written and read by Gladstone—more material, in short, that's merely passing through.

Harp glissandos seem to go directly with the mottled stripes, and the kind of visual drift that characterizes most of the film can turn into a kind of ecstatic contemplation when it focuses on two little boys tossing up clouds of sand—magical emanations that are partially separated by jump cuts. It's nice to see how Gladstone, like those kids, can be structural and non-possessive at the same time.

JEAN-LUC GODARD is as major an omission as I can imagine, largely necessitated by the philistinism of a country that isn't even interested in his prodigious work for French TV. (The little that I've seen, particularly of the second series done for French TV, **France tour détour deux enfants,** surpasses any recent American programming about anything that comes to mind. The British Film Institute owns videotapes of both of Godard's series, and has even gone to the trouble of having them translated for classroom purposes. But the much wealthier American Film Institute apparently couldn't care less.) Regarding **Passion**, his last feature—which Chantal Akerman told me was the most exciting film by anyone she's seen in years—we'll have to wait until Godard agrees to let the film be shown in the U.S.; it's already had some commercial runs in Europe.

And what about **GEORGE LANDOW**, a particular favorite as well? Three years ago, *Soho News* commissioned a piece from me entitled "Getting Ready for Landow" (May 28, 1980)—specifically, in preparation for the New York premiere of his 1979 film, **On the Marriage Broker Joke as Cited by Sigmund Freud in Wit and Its Relation to the Unconscious, or Can the Avant-Garde Artist Be Wholed?** But such are the contradictions of being a non-wholed journalist that I had to miss the film's actual premiere (at the Collective for Living Cinema on June 6), and haven't been able to catch up with it since. In the meantime, I can only recommend **Institutional Quality** (1969), **Remedial Reading Comprehension** (1971), **Wide Angle Saxon**, and **New Improved Institutional Quality: In the Environment of Liquids and Nasals a Parasitic Vowel Sometimes Develops** (both 1975). These movies get their well-earned howls (and titles) by starting from the structural nightmares imposed by different forms of institutional rhetoric—childhood perception tests, TV ads and newscasters, speed-reading techniques, and even structural films (when Landow parodies himself, Snow, Frampton, and Sitney).

I've seen only one film by **ROSE LOWDER**, and it is mentioned elsewhere in this book—both in the section on Peter Gidal and in the conversation with Gidal that comes at the end. Lowder has been making films only since 1978, and **Retour d'un repère composé (Composed Recurrence)**, made in 1981 and 59 minutes long, was shot in a single day, frame by frame, using a rotational system in which seven separate focus points where chosen. The setting filmed is a tree branch by a duck pond which Lowder has mentioned having looked at for years—it was where she sat and had coffee—before she thought of making the film. The original length of what she shot, comprising 60 separate bits of film, was 2½ seconds; the complex system of repetition in the film, as in many of Gidal's films, is not experienced as repetition. As Lowder explains in her program notes, "The same material is presented successively in three versions: a simple single print, a double print printed slightly differently twice onto the same piece of film stock, a triple print printed slightly differently thrice likewise, each version providing a configuration of rhythm of its own."

Born in Peru of British parents, and presently living in Avignon where she moved from London, Lowder in a way seems as elusive to a precise nationality as Gidal or Straub. She sees her film as "a vehicle to go somewhere else" (as she put it at Millennium Film Workshop on November 20, 1982), not as "a beautiful object." Yet insofar as she focuses for an hour on the same subject and processes, one can certainly find aspects of beauty in the experience of watching it. At times the colors seem to function like musical phrases that mix and thicken, growing sumptuous in spots that made me think of Berlioz. But this rich diet of rushing images eventually begins to take on a reef-like underwater appearance, emphasized by the oscillation between sharpness and blurriness in separate images. Process eventually overtakes everything, so that the images become more and more decomposed, and the very notion of surface seems to become undermined. If there's a more rigorous film of this kind available anywhere, I don't know what it is.

PAUL MORRISSEY would not ordinarily belong on this list, were it not for the remarkable film version of **Forty Deuce** (1982), which as I write has yet to receive a public screening anywhere in this country, to my knowledge. (I caught it at the Toronto Festival of Festivals.) Morrissey's starting point is a brilliant literary construction, a play by Alan Bowne written in a mainly invented male hustler lingo, set around 42nd Street. Simply as a theatrical object, the writing has the kind of giddy power that makes Wallace Shawn's dramatic monologues, in **My Dinner with André** and elsewhere, seem to have all the combined finesse and corrosiveness of a Mickey Spillane by comparison. (Shawn's lackluster use of profanity in his plays was desperately succeeded by the vastly more successful, "cleaner" **André**, directed by Louis Malle—a film of some local historical moment insofar as it confirms with an audible sigh of relief that the true aims of the American art film are petit-bourgeois, a conclusion arrived at independently by Allen, Cimino, and Mazursky. Needless to say, this gospel was accepted with as much dutiful glee in The New Yorker as the patriarchal, macho Zeus stances of Brakhage and Coppola are unproblematically savored in The Village Voice.)

Aiming at something more nearly Elizabethan than *New Yorker*ish in style as well as at moral nuance, Bowne's play has some of the lyrical urban rage of Jack Gelber's *The Connection* (with the related theme of heroin addiction); but the passion that went into the jazz improvisations there are conveyed here directly through Bowne's remarkable poetic language, in which obscenities are mounted and relished like jewels in the midst of other verbal exotica.

Shirley Clarke's film of *The Connection* attempted unsuccessfully to deconstruct its own filmic terms much as the play had sought to undo certain theater conventions. Morrissey's film adopts the unexpected course of opening up the play's first half into long, loping takes across substantial portions of the title street and the adjacent Port Authority Bus Terminal, then compulsively closing in the second half—set mainly in one cramped hotel room—even further by filming all the action with adjacent cameras, and showing this double-action in simultaneous split-screen. The variable binocular effect of the latter has led to the charge of arbitrariness in some quarters, yet it seems a defensible as well as daring formal approximation of a vision that sees the whole world through a veil of cross-eyed and two-faced duplicity—a context where every act has at least two motives and hence potential cross-purposes, and every event becomes at once a moment of moral horror and an act of aesthetic perception. Triumphantly *sui generis*, **Forty Deuce** is said by Morrissey to have been influenced by Gance's **Napoleon** as well as Sartre's *No Exit*. Yet its rhythms, intonations and vocal colors—not to mention its intoxicating language—could not be more American.

Having already written at some length about and with great affection for the deliberately primitive and rather Jarryesque work of **LUC MOULLET** (*see* my article/position-paper in the November-December 1977 *Film Comment*), I want to mention him here only to point out that he's managed to remain active in recent years, although none of his movies since **Anatomy of a Relationship** (1975) have made it across the Atlantic. I've heard about at least three more completed Moullet films, all described favorably to me by various friends and acquaintances who've seen them in *Paris):* **Origins of a Meal**, a documentary about the sources of the ingredients in a meal; an autobiographical documentary of intermediate length (i.e., a featurette, like Driver's **You Are Not I**) about Moullet in his forties learning how to swim; and an episode for a French TV series about the change of government after the election of Mitterand—a series to which Godard and Jean-Louis Comolli, among others, also contributed episodes. (Godard, one hears, created something of a scandal by having himself stripped and beaten in his own segment.)

MAURIZIO NICHETTI is a name I happen to know strictly by chance. My last trip to Europe (and only trip to Italy) consisted of three days at the Venice Film Festival in 1979, where I was invited to participate in a conference devoted to Cinema in the Eighties. And as I noted in an account of that conference in the December 1979 *American Film*, one film that I happened to see during those three days, Maurizio Nichetti's **Ratataplan**— a first feature with an onomatopoeic title based on the sound of a drum cadence—may have actually suggested more about the subject of the conference than any of the lectures I heard. Since then, **Ratataplan**, a popular favorite of sorts at Venice, has gone on to become a monster hit in Italy, and I'm told has already occasioned one or two follow-up comedy features from Nichetti. But despite some initial interest in opening the film in the U.S.—to the point where I even recall seeing a coming-soon poster for it in a Manhattan arthouse cinema in the early 1980s—American audiences have been deemed not ready for it.

In addition to writing and directing, Nichetti plays the central character, a shy, unassuming café waiter named Colombo. (Nichetti played a substantial part as an orchestra conductor in the live-action portions of the animated feature **Allegro Non Troppo**, and some American spectators may recall his wiry frame and mousy mustache from that film.) In an early sequence, a participant at an international conference in a skyscraper has a heart attack, and Colombo—who operates a refreshment stand on a hilltop on the other side of the vast metropolis—is summoned by phone to bring this poor, suffering fellow a glass of mineral water. Colombo goes hurtling down the hill with his tray, and his convoluted journey across Rome— during which his glass of water gets sprayed by exhaust fumes, covered by a policeman's cap, and speckled with white paint, before a bee unceremoniously drowns in it with a Tatiesque fizzle—becomes an epic, absurdist poem about contemporary urban life, concocted out of nearly equal bits of Clair, Tati, and Lewis crossed with some of the literary madness of a Carroll, a Gogol, and a Sterne.

Later, this poem turns nightmarish when Colombo puts together a robot duplicate of himself inside his dingy tenement flat, using various odds and ends from the city dump, including a video camera that fits neatly inside the headpiece. Guiding his suave, remote-control better self out the front door with a fixed steering wheel like a puppeteer, and picking up its precise viewpoint in a TV monitor, Colombo promptly gets his robot to score with the girl downstairs and take her out disco dancing.

Is **Ratataplan** avant-garde? Apparently it isn't in Europe, but fashion dictates that it assume that dubious position over here, where you can't see it because somebody assumes it will be bad for your health. Could it be the mixture of fantasy and whimsy with satire and comedy that scares off potential distributors and programmers? I could always be wrong about this, but I have a terrible suspicion that the adults who previewed **Ratataplan** neglected to bring their kids along; if they *had* brought them, they might have discovered how funny it is.

The only film I've seen by **ANDREW NOREN** is the feature-length **Charmed Particles** (1977), Part IV of his ongoing **The Adventures of the Exquisite Corpse,** which I've seen twice. Limited thematically, more or less, to the male-possessions vantage point, the film nonetheless has so much to "say" about light and texture—something that affects all our daily visual experience, a subject that spreads out over our lives as blandly, as completely, and, most of the time, as unmemorably as a picnic tablecloth over a patch of ground—that I can't really ignore it. So black and white it can make you forget that color films exist, and so sensually rich it may make you want to go on a movie diet afterwards, this exquisite chroni-cling of Noren's self-confessed activity as a "light thief" and "shadow bandit," mainly within the limited yet limitless confines of a small city apartment, is fortunately silent, too. It creates a visual music so concen-trated that I'm sure any musical accompaniment would be redundant or, even worse, reductive in effect.

Often evoking the luminous textures of certain European films in the Twenties (like the pulsating light patterns of F. W. Murnau's **Faust**), as well as the pantheism and "poetic structuralism" of Louis Hock—with smoke, hair, leafy textures and fabrics treated as delicately as brushstrokes, then mixed together in a sort of light blender that suggests Josef von Sternberg's teasing manner of dissolving his own glittering bric-a-brac—**Charmed Particles** can lead one off in many possible directions, most of them internal. Mottled shadows flicker across an eye, a horizontal wipe reveals clothes swaying on a line (like a glissando running up a keyboard), silvery light speckles a floor or atomizes on quivering water or turns a woman's hair into the Milky Way, wind blows snow crystals at night, fragments of fabric drift past an open window (in a peekaboo pattern remaining a basic rhythmic component throughout, a perpetual give-and-take of now you see it/now you don't), parts of human and feline bodies and diverse objects conspire in activities (walking, dishwashing, reading the paper, looking at a TV or a movie still, climbing stairs). If this is formalism, the least that can be said for Noren is that he makes the most of it.

More than an adaptation of dance to film, the 40-minute, Canadian **Shades of Red** represents a profound collaboration between filmmaker **DAVID RIMMER** and choreographer **PAULA ROSS;** the only precedent that comes to mind is Yvonne Rainer's assumption of both roles in **Lives of Performers,** where the overall effect of the private/public dichotomy is more fictionalized. The structure is carefully worked out through the interactions between the two artists, which start with Ross reciting a parable about a scorpion and a frog (also used by Orson Welles in **Mr. Arkadin**) followed by a performance of her dancers. As off-the-cuff autobiographical remarks later become juxtaposed with her rehearsal of a piece to be done with (as opposed to for) the camera, the brew becomes still headier. By the exhilarating end, a mutual choreography of dancers, camera, and lights achieves a happy union of intentions. The images thus created—funny slapstick writhings, a man moving a woman's body around like human clock hands in **Metropolis**, cross-currents of pedestrian traffic—are keyed to arrangements of color, text, costume, movement, and light that are deftly cross-referenced.

RAUL RUIZ "has known three kinds of marginalization," according to Ian Christie—introducing the second half of *Afterimage* No. 10 (Autumn 1981), devoted to "Myths of Total Cinema" (the first half focuses on Jean Epstein in the Twenties)—"all of them contributing to the present paradox of his considerable fame and influence, yet near-total inaccessibility." As a pioneer of Chilean cinema in the late Sixties, a European exile since the military coup of September 1973, and a filmmaker who has worked almost exclusively on television commissions since 1975, Ruiz is triply invisible, one might say. His most important film by reputation is the 1978 **L'Hypothèse du tableau volé (The Hypothesis of the Stolen Painting)**, celebrated in *Cahiers du Cinéma*. His most important recent film by legend is **The Territory** (1981)—a project that was inadvertently cut short by the last-minute decision to make Wim Wenders's **The State of Things** on the same location in Portugal with many of the same actors, cannibalizing in effect a film about cannibals so that another sort of film about survival could be made.*

The only Ruiz film I've seen, in fact, is an extraordinary short, **Le Colloque de chiens (Dog's Dialogue)**, shown in an excellent English version prepared by Michael Graham at the New York Film Festival in 1980, and, so far as I can tell, almost totally ignored in the press. To quote Ruiz himself on this wonderful film (from a *Cahiers* interview quoted in *Afterimage*):

> What interests me are all the possibilities of relations, misunderstandings, between what is seen and what is said. For Le Colloque I took a story from *Detective,* cut out various phrases and made a new story in which the same phrases were repeated in relation to different events. It runs through several times but it is always the same phrase that recurs.

---

*Ironically, Ruiz wasn't the only filmmaker cut short. Jon Jost, who was shooting a documentary on Ruiz making **Le Territoire** for the British Film Institute as a sort of follow-up to his **Godard 1980**, also wound up with an unfinished film. Ruiz's film, however, unlike Jost's, was completed in its "unfinished" form.

This is the whole trick. The title does not have much connection with Cervantes. I inserted shots of dog barking, originally with subtitles: 'Love,' 'Hate,' 'Violence.' I interlinked three kinds of film, one which is a kind of photo-novel (the main narrative is entirely in stills), another which has talking dogs, and a third which shows real places referred to in the photo-novel, the streets and monuments framed in a banal manner.

WERNER SCHROETER remains a key missing link in the contemporary German avant-garde as far as this country is concerned, apart from scattered screenings of **Eika Katappa** (1969) and **The Death of Marie Malibran** (1972), probably still his best films, and in spite of the writing of Gary Indiana in *Artforum* and an article by Timothy Corrigan in *Discourse* (No. 3). It is surely the narrative bias of the New York Film Festival that promoted a likably mediocre director from the same campy school, Daniel Schmid, while totally ignoring the remarkable non-narrative meditations of Schroeter, whose level of intensity seems equal at moments to the great silent directors. Unfortunately, for a fan like myself who was primed on this non-narrative work, the more recent forays of Schroeter into more respectable areas—**The Kingdom of Naples** (1978), **Dress Rehearsal** (1980), and **Wolfsburg or Palermo** (1981)—have all been disappointments. The latter, which seems more interesting from an experimental standpoint after the Felliniesque post-neorealism of the first and the personal documentary of the second (about a theater festival in Nancy, France)—a film that starts off in a neorealist mode and Italian location, and winds up in Germany and expressionism—fritters away most of its interest through an overextended narration that flattens out all of Schroeter's most interesting effects. The problem is, to judge from the eight or nine of his features that I've seen over the years, his essential gifts are not narrative ones; yet it is narrative art, alas, that the world apparently requires of him.

If you don't already know **WAYNE WANG's** first hit, **Chan Is Missing** (1980)—an independent black-and-white feature costing only $20,000 which deftly combines the detective story, the structural film, and an investigation into what it means to be Chinese-American in the present economic crisis—you should. Wang currently has two new features in the works for 1983, and I hope that the next volume in this series will have something to say about them.

ORGANIZING THE AVANT-GARDE:
A Conversation with Peter Gidal

Anything can be acquired in solitude, except character.
Stendhal

JONATHAN ROSENBAUM: I'm interested in asking you about two separate matters: (1) European avant-garde filmmakers of interest whom you're familiar with who aren't known in the U.S., and (2) the differences in communications within the respective avant-garde film communities in London and New York—communications between filmmakers and between filmmakers and the audience. There's a lot that Americans don't know, both about the work being done and about the information flow.

PETER GIDAL: Could you be more specific?

JR: I'm remembering some of the special screenings that used to be held in London at a theater on Russell Square to raise money for a distribution company, The Other Cinema—screenings of **Out 1: Spectre, Numéro Deux, Winstanley**. I can't imagine anything like this happening in New York outside a festival or a Coppola special event, and I'm wondering why. You couldn't find an equivalent to The Other Cinema here.

PG: Yes, but you couldn't find an equivalent of the London Filmmakers Co-op, either, or any of the British groups. Here there's a Co-op, but there's no distribution and exhibition—the closest equivalent to the London Co-op in New York is Millennium.

JR: How often does the London Co-op have screenings?

PG: Twice a week. For many years, it was once a week; it's only been twice a week, Wednesday and Friday, for the last three or four years. In England most of the groups have followed the pattern set by the Co-op in attempting to do distribution *and* screening, if not production. Everything's much more split here, where exhibition and distribution tend to be separate.

JR: This is true now, but I think it was less true 15 years ago. Can you think of places in London other than the Co-op where avant-garde films have been shown on any regular basis?

PG: Not The Other Cinema, and not the Gate, as you were suggesting earlier. The Gate happened to show a few Brakhage and Snow films because it's run by Barbara and David Stone, who, when they lived in New York, supported *Film Culture*. They didn't realize—as Annette Michelson didn't realize—that in England, where socialism is not a reds-under-the-beds concept, and where there's one Co-op that distributes experimental film and works hard to get work like Snow's shown, you don't want free enterprise. I have a letter from Michelson extolling the rights of free enterprise—which is why the Gate should be allowed to show Brakhage and Snow even if it means that the Co-op will have a smaller audience, because the Gate can afford to advertise, and since they mainly show Woody Allen crap, they can then lose a bit on the side showing avant-garde on Sunday afternoons. But in the end that could have been very detrimental to the whole experimental film distribution setup in England. We had endless battles, and Michael Snow, who is not that political, finally understood it and said he's made a big mistake letting Michelson convince him to allow the Stones to have his work, because he realized it was divisive. You *do* need a central structure and a planned culture, just liked a planned economy—you can't allow free-ranging, piratical capitalism.

JR: This seems parallel with some of the issues Jonas was involved with—the avant-garde having a fixed identity and place rather than having to depend on being picked up by different foster parents.

PG: That's right. You have your own structure—not your own in the sense that it's separate from the social/political context you're in, but it has to be run and structured and organized autonomously, or semi-autonomously. It isn't just begging the National Film Theatre to show a film one time. Once you have a structure, you can then *allow* that to happen at the NFT—these amazing experimental film festivals every five years where for ten days, day and night, you saw films by unknown, new, young, old filmmakers, from 16 countries. The NFT could only allow itself to do that because the structure of experimental film had its own power, its own group of people, its own interest groups and funding. Once you've got that *then* you can gain by making links.

It's the whole thing about separate practices. In a sense, my polemical problems, when I used to work at the Co-op in the Sixties and early Seventies, included a constant battle against The Other Cinema, who wanted to co-opt it as just one part of this general, liberal pluralistic thing—even to the point where they offered us free office space, we had practically no money, yet we didn't take it. And that's why the experimental film in England has its own identity—because it was never co-opted.

JR: In my dialogue with Jonas, I began by pointing out that a person from Kansas today who's made an avant-garde film and wants it shown in New York would have to choose between different institutions.

PG: It's a very interesting contradiction, actually. There are more venues here in New York. You can go to the Millennium or the Collective or the Museum of Modern Art. On the other hand, in London, you can only go at this point to the Co-op or to Four Corners—Four Corners being a group of people in the East End, men and women but mainly women, who make films there, distribute (or, rather, publicize the distribution of another group called Circles, run by Felicity Sparrow, which has a whole range of feminist films, including avant-garde). It's almost like a collective effort to get the work distributed, even though Four Corners actually have production facilities *and* they have screenings two or three times a week.

JR: Do they compete with the Co-op?

PG: No, because first of all, their main interest is with certain issues and themes. Secondly, although they have the hardest time with it in terms of their audience, they still accept that one can make experimental films which come out of the Co-op tradition, the way that Lis Rhodes has (and admits she has), or the way that Sally Potter has (and a bit belatedly admits she has). Lucy Panteli comes out of that tradition, and Joanna Millet. Four Corners shows these works. Mary Pat Leece and Jo Davis, who run Four Corners, are also filmmakers whose work comes out of a tradition that is not separable from Co-op-type work, even though there's no question that they've made a radical break, because if there's one thing the Co-op films didn't do, they didn't engage with questions of feminism—certainly not ten years ago. So the split happened about five years ago.

Most Co-op filmmakers don't make a living in commerce; their practice is as experimental filmmakers *all the time*. Maybe they teach for a living, or paint houses, or build flats or sort letters in the post office five months a year; but they don't make Ivory Soap commercials. And that's something in England that is the case only with Co-op filmmakers—there's a real attempt not to mix practices. Nevertheless, the Co-op didn't fulfill certain expectations, especially for women filmmakers who have feminist political positions which they wanted to have problematically worked through their experimental film practice, but not at the expense of their feminist practice. And that meant a split was needed. So that the most productive members of Four Corners left the Co-op and started a powerful new group, which is not in competition but fulfills a different need. The result is that the Co-op has now had to come to terms with this, and the relations between the two groups is very good. Lis Rhodes and Mary Pat Leece are, if anything, the strongest defenders of the kind of socialist organization that the Co-op is. It's interesting, because those who split did so for very real and objective political, aesthetic reasons, and also realized the strength of the other organization—because it *doesn't* co-opt them. I think the much bigger danger happened with The Other Cinema, where everyone wound up co-opted: they talked socialism but they paid their floor cleaners and their so-called collective members starvation wages and didn't let them vote. The people who cleaned the cinema and showed you to your seat were members of the so-called collective but they couldn't vote, while the voting directors—Steve Dwoskin, Marc Karlin of the Berwick Street Collective, Nick Hart-Williams, and Peter Sainsbury, etc., the big boys—made all the decisions.

JR: Where does someone like James Scott fit within this configuration? I remember him as one of the more interesting figures, whose **Coilin & Platonida** I reviewed for *Monthly Film Bulletin* in 1976—one of the most original English films I saw when I was living in London. Even the kind of film that it was—a partial adaptation of Leskov inspired by Walter Benjamin's essay on the storyteller—made it exceptional.

PG: He's an interesting case—the most talented, visual and filmically sophisticated member of the Berwick Street Collective. He's made about ten films for the Arts Council about living artists—that's been his meat and potatoes: documentaries, but not uninteresting documentaries. His Richard Hamilton film is, in that genre, probably the best. On the other hand, it's as if that practice informed Berwick Street's "other" practice. I have nothing but contempt aesthetically for their work: I think it's recuperative, it's a ripoff, it's substandard—it's everything I loathe about certain avant-garde films: a little avant-garde, a little political, a little good-conscience soundtrack, a little bit grainy Cassavetes stuff...and, without knowing it, it's tailor-made for *Screen* academicism. Which the Co-op never was—which is why the Co-op films never got dealt with by *Screen*.

Anyway, to answer your original question, there are only two places that might show your hypothetical avant-garde film in London. The main difference is, if you have a film, you can probably show it. Here, as you know—except for Millennium, who are really good at this—I have the feeling that there's much more of an elitist system in terms of who gets a show, who you know, and so on. And this isn't sour grapes, because I've had more than my fair share of shows in New York, more than I deserve.

JR: You mean there's more star orientation.

PG: *Much* more. It's unbearable. If anything, I find it terribly oppressive here on every level, that climbing up ladders at no matter whose expense to get wherever you are. And then where you are, like Warhol says, is nowhere: you're a star for five minutes and then comes the next person anyway.

JR: I'm remembering that a lot of the original footage for **Coilin & Platonida** was shot in Super-8. Is there much English work being done in Super-8?

PG: There's no need for Super-8, because you have the means of production in 16. The Co-op has had the means of production to do superb 16mm work since 1968. Who needs Super-8?

JR: Who put up the initial money to get the Co-op started?

PG: Well, this is the contradiction of even British quasi-socialist capitalism: at the beginning, someone had to give the equipment. And it was very grotty, bits and pieces, it was like £2,000 worth in 1968, when the first pieces came trundling in. Actually a person from Paris who owned cinemas, Victor Herbert, gave the £2,000 to this group of people who started the Co-op, Simon Hartog, Steve Dwoskin, David Curtis, Malcolm Le Grice, and some others. There were no state support grants, and no private funds from a grant institution.

JR: What about Annabel Nicholson? The first Co-op show I ever attended was hers, in the mid-Seventies. She showed her sewing machine projection piece—in which a film is actually run through a sewing machine.

PG: She's been active since the late Sixties. And she's an important teacher.

JR: Could you speak about some recent English avant-garde work of interest that hasn't gotten to the U.S.? More generally, I'd be interested in hearing why you think some work comes over here and some doesn't.

PG: That's a difficult one. There's a three- or four-year period of graduates from St. Martin's and the Royal College of Art that's about 50% of the new filmmakers. And then there are filmmakers who aren't from these schools and have been making films for years and haven't been heard about. Like David Parsons, an incredibly important filmmaker—I don't know if he's ever shown in America. I've no idea; he teaches at Northeast London Polytechnic. His films are probably the most extreme form that uses film and the apparatus and the machinery as its subject matter—whereas most experimental films about the film process are in fact journalistic parodies (maybe that's what J. Hoberman thinks experimental film should be, but it's not). Parsons's **Picture Planes II** actually does that, but does it totally: the subject matter and content *is* the filters, the camera, putting a lens onto a camera which is running without a lens, and having an image take place, and then disappear, and then change color when the color filter is put up in front; switching to negative and doing the same operation in negative-reverse—there's a symmetry of form. At first you can't decipher what's going on at all, then you realize that it's something you've seen before, but "opposite."

The trouble with this kind of description is that it always reduces it to seeming as if it were an illustration of the machinery. It isn't that; it's a visible and visual transformation of the material world via a series of film components. It's almost like the feedback on a single note played by a guitar, which transforms the sound and transforms what sound is *in its specificity* for the listener. In the same way, that kind of operation, if it's done very precisely, with a great deal of knowledge about when cliché might start—you can actually come up with a film that through the viewer actually becomes the visible process of that experience. I've only seen it done well once, and that's in this film. Usually, it's cliché, it's redundant, it's kind of illustrative, it's something you could say in words much more succinctly. It's sort of like saying a painting's about color. Well, a lot of awful paintings are about color, but not all paintings about color are awful. A good Mondrian is a good Mondrian—and you can explain why. The same with Popova.

I think the British experimental film since the Sixties is actually what I would call genuinely experimental. Which means you really sit down with the whole apparatus—making, visualizing, memories of things, trying to experiment with cinema the way one accepts totally experimenting with painting, cubism or early Kandinsky. It's as if the British fits into a tradition of twentieth-century experimental avant-garde work, whereas in fact the American tradition, as in so many other things, has become aberrant, yet given over as the norm because of power. The American experimental film is still always stuck with the notion of an image, the power of the image. The aberrance goes back to Abstract Expressionism, which learned everything from surrealism. It was a very powerful movement where a lot of the work was what I would call materialist work, but the way it was exploited was as the grand image. They still talk about Jackson Pollock's pictures as somehow his transcriptions of the fluttering light on the leaves behind his garage. The American avant-garde filmmakers bought that and started producing "a different kind of image." But the notion that you still produce an image rather than experiment with time and space and imagery and contradiction and the viewer's imbrication in meaning—all that was still much more separate from the viewer, producing in America, on the wall, a different image or structure or concept. But somehow, I think in Britain, because the means of production were in the hands of the people making the films—I'm not saying there was some kind of superior socialist mind, I'm just saying that the actual, objective history of Britain, and of cultural production in Europe, was such that it led to that being much more possible. So that you were more concerned with the whole process than with the final image. Actually, I would give quite a few of the Action painters full credit for investigating process.

JR: Let's bring up the question of magazines devoted to avant-garde film, which I also discussed with Jonas. There seem to be two major English journals. One is *Afterimage*, which I think could presently be called superior to any American avant-garde film magazine that appears with any regularity. And now there's also *Undercut*, which I don't know as well but which looks pretty lively *and* substantial.

PG: Yes, now that they've been going as a quarterly for nearly two years, they've attempted to avoid the over-academicism and pro-narrative literarization of *Screen*, but at the same time take up some of the kind of post-Althusserian and radical feminist ideas which are necessary to problematize avant-garde and experimental filmmaking—otherwise it really *does* become formalist filmmaking, in the weakest sense of formalism.

JR: Doesn't *Undercut* have certain links with the Co-op?

PG: Yes, in the sense that the collective which produces it produces it at the Co-op. But obviously there's a lot of interchange *and* lack of interchange between filmmakers—it isn't as if it's an unproblematic discourse from the Co-op. But without that engagement and those interventions, avant-garde will remain purely imagistic—not Soviet formalism but a kind of bad *Artforum* formalism. The one thing one has to give people in England credit for, whatever side they were on, or whoever they were— Noël Burch or *Screen* or the Royal College of Art or St. Martin's or the Co-op or Four Corners or even The Other Cinema (though less there than anywhere else)—there *was* a thing about wanting to deal with certain issues of one's practice. Here, every time you go to a screening, there's a constant aim to get out afterwards and go to a restaurant. I've seen question and answer periods that lasted eight minutes—six minutes—four minutes! There's almost no interest in actual film issues. You can see here at any venue, at almost any university or conference, at least six different positions, all contradictory, that are not taken up as contradictions. It all depends on the hierarchy of the writer, and you just consume it, with no mental, conceptual, philosophical, or political headaches. There's no need to engage, because next week something new will come up which you can also consume.

JR: There's a total contradiction at the base of this, because the one time one encounters a film that really overturns one's way of thinking, it actually stops the consumption flow—which *isn't* supposed to happen. Which makes me think of Rose Lowder, whose most recent film we both saw recently at Millennium—**Retour d'un repère composé [Composed Recurrence]**—and which you had such a strong response to.

PG: Yeah. Her film and Lis Rhodes's **Light Reading** and Lucy Panteli's **Motion Picture** and Joanna Millet's **House Light** and Michael Maziere's

Film Work, and David Parsons's **Picture Planes II** are a solid body of work which I don't really think is being dealt with yet, for the issues raised and even the way the films' presences operate on you as a spectator. It's just the beginning now of an attempt to figure out what that post-Co-op, feminist, anti-narrative work really is.

JR: How does feminism figure in these films? A lot of people are going to wonder how this is possible without any reference to a narrative tradition.

PG: I think rather than me trying to answer that—because it's up to the women making and theorizing the films to do that—I should refer to an essay by Nancy Woods on Lis Rhodes's **Light Reading** which will be appearing in the English avant-garde issue of *Afterimage* around the same time that this book appears, which attempts to address precisely those issues. And in *Undercut* No. 4, an article by Michael Maziere attempts to address those issues in relation to Lucy Panteli's **Motion Picture.** And I think, from what I know, the upcoming film issue of *Heresies,* an American journal, will have an article by Lisa Cartwright on Rose Lowder's film. So those three pieces might answer that question better than I can.

JR: I'm wondering how you feel about the relation between your own film work and Lowder's, which seems problematic.

PG: Absolutely—because she's taken certain things much further than I have, and therefore the film's very interesting to me. It's also very powerful—like seeing **Wavelength** or **The Chelsea Girls** for the first time.

JR: But isn't this different? Those other films introduced you to new kinds of discourse, whereas Lowder's kind of discourse is something you're already familiar with.

PG: Yeah, that's why it's surprising that it's so powerful—because it *isn't* the unknown. And yet it feels like reading Gertrude Stein for the first time, or first hearing Billie Whitelaw speak Beckett—that kind of feeling. But you're right; it's weird when it happens in a discourse that you're engaged in yourself and theorizing and writing and making films. It makes me in a sense almost scared—that I have to be very careful not to get sloppy!

JR: I'm wondering what you mean by "powerful" in this context.

PG: Like reading Marx's *Critique of the Gotha Program,* or Christine Delphy's *The Main Enemy*—really powerful. It's like a strong, important, aesthetic, political moment. And it *is* power—it's against other things.

JR: It's "correct." But I'm wondering how much a negativity can be turned into something positive. As she puts it, "I do not want to make beautiful objects." Is that *in itself* powerful?

PG: "Powerful" means forceful, strong, complex, problematical, and contradictory, but also engaging in the sense that one can't separate one's self from it and become a pure consumer of it. And also power means oppositional—against a whole series of other cultural political manifestations that exist.

Name Index

Film Title Index